Hungry,
Thirsty,
a Stranger

Hungry, Thirsty, a Stranger

THE MCC EXPERIENCE

**Robert S. Kreider and
Rachel Waltner Goossen
Foreword by John A. Lapp**

HERALD PRESS
Scottdale, Pennsylvania
Kitchener, Ontario

LIBRARY OF CONGRESS
Library of Congress Cataloging-in-Publication Data

Kreider, Robert S.
  Hungry, thirsty, a stranger : the MCC experience / Robert S.
Kreider and Rachel Waltner Goossen ; foreword John A. Lapp.
      p.   cm.
  Bibliography: p.
  ISBN 0-8361-1299-7 (pbk.) : $14.95
  1. Mennonite Central Committee—History.   2. Mennonites-
-Charities—History.   I. Goossen, Rachel Waltner.   II. Title.
BX8128.W4K74   1988   88-692
361.7'5—dc19   CIP

HUNGRY, THIRSTY, A STRANGER
Copyright ©1988 by Herald Press, Scottdale, Pa. 15683
      Published simultaneously in Canada by Herald Press,
      Kitchener, Ont. N2G 4M5. All rights reserved.
Library of Congress Catalog Card Number: 88-692
International Standard Book Number: 0-8361-1299-7
Printed in the United States of America
Cover: MCC Photo by Jim King
Design by Gwen M. Stamm

95 94 93 92 91 90 89 10 9 8 7 6 5 4 3 2 1

Contents

Series Preface

"Did you ever in all your days read in the Scriptures that an orthodox, born-again Christian continued after repentance and conversion to be proud, avaricious, gluttonous, unchaste, greedy, hateful, tyrannical, and idolatrous, and continued to live after base desires of the flesh? You must say no, must you not?" So wrote Menno Simons in 1541. Obedience is the fruit of repentance and conversion. This is the taproot of Mennonite Central Committee (MCC) life and its motto, *In the Name of Christ*.

At the heart of this life in Christ is the unity of word and deed. Sharing the faith by speaking it and living it has been a great biblical and Anabaptist-Mennonite heritage. Giving a cup of cold water to a thirsty person is a good deed in itself, but most Mennonites have always expected MCC to be more than a welfare agency. Obedience to the words and deeds of Christ still means love, grace, witness, compassion, and community.

There have been times when Anabaptist-Mennonites defined community to include their own in-group people only, but MCC has rejected this narrow definition from the time of its first work in Russia in 1920 to the present. Help is indeed given to the "household of faith," but to others too, as possible.

In 1547 a group of Hutterite elders drafted "Five Articles of the Greatest Strife Between Us and the World," in which they stressed in-group community. But they also quoted Luke 10:27b, "You shall love your neighbor as yourself," and added: "Whoever wants to do this must share at all times with his brother and neighbor.... Otherwise, it is not loving as he loves himself, but only a pharisaical, heathen, and despicable love."

The chapters of this fifth volume in *The Mennonite Central Committee Story Series* (see listing at back of book) present a marvelous panorama of this love of neighbor. The vast global dimensions of the MCC program are gratifying, yet not more so than the accounts of intimate, personal encounters one on one. We see a great God using a small group of believers to bring hope and healing in most unusual ways. The often inadequate and fumbling efforts of inexperienced lay workers bear fruit beyond expectation under the guidance of the Spirit. Little signs of the kingdom appear in the wilderness of suffering and despair.

So we thank God for MCC, for every loving word and deed. Who knows what tomorrow may bring? "But you shall receive power when the Holy Spirit has come upon you; and you shall be my witnesses in Jerusalem and in all Judea and Samaria and to the end of the earth" (Acts 1:8, RSV). This, it seems to me, is a good text for the MCC family, workers, clients, all of us.

—Cornelius J. Dyck, Elkhart, Indiana

Authors' Preface

Among Mennonite institutions Mennonite Central Committee (MCC) is a large organization with a thousand workers, ten thousand part-time volunteers, ten thousand worker alumni, programs in fifty countries, and an annual operating budget exceeding thirty-three million dollars. MCC's many activities fan out from two headquarters located at Akron, Pennsylvania, and Winnipeg, Manitoba.

With a thousand workers in fifty countries—many of them in international crisis areas—MCC generates countless stories: some written, some told orally, and some simply remembered. We have selected from the sixty-eight years of MCC''s history thirty stories or "case studies."

Hungry, Thirsty, a Stranger is not a historical survey, although the volume contains much history. We offer a series of selected scenes from a complex drama. Presented here are significant episodes from six continents and from each decade in the MCC experience.

Implicit and explicit in each episode or case study are questions that invite the reader to ponder, "What would I have done had I been there?"

These questions involve morality and faith: To be prudent or to be prophetic? To be pragmatic or to be faithful? Can one be both? With the gift of hindsight, what should have been done? Are these issues akin to contemporary ones in the home congregation and community? This volume is an invitation to dialogue.

Hungry, Thirsty, a Stranger is intended for MCC workers and friends who wish to gain understanding of the larger MCC experience, for persons contemplating MCC service, and for those who are curious about an agency that is present in diverse and faraway places. The volume is designed particularly for study groups, who are encouraged to identify the critical issues in each chapter and discuss them. In many communities, former MCC workers may be invited into the circle of discussion to add descriptions and to offer alternative perceptions.

This volume is fifth in the series "The Mennonite Central Committee Story." *From the Files of MCC*, the first three in the series, provide a wealth of rare source material: documents, reports, minutes, and letters. The fourth volume, *Something Meaningful for God*, offers biographies of fifteen women and men who have shaped the character of MCC.

MCC means different things to different people: to some, emergency relief or agricultural development; to others, aid to refugees, advocacy for the conscientious objector, help through Mennonite Disaster Service, administration of psychiatric centers, and much more. In this volume we have sampled many of these significant experiences, but not all. Some programs not included in this volume have been described elsewhere.

Many individuals acknowledge that MCC symbolizes their sense of Mennonite identity. Some who emigrated from Russia tell of how MCC food relief saved their lives. Others recall with gratitude that MCC service led to a redirection of life plans.

Some see MCC as a companion of missions in sharing the good news of Christ. But not all Mennonites feel this affection. Some see MCC as captive to social activism; others see MCC as conservative and restrictive in its personnel policies. Some perceive MCC as a big, powerful, sophisticated agency with more abundant financial resources than other church agencies, more mobility, more aggressive communication efforts—elements which, taken together, may intimidate. Those who read these case studies bring differing perceptions of MCC that can add to the delights of discussion.

MCC has its own special vocabulary, folklore, and organizational maze. Introduced in this volume is a special set of MCC acronyms: VS, TAP, CPS, 1-W, Pax, MDS, CROP, MMHS, MEDA, and many more. MCC has a way of spinning off quasi-independent agencies that hover near the MCC. A timetable of MCC's international programs and suggested books for further reading (at the back of this book), as well as an organizational chart (inside back cover), may help one understand these complexities.

These studies have been written for a broad readership. No footnotes appear. The background notes and papers for each study are deposited in the MCC Collection at the Archives of the Mennonite Church in Goshen, Indiana.

Readers will find in these case studies more than one use of the term "MCC." It may refer to Winnipeg and the headquarters of MCC Canada or it may mean Akron and the headquarters of the binational MCC. It may mean a regional center such as the Central States office at Newton, Kansas, or a provincial MCC office such as the one in Calgary, Alberta. Thus, in MCC circles one hears shorthand language: "What does Winnipeg say?" or "We ought to check with Akron."

We gathered information but did not include a chapter on the administrative structure and procedures of a church agency. Such a study would chart the flow of activity through a headquarters office: incoming and outgoing mail, phone calls,

Telex messages, committee meetings, reception of visitors, orientation of outgoing workers, debriefing of returning workers, processing of supplies, the stream of publications from the production room. This would contrast with the daily rounds of an MCC volunteer in a tribal community on the edge of the Sahara: no telephones, little paperwork, much sitting and listening. Both are MCC.

One should read these studies from the MCC experience while keeping in mind the question: What other episodes should be described and analyzed? The studies should also be read with an eye to a host of critical questions: Which national and world developments envelop the particular MCC story being told? With so much need, where can we best serve? How can we minister to those in need? How can we allow others to be sisters and brothers to us in our need? Are these programs central to the mission of the church of Christ in the world?

The reader may ask, "What gives the MCC its particular character?" One observes a wide range of conference bodies working together. Much of MCC"s support comes from its own church constituency. It has few salaried staff members. It draws its strength from volunteers, yet increasingly is using professionals. Its program is sprawling and diversified. With a flow of workers through its programs, MCC may be called a center of nonformal education. Forty percent of the applicants for service come from beyond the MCC church constituency. Recognizing that businesses and institutions come and go, is there a continuing vocation for Mennonite Central Committee? If so, in what form?

Hungry, Thirsty, a Stranger issues an invitation to dialogue on issues of life and death, war and peace, wealth and poverty, justice and injustice, faith, hope, and love.

—*Robert S. Kreider, North Newton, Kansas*
—*Rachel Waltner Goossen, Goessel, Kansas*

Acknowledgments

We are indebted to scores of people for candid and thoughtful counsel in the preparation of these studies from MCC experience. Virtually every administrator at the Akron and Winnipeg offices contributed helpful information and criticism. Many present and past program directors and other MCC workers shared counsel. In response to their suggestions, and because of space limitations, we revised and condensed manuscripts on complex subjects. Despite this effort to integrate data and the insights of numerous readers, responsibility for the final text with its faults is ours.

We are particularly grateful to the following persons for writing the original revisions of the following: Bob and Judy Zimmerman Herr, the Transkei; Fred Kauffman, Kampuchea; Martha Wenger, the West Bank; Mary Sprunger, Lebanon, Bolivia, and Botswana; and Linda Shelly, Honduras. Harold Nigh contributed substantially to the Crete study.

We are grateful to Tina Mast Burnett and her Information Services staff for assistance in selecting the posters that are shown at the end of chapter 15 and for providing the commentary on them. We appreciate the careful work of Scott Jost and Kim Garret on the graphics, including the maps. Mennonite Central Committee provided grants which defrayed a substantial portion of the costs of writing and editing this volume.

We appreciate the wise counsel, gentle nudging, and abundant patience of the other members of the editorial committee, John A. Lapp and Cornelius J. Dyck. We are grateful for the opportunity of entering into the lives of a multitude of MCC workers who have shared abundantly of their experiences with us.

Finally, we acknowledge the presence of a host of MCC friends and colleagues—drivers and receptionists, typists and hosts, archivists and researchers—who have made this task a pleasant one. We are grateful for the research done years ago by two students, Linda Schmidt and Martha Wenger, and particularly for the information gathering of Marion Keeney Preheim. Leonard Gross, Rachel Shenk, and others of the Archives of the Mennonite Church at Goshen, Indiana, served far beyond the call of duty, as did David A. Haury and his colleagues of the Mennonite Library and Archives, North Newton, Kansas.

—Robert S. Kreider and Rachel Waltner Goossen

Foreword

There is a new game on the market called "Scruples." Players of this game work at moral dilemmas, posed to reflect human experience. At Mennonite Central Committee (MCC) there are few days that we do not confront a series of "Scruples." The problems are compounded by the fact that we represent an increasingly diverse constituency and work in a variety of cultural situations.

This set of case studies might be viewed as MCC "Scruples." These cases represent the diverse expectations constituents bring to bear on the organization. And they illustrate the complex entanglements in which the organization gets involved. This is indeed Mennonite Central Committee—concerned constituents putting resources, primarily personnel, in the midst of human need. In 1986 MCC had 1,010 workers directly involved in a rich variety of human situations. Thousands more volunteered their time in generating resources and hammering out policies essential for this ministry. Although rooted in churches located in Canada and the United States, MCC works in fifty-one countries.

Case studies are a wonderful way of getting inside a situation, feeling the tensions and speculating on a course of action. But there are numerous intangibles that grow out of conviction and circumstances. MCC is a constituency organization. We are dependent on vision, personnel, and financial support supplied by the Mennonite and Brethren in Christ peoplehood. As an organization representing the church we are very conscious that it is God who "gives us grace to practice mercy," a phrase from early MCC leader B. B. Janz.

Being personnel-intensive means that people on the scene, led by God's Spirit and local friends, usually have an angle of vision for decision-making better than those of us in comfortable offices in Akron and Winnipeg. We are well aware that our efforts are small and sometimes ineffectual. We trust that what we do can be seen as signs pointing toward the loving community God wills for the earth.

While this volume supplies considerable information, much more could be said about each case. Further inquiries are welcome. But more importantly, we hope readers will begin to see the drama, opportunity, and problematic character in everything we do. We hope this book will inspire your interest in meeting human need wherever it is and encourage your prayers for people serving God through MCC.

Robert S. Kreider, who coauthored and edited this volume, has been part of MCC since the early 1940s. He served as an administrator in postwar Europe and as the architect of Teachers Abroad Program (TAP) in the 1960s. As a longtime member of the MCC Executive Committee, he frequently filled special assignments overseas and carried out a major self-study in 1973-74.

For the editor, these case studies are not academic exercises or heroic stories but part of the faithful wrestling of an MCC administrator and policymaker. On behalf of MCC and all readers a special word of appreciation to Robert Kreider and to Rachel Waltner Goossen, his author-editor colleague, for bringing these cases to us in an authentic and powerful way.

—*John A. Lapp, Akron, Pennsylvania*

In the Beginning

In his history of Mennonite Central Committee Canada, *Parters in Service*, Frank Epp wrote of MCC's beginnings: "There is a sense in which the foundations of the partnership called Mennonite Central Committee Canada go back to creation and the origin of the human family. In the beginning, God willed that God and man, divinity and humanity, should be full partners in the stewardship of creation."

The story moves on to the coming of Jesus, the Christ, whose followers were given the ministry of reconciliation and were called to proclaim the good news. Symbols of mission became the cup of water, loaf of bread, basin, towel, and cross. The church Christ founded became a community of believers who shared, served, and loved even their enemies. Members of this blessed community refused the oath of loyalty to earthly rulers and declined to take the sword to fight for country and faith. They were citizens of a Peaceable Kingdom.

Epp traced a story which leads to the gentle St. Francis of Assisi and the Waldenses, who lived for the sake of others. In the sixteenth century came the Anabaptist-Mennonites, among whose leaders was one Menno Simons who wrote: "True evangelical faith cannot be dormant. It clothes the naked. It feeds the hungry. It comforts the sorrowful. It shelters the destitute. It serves those that harm it. It binds up that which is wounded. It has become all things to all men."

From the days of the Anabaptists come stories of faith in action. In 1553, Anabaptists in Wismar on the Baltic aided Calvinist refugees escaping from imprisonment or death in England. In 1569, the Anabaptist Dirk Willems rescued his captor only to be seized again and burned at the stake. The Hutterite colonists in Moravia provided shelter and food for the homeless.

In 1710 Dutch Mennonites formed the Dutch Relief Fund for Foreign Needs to aid those fleeing persecution in Switzerland and immigrants from the Palatinate seeking new homes in Pennsylvania. In the 1870s relief committees were formed in Canada and the United States to assist eighteen thousand Russian Mennonite immigrants arriving in the prairie provinces and states.

Etched in the consciousness of those who established MCC and MCC Canada are the words of Christ: "For I was hungry and you gave me food, I was thirsty and you gave me drink, I was a stranger and you welcomed me, I was naked and you clothed me, I was sick and you visited me, I was in prison and you came to me" (Matthew 25:35-36, RSV).

1

MCC Is Born

*Etched into their Mennonite consciousness was
the call of Christ to minister to the hungry,
the thirsty, the stranger.*

Mennonite Central Committee was born on July 27, 1920. Mennonites had been hurt by the war that had ended twenty months earlier. Of the estimated two thousand Mennonite young men drafted in the United States, 138 had been court-martialed and sentenced to federal prisons for their refusal to obey military orders. An estimated one thousand Mennonites and Hutterites had fled to Canada, where young Mennonites who could show certificates of church membership were granted "postponements" of service. In many communities, Mennonites had been coerced into buying war bonds. Some who refused had been publicly taunted and harassed. During the fervor of war, Mennonites had not found it pleasant to be a people who spoke the language of the enemy. Despite the hurts of war, Mennonite farmers had prospered and had money to give.

Many Mennonites, accustomed to isolated, rural living, felt rudely yanked by the war into an American society which was experiencing turbulent changes. By 1920, one in thirteen

Americans owned an automobile. Soon they would be listening to radio broadcasts. The behavior of women was unsettling to many: some were cutting their hair and smoking in public. A fear of Bolshevism was abroad in the land. Americans discovered a place called "Hollywood" and talked of movie stars and professional athletes like Babe Ruth and Jack Dempsey.

Meanwhile, Mennonites were experiencing stress. An older generation of leaders who had introduced Sunday schools, revival meetings, publishing houses, and missions dug in their heels to brake the tempo of change. Young people who had left home for college or the draft called for change and for a share in the responsibilities of the church. Due in part to outside Protestant influences, theological positions became polarized: alleged fundamentalists were mutually at odds with alleged modernists. Among Mennonites this was a judgmental period. Many were highly suspicious of any activity which brought Mennonites together and thus compromised separateness and purity. And yet, during the twenties, Mennonites prospered, sent missionaries abroad, and experienced church growth.

Thirteen men attended the meeting on July 27 and 28, 1920, when in a Mennonite meetinghouse on Prairie Street in Elkhart, Indiana, Mennonite Central Committee was established. It was not a broadly representative group: a Mennonite bishop and his two sons, two persons from the Scottdale Publishing House, three from Kansas, plus additional persons from Indiana, Pennsylvania, Minnesota, and Iowa. Influential Daniel Kauffman, member of a dozen conference boards and committees, was not present. No photograph survives of this momentous event. The reporting in Mennonite papers was modest. In fact, some influential Mennonites feared such meetings where one could be unequally yoked with other Mennonites who did not dress, speak, and act as one did. In 1920 Mennonites from different conference groups did not know each other very well. MCC was not a marriage born of affection, but a cautious contract born of necessity.

At Elkhart, the Mennonite representatives devised an arrangement that met the needs of each group. They selected as secretary Levi Mumaw, who was also secretary of the Mennonite Relief Commission for War Sufferers. Mumaw represented the largest conference, the Mennonite Church. They chose a representative of the Emergency Relief Committee of the General Conference, H. H. Regier of Mountain Lake, Minnesota, for the second member. (Regier was succeeded at the next meeting by Maxwell Kratz, a General Conference attorney from Philadelphia.) For chairman they selected a Mennonite Brethren educator from Hillsboro, Kansas, P. C. Hiebert.

Aware that many were reluctant to engage themselves in inter-Mennonite activity, they acknowledged that the newly-formed MCC was a temporary arrangement to facilitate emergency relief work for a limited period of time. The representatives at Elkhart did not see the proposed MCC as displacing existing Mennonite relief agencies:

> We ... deem it well and desirable to create a Mennonite Central Committee, whose duty shall be to function with and for the several relief committees of the Mennonites, in taking charge of all gifts for South Russia, in making all purchases of suitable articles for relief work, and in providing for the transportation and the equitable distribution of the same.

In fact, immigration work was not to be in MCC's portfolio. Two months after the formal organization of MCC, the Mennonite Executive Committee for Colonization (MECC) was created at Newton, Kansas, with five members, none of whom were members of MCC. MECC never got off the ground, presumably because the United States was accepting very few immigrants.

On September 27, 1920, MCC held its first official meeting in Chicago with representatives from seven conferences and relief organizations. They accepted the plans that had been adopted by the Mennonite Relief Commission and by the group of workers traveling to Constantinople. Thus the "old" Mennonite agency provided the policy and personnel for the launching of the MCC program in Russia.

Two months later the first MCC workers, Orie O. Miller and Clayton Kratz, arrived in South Russia. Russia's civil war was still raging. Miller returned to Constantinople and Kratz remained at Halbstadt in the Molotschna Mennonite colony. When the Red Army arrived, Kratz was arrested. He was never heard from again, and became the first MCC martyr. Not until December 1921 could the first relief be distributed by MCC in South Russia. With resources totaling $1,300,000, MCC completed its relief work in Russia by 1925 and in Siberia by 1926. In an eighteen-month period from March 1922 to August 1923, MCC fed seventy-five thousand people, including sixty thousand Mennonites. Nine thousand Mennonites are said to have been saved from starvation. By 1924, Mennonites in America talked of disbanding MCC.

The thirteen men who met at the Prairie Street church on July 27, 1920, were not the reluctant ones. They were ready to act, ready to work together in response to the need in Russia. Etched into their Mennonite consciousness was the call of Christ to minister to the hungry, the thirsty, the stranger. The constitution of the Mennonite Relief Commission for War Sufferers included the words from Matthew 25 (KJV): "For I was an hungred, and ye gave me meat: I was thirsty, and ye gave me drink. . . ." They knew also the words from 1 John 3:17 (KJV): "But whoso hath this world's good, and seeth his brother have need. . . ." There was no question in their minds that to be biblically faithful one must relieve human suffering. They also remembered that in past generations Mennonites had responded instinctively to crises.

Historian James C. Juhnke has gathered evidence that American Mennonites, who had prospered during the war, experienced a tinge of guilt that they had not suffered or sacrificed as much as others. The college-age youth Clayton

Kratz of Perkasie, Pennsylvania, wrote on his application for service that he wished to help persons in need "because this great world catastrophe has not caused me any inconvenience." In 1918, the Franconia Conference bishops sent out solicitors to "collect an amount of money for relief purposes that would seem consistent with the sacrifices that some of the other people are making."

On the morning of November 11, 1918, President Woodrow Wilson had penciled on White House stationery a three-sentence message with this concluding line: "It will now be our fortunate duty to assist by example, by sober, friendly counsel, and by material aid in the establishment of just democracy throughout the world." In the giving of "material aid," Mennonites could again be seen as patriotic Americans.

The thirteen who met at Elkhart knew that a number of Mennonite relief committees were aggressively probing ways to engage themselves in overseas relief efforts. The oldest of these was the Emergency Relief commission of the General Conference, which dated back to 1899 when it mobilized famine aid for India. In 1919 a Pacific branch of the Commission gathered clothing and forty-four thousand dollars, and sent M. B. Fast and William P. Neufeld, both of Reedley, California, to Siberia, where they planned to distribute aid among destitute Mennonites in distant Omsk. Halted at Vladivostok in their effort to reach Omsk, Fast and Neufeld returned to North America and told of the suffering they had witnessed in Russia. People, captivated by their reports, "streamed together in large numbers to get all the information possible, and also to find an opportunity to share in the mission of benevolence."

One such appeal led to the formation in January 1920 of the Emergency Relief Committee of the Mennonites of North America, a joint committee that included the Krimmer Mennonite Brethren, the Mennonite Brethren, and the General Conference. When further work in Siberia was blocked, the Emergency Relief Commission turned its assistance to Austria and Germany.

In 1917 two relief committees were organized. First, in Ontario, Mennonites and Brethren in Christ formed the Non-Resistant Relief Organization. In December of that year, the "old" Mennonite Church organized the Relief Commission for War Sufferers. It contributed funds and assigned thirty-one workers to Near East Relief. It also sent sixty workers to Europe with the American Friends Service Committee (AFSC), established in June 1917, which sponsored reconstruction teams in France and child-feeding programs in Germany. In April 1919, the Quaker AFSC sent invitations for cooperation in sending a unit of relief workers to Russia. A Mennonite worker with the AFSC team in France wrote home, "The future of the Unit lies in Russia." The young Mennonites in France saw in the AFSC a model that could be replicated by the Mennonites. The Relief Commission appointed three of its workers in France—Alvin J. Miller, Roy Allgyer, and A. E. Hiebert—to investigate need in Europe and Russia. On December 4, 1919, they cabled to the home office in Scottdale: "Appalling need for clothing, bedding, hospital supplies, fats, milk. Recommend unit for Russia and cooperation Central Europe."

Mennonite newspapers took up the call for relief to Europe and Russia. In addition to the articles that appeared in official conference periodicals, several Mennonite newspapers were particularly active in telling of the need: *Vorwaerts* of Hillsboro, edited by the invalid J. G. Ewert: *Die Mennonitsche Rundschau* of Scottdale; and *Der Herald* of Newton. North American Mennonites waited anxiously and expectantly for news from their sisters and brothers in civil war-stricken South Russia.

In the summer of 1920 came eyewitness reports from a delegation, a *Studien Kommission* (Study Commission), dispatched by the Russian Mennonites. Leaving Russia on January 1, 1920, via Constantinople, they spent five months in Germany and the Netherlands, and arrived in New York on June 13, 1920. The three representatives, Benjamin Unruh and A. A. Friesen of Halbstadt, and K. H. Warkentin of Waldheim, asked for assistance for suffering Mennonites in Russia and for an investigation into the possibilities of migrating from Russia. They told of the atrocities of revolution and counterrevolution and of the epidemics that were sweeping Russia. The famine was yet to come. In Berlin the delegation met A. J. Miller of the Relief Commission, and in Basel, Switzerland, met Orie O. Miller and Chris Graber, who were returning from assignments with Near East Relief. Johann Esau, former mayor of Ekaterinoslav, then living in Berlin, joined the delegation for the trip to America.

On July 13, 1920, the Study Commission arrived in Newton, Kansas, to report to an inter-Mennonite group from Kansas and Oklahoma. The commission asked that North American response to needs in Russia not be fragmented into separate conference projects but be a strong, united, all-Mennonite effort. The delegation carried this message to Canada, and on October 18, 1920, at Regina, Saskatchewan, the Central Relief Committee (CRC), predecessor of the Canadian Mennonite Board of Colonization, was formed. David Toews collected and sent the first $3,500 to the young MCC. CRC sent out two appeals in 1920 for Russian relief. At Herbert, Saskatchewan, in December 1920, Mennonites raised $1,100 in an auction of contributed goods—certainly the first MCC relief sale on record.

The Kansas-Oklahoma inter-Mennonite group appointed a five-member Committee on Information. A week later, this committee met in Hillsboro and issued a formal call for a meeting to be held the following week in Elkhart, Indiana, of representatives of Mennonite relief organizations. Immediately, a group of Mennonite leaders saw this as a significant meeting and made plans to attend. The action suggests that in the summer of 1920 there was in the North American Mennonite consciousness a sense of anticipation and urgency.

No other project in North American Mennonite experience had captured Mennonite attention as did this Russian relief effort. Here was high drama: war, revolution, drought, famine, and distant kinsmen starving. Bolshevik bureaucracy thwarted emergency relief aid. Meanwhile, the time clock of death was ticking. When the doors opened, Mennonites burst forth with generous giving. From 1921 through 1923, church periodicals carried articles on the Russia program and filled pages with donor's names, addresses, and dollar amounts. The outpouring of gifts lay exposed for all to see.

The study which follows tells of MCC's first relief program in Russia. By 1925 MCC program had concluded, except for work in Siberia. Thousands of Russian Mennonites had emigrated to Canada. With the emergency past, most Mennonites considered MCC's job to be done. North American Mennonites could take leave of inter-Mennonite activity and return to separatist conference ways of doing relief.

However, in 1923, when MCC was concluding its Russia operations, chairman P. C. Hiebert issued through conference periodicals an invitation to establish continuing inter-Mennonite "Relief Machinery." At the December 1923 MCC meeting, he reported favorable responses from a number of conferences. The largest group, the "old" Mennonite Relief Commission, however, in May 1924 rejected Hiebert's proposal and pointed out that the Mennonite Relief Commission, a constituent member of the MCC, was to disband when the emergency was past. In the January 10 issue of the *Gospel Herald*, the editor had counseled that relief work should be folded under the mission board. Since this appeared to spell an end to MCC, in December 1924 Hiebert and others formed a new agency, the American Mennonite Relief Commission (AMRC). Orie Miller and Levi Mumaw, members of the "old" Mennonite Relief Commission, "were accorded the privileges of the meeting." Mumaw was even elected secretary. He continued as secretary of MCC and together with Miller worked quietly behind the scenes to avoid a break between the "old" Mennonite Relief Commission and the MCC. The new organization took form and adopted a constitution, but never really functioned. The AMRC held its last meeting in December 1926.

MCC, meanwhile, lingered on. The last MCC worker, A. J. Miller, did not return home until May 1927. A book on the Russia relief story, commissioned in 1924, appeared five years later entitled *Feeding the Hungry*. MCC remained relatively inactive until late 1929 when Mennonite refugees arrived in Germany from Russia, and a call came to MCC to resettle thousands in the Paraguayan Chaco.

The story of MCC's origins suggests the fragility of inter-Mennonite relations in the 1920s. One observes how church programs are unexpectedly propelled by the distant forces of national and world events. Moreover, a few persons of conviction can move institutional mountains. People can transcend their suspicions of each other when external needs compel them to work together. The first decade of Mennonite Central Committee reveals both conviction and hesitation, and in so doing, reveals much of the character of Mennonite people.

2

Feeding the Hungry:
Russia

*A time of dying is now beginning for us
Mennonites. . . . In Russia there are few that are
living, many that are vegetating, and the vast
hungry South is dying. What a smell from the
cadavers will rise towards heaven by May.*
                    —B. B. Janz, March 1, 1922

B. B. Janz, Mennonite leader in South Russia, had just
surveyed the needs of his people and knew their plight. He and
his people had lived through five years of revolutionary
change. From 1917 to 1920, the outside world knew little of
what was happening in Russia. German troops occupied briefly
the Ukraine. With the collapse of Germany in 1918, South
Russia became a battleground of Red, White, and bandit
armies. In 1919 and 1920, typhus epidemics in Mennonite
areas killed a tenth of the population. During the fall of 1920,
drought descended on the southern Ukraine. Livestock died.
Many families rationed their food supplies. Others were driven
to begging. People took clothing, furniture, and farm imple-
ments to the village bazaar, *toltchok* (jostling place), to exchange them for food. Some families ground leaves, bark,
cornstalks, or thistles into flour and ate cats, dogs, gophers, or
birds. It was a time of dying.

No food came from Mennonite Central Committee during

the famine winter of 1920-21. Not until December 1921 did the first trickle of MCC food arrive in the Volga, Orenburg, New Samara, and Old Samara districts. In March 1922, twenty months after the founding of MCC, the first feeding kitchens opened in the populous Chortitza and Molotschna Mennonite communities of South Russia. Why the long delay? The Soviet government, plagued by counterrevolutionary armies, sought to keep out agencies from capitalist countries. Food was power; the side with the food could claim the power. The young, self-reliant revolutionary government found it embarrassing to admit domestic catastrophe.

At first, entrance into Russia looked easy. On September 27, 1920, the very day that MCC was organized in Chicago, the first three Russia-bound MCC workers arrived in Constantinople: Arthur Slagel, Clayton Kratz, and Orie Miller. They conferred with officials of Near East Relief, the American Red Cross, Russian YMCA, and the American Embassy. Admiral Bristol of the American Embassy arranged for Miller and Kratz to board a U.S. destroyer bound for Sebastopol, Crimea, and gave them a letter of introduction to his colleague, Admiral McCully in Sebastopol. Upon their arrival on October 6, Admiral McCully put them in touch with the staff of General Wrangel, commander of the White armies controlling the region, who provided them with free transportation and an interpreter for their trip north to the Molotschna.

In Melitopol, at the home of miller Jacob Neufeld, they learned that the battlefront had shifted more than twenty times in two years through some Mennonite villages. They heard about the dreaded black typhus and the terrifying raids of bandits led by Nestor Machno. They learned that most colonies lacked medical supplies, clothing, bedding, and soap. In Orloff and Halbstadt they met with Mennonite colony leaders, but were unable to go beyond the Dnieper River to the Chortitza colony because Wrangel's army was retreating. They agreed that Kratz should remain in Halbstadt and Miller should return to Constantinople to procure relief supplies. When Miller and Kratz parted in the Alexandrovsk (Zaporozhe) railway station, it was the last time Miller saw his MCC colleague.

In Constantinople, Arthur Slagel assembled the first MCC shipment, which included "one thousand yards of flanellette, twelve sewing machines, fifty cases of milk, one hundred cases of soap, one thousand yards bed-ticking and one ton Ford truck with complete equipment and spare parts." Slagel arrived with the shipment in Sebastopol on November 14, just as thousands of Wrangel's defeated troops were comandeering ships for flight. The ship's crew presumably dumped that first MCC relief shipment overboard to make room for panic-stricken soldiers: somewhere on the bottom of the Black Sea lies MCC's 1920 model Ford truck.

By November 21, more than one hundred thousand refugees, including some Mennonites, had poured into Constantinople. While the door to relief work closed in Russia, another door for MCC opened in Constantinople. MCC and other American relief agencies joined in an emergency program. MCC workers opened a shelter for a hundred children under MCC worker Vesta Zook, established a clothing distribution center under J. E. Brunk, and visited regularly four refugee camps. Brunk and B. F. Hartzler opened a hostel for two hundred Russian refugees, two-thirds of whom were Mennonite. A Russian women's home accommodated up to fifty-five women. MCC workers provided transportation loans to persons wishing to migrate to Germany, Palestine, and other places. They made "every effort . . . to help without pauperizing," which led to an emphasis on loans to establish people in trades. MCC workers remained in Constantinople until July 1, 1922.

On January 29, 1921, Alvin J. Miller joined the MCC unit in Constantinople with the assignment of contacting Soviet authorities. On April 6, Miller and Slagel obtained passage on the *S.S. Albatross* to Novorossiysk, a port city overcrowded with refugees and showing the "ravages of revolution and neglect." They sought out Comrade Frumkin, Assistant Commissar of the regional capital of Rostov, who permitted them to live in his private railway car during their stay. However, he explained, the Commissariat of Foreign Affairs in Moscow would have to authorize the relief program. After hearing no response from Moscow, the two men telegraphed Moscow that they were coming. Moscow wired back, forbidding them to come. In June of 1921 they departed for Constantinople, feeling a sense of failure. Meanwhile, they met a Mennonite named A. J. Fast from the Kuban, who relayed to Halbstadt that two MCC workers were hoping to bring relief.

After eight months of attempting to penetrate Russia from Constantinople, A. J. Miller decided to try to enter Russia from the north. He took a train to Paris. At a station on the Italian-Swiss border, he picked up a newspaper and read that the American Relief Administration (ARA), headed by Herbert Hoover, had been asked to give relief aid in Russia, and that an ARA official was leaving for Riga to confer with Soviet officials. Two years earlier, Miller and three other Mennonites had met with Hoover in his Paris office.

Arriving in Paris, Miller phoned the London office of ARA and made an appointment to meet with Lyman Brown, chief of the ARA program in Europe. Miller then booked a seat on a six-passenger airplane headed for London; this, undoubtedly, was the first use of air travel by an MCC worker. He met with Brown and told of MCC's two efforts to enter Russia from the south. Brown discussed with him how MCC might be part of a larger ARA effort in Russia, an understanding to be negotiated in Riga. English Quakers in London introduced Miller to a Mr. Klishko at the Soviet Embassy who showed enthusiasm for MCC plans and gave Miller a letter to present to the Foreign Office in Moscow. En route to Riga, Miller attended in Geneva, Switzerland, a conference of thirty international relief organizations concerned about the Russian famine. He then headed for Moscow via Riga, Latvia, and arrived on August 27, 1921.

In the formerly elegant Savoy Hotel, Miller took a room that also became his office. Nearby was the Foreign Office and the headquarters of the Cheka, the dreaded secret police. On Monday, August 29, Miller appeared at the Foreign Office with a request that MCC be permitted to begin a relief program in the south "within reach of the railroad line from Sevastopol to Militopol, Alexandrovsk, Ekaterinoslav and Kharkov." He presented plans to assist the Russians in their relief program and requested between fifteen and twenty workers. He asserted that the MCC was prepared to enter Russia under the same terms as those of the ARA. He further pledged that the MCC would "refrain from all political activity, and carry on the work of relief in a spirit of fairness and openness in cooperation with the local committees."

Each night for nearly a month, Miller appeared at the Foreign Office to meet officials. The new Soviet officials preferred to work from midnight to seven in the morning. Eventually, Miller met Leo Borisovich Kamenev, member of the Politburo, president of the Moscow Soviet and president of the Central Commission for Combatting Famine. In those early days of the Lenin era, the aggressive Miller found open doors to the highest officials of the Soviet Union.

On October 1, Kamenev and Miller signed a contract permitting the American Mennonite Relief (AMR, the Russia-based branch of MCC) to operate. Miller had pressed hard for independence from government controls. Jacob Koekebakker, a Dutch Mennonite, arrived in Moscow and requested recognition for a Dutch agency. The Soviets instructed the Dutch Mennonites to operate under the umbrella of the AMR (MCC).

The authorization of the proudly independent Ukrainian Socialist Soviet Republic was still needed. Mennonite leader B. B. Janz arrived from Kharkov and accompanied Miller back to the

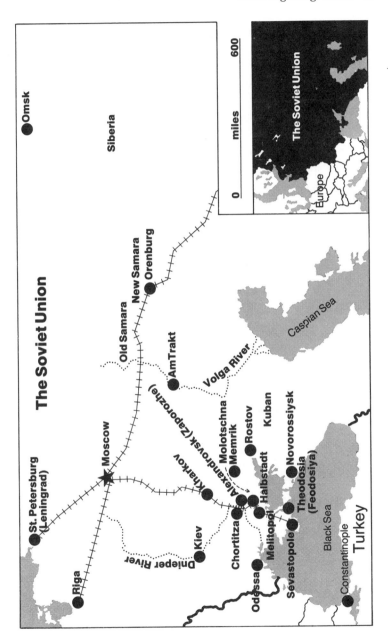

Ukrainian capital to negotiate the second contract. In Kharkov Miller and Janz entered the home of a friend of Janz, a Jewish doctor, who had been expelled from the Communist Party. Two Cheka secret police were also house guests, which surely contributed to interesting breakfast conversations. On October 21, 1921, the two highest Ukrainian officials, B. Yermostchenka and Khristian Georgiyevich Rakovsky, signed a contract with Miller, as well as a contract for the Dutch Mennonite agency.

In the sprawling city of Moscow were two Mennonites, Cornelius F. Klassen and Peter Froese, who had represented the Mennonite communities of East Russia and Siberia in negotiations with authorities. Klassen had served on the All Russian Relief Committee, on which the daughter of writer Leo Tolstoy was also member. The day Miller arrived in Moscow, the Cheka had dissolved the committee and temporarily imprisoned Klassen, Countess Tolstoy, and others. Peter Froese located Miller in the city and a close partnership of these Russian Mennonites and the American began. MCC needed information on community distribution networks among the scattered Mennonite communities in the Volga region and east toward the Urals. B. B. Janz had gathered such data and set a distribution system into motion. As winter set in, Klassen journeyed east to plan for the relief program.

Essential to the effectiveness of the MCC program was the work of Janz, Klassen, Froese, and scores of other Russian Mennonites who had organized committees. Of his colleagues, Miller later wrote: "Their achievements were monumental. And yet, in spite of all the hard fought struggles with government leaders . . . they have remained courageously at their posts . . . representatives of the Mennonites during more than eight years—when even the Communist Party leadership shifted. . . ."

With contracts signed, Miller sent cablegrams to the MCC office in Scottdale, Pennsylvania. Miller waited. He did not hear from Scottdale. Meanwhile, ARA relief aid became caught in a bureaucratic bottleneck that required all shipments to pass through Baltic ports, where ship after ship was tied up in icy harbors. MCC's buildup of relief supplies in Constantinople could not enter from the south. Miller left for Berlin to communicate with Scottdale. He learned that AMR had to operate under ARA with only one worker. The separate AMR agreements meant little to ARA officials who controlled the entrance of supplies and personnel. Returning to Moscow, Miller negotiated with Colonel William N. Haskell, chief of the ARA mission, who "was not acquainted with the American Mennonites" and dismissed their intended effort as one of minor importance. However, MCC gradually earned the respect of the ARA under whose umbrella it conducted most of its program.

The tangled exchange of correspondence among MCC Scottdale (Levi Mumaw), AMR Moscow (A. J. Miller), and ARA offices in London, New York, and Moscow suggest the inevitable problems experienced by isolated workers in the field, agonizing silences in intercontinental communication, and the discomfort of a small agency operating under an inattentive giant agency. Miller's intense feelings of frustration and exasperation, however, were soon alleviated by a flood of significant relief activity.

A cable arrived from MCC, authorizing the purchase of food in bulk. Two Russian Mennonites arrived from Am Trakt near Saratov with a report of need. They returned with authorization to draw from an ARA warehouse certain quantities of white flour, sugar, evaporated milk, rice, lard, and cocoa—the first MCC relief distribution in the Soviet Union. C. F. Klassen, meanwhile, returned from his inspection tour of the Volga regions. He told of "starving people clinging desperately to life." Miller directed relief allocations to the New Samara, Old Samara, and Orenburg settlements and to a group near Ufa. Some of the food, carried in sled caravans, arrived in time for Christmas 1921.

Farther south in the Ukraine, no MCC relief arrived by Christmas. B. B. Janz repeatedly begged for assistance for his people. Finally, he sent two men to Moscow to describe the suffering in the Molotschna and Chortitza colonies. "With bitterness in my heart," wrote Miller, "I had to send them back with nothing more than the promise to come as soon as possible." The delays were rooted in an upsurge of Ukrainian identity. Although AMR had an agreement with the Ukrainian government, ARA did not. Kharkov officials refused to allow ARA to operate in the south until there was also an understanding with their government.

The dispute was finally resolved. On February 24, Miller and Slagel met with the Mennonite relief committee in Alexandrovsk to select the neediest communities; on March 3, seven carloads of food from Constantinople arrived; on March 11, six carloads of food from the north arrived at Alexandrovsk; and later that month, AMR kitchens began feeding people in Chortitza, the Molotschna, and Gnadenfeld.

Arthur Slagel supervised the Ukrainian feeding programs. The MRA bought food at cost from the ARA. The Soviet government provided free rail transportation. Most of the food was distributed through AMR kitchens. In April and May, the feeding extended to seven additional districts (*Volost*), each with from five to twenty villages. The standard ration was 778 calories: a quarter-pound bread biscuit, cocoa twice weekly, beans once or twice weekly, rice or cornmeal cooked with sugar and milk. At first, the rations were limited to "families that had no food, no possibility of procuring any, and not more than one cow." Later, children, the elderly, the sick, and nursing and expectant mothers were given priority.

By fall of 1922, the need for clothing intensified. In the AMR area of operation, seventy thousand persons submitted a detailed wardrobe inventory to qualify for clothing distribution. Each person was assigned a credit unit on assessment of need, and each garment was assigned a unit value. With a network of village committees, AMR sought to distribute scarce clothing equitably.

ARA had developed a food and clothing remittance system: donors could pay ten dollars for a package containing 130 pounds of food which would be delivered to a recipient in Russia. For twenty dollars, a clothing remittance would provide thirty-two yards of cloth delivered to a designated relative or friend. Mennonites in North America contributed an estimated two hundred thousand dollars for this forerunner of the "Care" package.

The drought brought not only hunger and starvation but also destroyed the resources for recovery. Fields lay unplowed and unplanted. In 1922, Ukrainian acreage under cultivation had declined to 32 percent of 1914 levels. By 1922, the number of horses had dropped to 20 percent of 1914 levels. In distant Whitewater, Kansas, a Mennonite farmer heard about the problem and offered to pay for a tractor and plow. In Hillsboro, Kansas, the bedfast editor of *Vorwaerts*, J. G. Ewert, rallied Mennonite interest in contributing to a fund to buy tractors, and Midwesterners assembled funds to buy fifteen tractors. The Canadian Mennonite Board of Colonization took up the cause. On June 24, 1922, the MCC decided to purchase tractors. Levi Mumaw went to Detroit and on special terms bought twenty-five Fordson tractors and Oliver gang plows with twelve-inch shares, together with spare parts. On July 24, the shipment left New York; by September 23, all twenty-five tractors were in operation in Alexandrovsk and elsewhere. In six weeks, 4,327 acres had been plowed, including 714 acres planted in rye by the AMR.

"Wonderthing," people called the Fordson tractor. Besides the opening of the first food kitchen, the most exciting community event in Halbstadt was the first plowing. The Halbstadt Tractor Committee wrote: "Next to the blessings of God, it will be the tractors that will rebuild Russian farm industry .... through the tractor work the axe is put to the root of the famine." On October 23, 1922, Miller cabled MCC: "Rush second tractor shipment.... Should include equipment for lights." On December 23, the second shipment of twenty-five Fordson-Oliver outfits, together with a Ford touring car, left New York. Three MCC workers, G. G. Hiebert, Howard Yoder, and Dan Schroeder, went to Russia to oversee tractor usage and maintenance. Enthusiastic Soviet officials offered the AMR large tracts of land for grain production. MCC, thus, played a role in the mechanization of Soviet agriculture.

MCC identified the tractor project as "reconstruction," signifying a shift from emergency relief to long-term development. In August 1923, the last feeding kitchens in the Ukraine closed. MCC's attention shifted to needs in Siberia. With many experiencing hunger in Siberia but few starving, the MCC emphasized "helping the needy to help themselves" and facilitated seed loans and horse and cow deliveries. In 1924, the arrival of 139 MCC-imported sheep in Siberia gave impetus to spinning, weaving, and the production of clothing.

Meanwhile, in 1923 and the years following, trainloads of Mennonites left the colonies and emigrated to Canada. On December 30, 1924, the MCC acknowledged that "the work for which the committee was organized has about come to a close" and "certain organizations supporting the work have taken action for disbanding." MCC instructed A. J. Miller to close the program.

On July 12, 1926, Miller left Moscow. He recuperated for some months in the French Alps, and returned home on May· 14, 1927, to report to the Executive Committee at Scottdale. Participants looked back with satisfaction on an undertaking well done. These feelings were reflected in the reports of MCC workers included in *Feeding the Hungry*, a 465-page summary of the Russian relief experience, edited by MCC Chairman P. C. Hiebert. Soviet officials evaluating the operations of all foreign relief agencies stated that "judging from the quality of the products which were delivered, the first place goes to the

French Red Cross, then the second place goes to the Mennonites."

In the MCC program and in the parallel Canadian Mennonite assistance to twenty-one thousand immigrants from Russia, Mennonites manifested the greatest outpouring of corporate benevolence in their history. MCC had spent $1,300,000 in Russian relief, feeding in 1922 and 1923, seventy-five thousand people, including sixty thousand Mennonites. Nine thousand Mennonites may have been saved from starvation. North American Mennonites gained confidence in their ability to undertake major projects. Trust among separated groups grew. Horizons of awareness of wars, revolutions, and world problems broadened. Patterns for doing relief and reconstruction etched themselves into the minds of a people. The shared experience of famine, feeding, and exodus focused in MCC as an enduring symbol of what it meant to be a Mennonite.

3

Settling Refugees:
Paraguay

During the last months of 1929, more than ten thousand Mennonites in the Soviet Union found temporary lodging in Moscow and its suburbs, hoping to escape the terror of Stalin's collectivization drive. Canadian historian Harvey Dyck recalls that as a boy growing up in British Columbia, he discovered a photograph of a frightened-looking man whom he learned was his Uncle Peter. Little was known about Peter:

> My uncle, and thousands of other Mennonites in Russia, had tried to flee from . . . Stalin, who didn't want them to be Christians any longer. He wanted to jail and even to kill some. They had flocked to the capital city of Moscow, hoping that Canada, where many of their relatives lived, would give them a new home. But Canada had refused. Most of the Mennonites at Moscow had then been shipped off to frozen Siberia as slave workers . . . the lucky ones [escaped]. They finally were able to find a new home for themselves in a jungle . . . called Paraguay. A few even managed to get to Canada. . . . Uncle Peter apparently just missed being one of them.

The 1930-32 migration of more than fifteen hundred Mennonites to Paraguay is a story of significance in MCC history, for it was the plight of these desperate families, huddled in

German refugee camps, which thrust the fledgling Mennonite Central Committee into a new burst of activity. Established as an emergency relief agency in 1920, the Russia relief program had concluded in 1925, leaving the young MCC without an agenda. The 1929 crisis in the Soviet Union, however, in which some thirteen thousand Mennonites fled the countryside under political and economic repression, pulled the agency into a massive effort for refugee relocation. Twenty years later, after the devastating events of World War II, Mennonites again fled the Soviet Union hoping to join relatives in Canada. Again MCC transported and settled Mennonite refugees in Paraguay.

Today, more than five decades after the first European Mennonite families arrived at Puerto Casado on the Paraguay River, MCC continues to assist refugees. What forces in 1929 and 1930 awakened the dormant Mennonite Central Committee and led so many German-speaking persons to the formidable Chaco of Paraguay?

In 1929 the international press picked up the story of the desperate refugees fleeing their homes for Moscow. Soviet authorities clamped down on the more than ten thousand "counter-revolutionary" Mennonites by refusing rail tickets to colonists and by seizing refugee passengers from Moscow-bound trains. The fleeing Mennonites believed that if only they could reach the safety of Germany, Canada would welcome them. But Canada, which had allowed twenty thousand Mennonite immigrants to the prairie provinces from 1923 to 1927, now cited agricultural depression and high unemployment as reasons for closing its gates to new immigrants; undoubtedly, nativism also played a role.

In Germany, however, a rising tide of anti-Soviet sentiment, together with nationalist and humanitarian concern, kept the plight of these fellow "Germans" in the national spotlight. "The fate of a German is the concern of every German," many cried. German foreign office officials intervened, persuading the Soviet government in November of 1929 to allow the remaining Mennonites in Moscow to enter Germany. By this time, however, Soviet officials had arrested many of the refugees, forcing them back to their villages to face starvation or banishing them to Siberia. Many of the eight thousand loaded onto trucks and trains died along the way. By the time Soviet authorities changed their policy to permit Mennonites to enter Germany, only 5,600 remained in Moscow to receive their passports. Germany would accept the refugees temporarily to keep them alive, but because of the deep economic crisis facing the country, the refugees needed to find a permanent home immediately.

Early in the fall of 1929, Mennonite Central Committee and the Canadian Mennonite Board of Colonization had promised the German government that they would do everything possible to resettle the refugees. Benjamin H. Unruh, a Mennonite leader in Karlsruhe, Germany, served as emissary between North American agencies and German government officials. *Bruder in Not* (Brethren in Need), a newly formed interfaith welfare council in Germany, mobilized German sentiment in favor of the refugees. Moreover, as historian Frank Epp described in *Mennonite Exodus*, the Canadian Mennonite Board of Colonization made strong appeals to the Canadian government, promising to support fully "any Mennonite emigrants from Russia who may be admitted into Canada toward the end that they may not become a public charge or a burden on any government."

In early December 1929, after the government of Canada had announced its decision to deny entry to all but a few Mennonites, Mennonite Central Committee met in Chicago and appointed a study commission of three—P. C. Hiebert, Harold S. Bender, and Maxwell H. Kratz—to explore other alternatives for resettlement. Within a month the commission recommended Paraguay, basing its decision on reports from Canadian Mennonite leaders of the newly formed Menno Colony settlement in the Chaco, from Mennonite missionaries in South

Bolivia

Brazil

Chaco

Puerto Casado

Fernheim Menno
Neuland

Paraguay

Paraguay River

Concepción

Volendam Primaveria
Friesland

Argentina Asunción KM 81 Sommerfeld
Bergthal

0   miles   150
___ Trans-Chaco highway
□ Mennonite colonies
  c. 1948

Peru
Bolivia   Brazil
Chile
Paraguay
Argentina
Uruguay

Parana River

America, and from an American official in Asuncion who had once visited Menno Colony in the Chaco for a few hours.

In 1930 Paraguay was an isolated country with a population of less than a million. Most Paraguayans lived east of the Paraguay River. To the west of the river lay the vast, dry Chaco populated by only a few nomadic Indians and the newly established Menno settlement. Paraguay had a history of political instability and civil war. Comparable in size to California, landlocked Paraguay was unquestionably poor. In the 1930s Orie O. Miller of MCC compared its gross national product with that of Lancaster County, Pennsylvania.

The Paraguayan government had offered to accept the penniless refugees, including the elderly and those with physical and mental disabilities. The MCC-appointed commission noted the contrast between this open-ended invitation and the more stringent Canadian immigration policies. In addition, the commission considered Paraguay attractive because of its 1921 *Privilegium*, a law promising all Mennonite immigrants freedom of worship, exemption from military service, rights of inheritance, and autonomy to maintain Mennonite-administered schools. In 1926 and 1927, the *Privilegium* had drawn 1,770 conservative Mennonites from Manitoba and Saskatchewan to the Paraguayan Chaco. Despite hardships, these earlier Mennonite colonists were surviving, and Paraguay's *Privilegium* now beckoned the majority of refugees clinging to each other in German camps.

Early in 1930, Mennonite Central Committee sent Harold S. Bender to Germany to make arrangements for transport. During the next two years, more than two thousand Mennonites who had fled Moscow in late 1929 entered the Paraguayan Chaco. Approximately a thousand other Mennonites went to Brazil as a result of negotiations through the German government. Before Canada closed her gates completely, another thousand entered Canada. Never before had MCC undertaken or even considered such a massive relocation effort.

Two major components of the Paraguayan settlement were financial backing—with MCC raising $100,000 among U.S. Mennonites and securing loans from the German government—and overseeing the logistics of relocation. Refugees sailed from German ports to Buenos Aires, continued the journey by riverboat to Asuncion and Puerto Casado, and finished the journey by wagon into the heart of the Chaco. More than three hundred immigrants from Siberia followed an eastern route of escape to Harbin in Manchuria, finally joining their Mennonite kin in the Chaco.

Beginning in 1931, MCC assumed a partnership role with the colonists and helped them to develop new communities. The new settlers needed land. Even before their arrival MCC had secured parcels from the Corporacion Paraguaya, a holding company which several years earlier had helped to settle the Menno Colony. With MCC's assistance the new colonists founded *Kolonia Fernheim*, meaning "a faraway home." They reproduced the land settlement patterns established in Russia and formed villages of approximately twenty-five families apiece, with a central road running through the colony. MCC's Orie O. Miller helped the colonists to negotiate land prices, originally set at eight dollars an acre, down to three dollars. As the wordwide Depression wore on, however, land prices dropped, and in 1937 MCC bought the Corporacion Paraguaya at a renegotiated price of forty cents an acre.

Miller, returning from a 1931 trip to the Chaco, saw the new settlement as promising:

> On the third day of our visit about two inches of rain fell, the first season, and as if by magic the whole landscape changed from winter with its dust and desert-like appearance to the green freshness of spring. At once everyone went to work, plowing, spading, and planting. We also visited [colony center Filadelfia... A steam engine, a sawmill, an oil press, several small mills for grinding flour and feed, all of which were purchased in Germany last year by the Mennonite Central Committee, are already on the spot and being set up.

Others viewed the situation more grimly. The isolated Chaco lacked commercial markets and transportation networks for cotton, the Mennonites' chief crop. S. C. Yoder, writing of early conditions in *For Conscience' Sake*, asserted that "from the beginning there were those who saw no future in the Chaco, and were discontented." Some disillusioned colonists, convinced they had been pushed into a bad situation, directed their anger at MCC. They felt that MCC had abandoned them with too little continued support. In North America, however, Mennonites were experiencing the grinding poverty of the Great Depression.

MCC's decision to settle the refugees in Paraguay appears to have had rational grounds, namely the time constraints and limited options. A few more refugees might have entered Canada if they could have stayed longer in Germany. Brazil was an alternative but only at the price of compulsory military service. And in Paraguay, the already established Menno Colony had modeled the possibilities of a "new start" in the wilderness. One student of the migration comments:

> The questions about the decision . . . were only raised after the immigrants were there. . . . It was probably inevitable that, after the first joy of escaping Russia and finding a new home, disillusionment would set in in the face of hardships. The easiest scapegoat for that frustration and anger was MCC.

Throughout the 1930s the colonists struggled with harsh frontier realities. Ninety-two members of the Fernheim Colony died the first year, many of a typhoid epidemic. The Chaco had repeated crop failures, droughts, and grasshopper attacks. The Bolivian-Paraguayan War raging from 1932 to 1935 in the Chaco threatened the land the Mennonites had so recently acquired. Colony villages viewed with apprehension the Chulupi and Lengua Indian groups who also lived in the Chaco. Mennonite farmers saw their incomes pushed down even further as wartime inflation devoured foreign payments for their cotton.

In 1936 one settler declared the Chaco frontier experience "a time of bitter testing." In 1937 Fernheim was weakened further when 748 colonists splintered away, moving east across the Paraguay River to what they believed would be more fertile soil. There the group formed Friesland Colony.

During the 1940s MCC continued to channel resources to the Fernheim Colony, as well as limited assistance to Friesland. On a 1941 trip to Fernheim, Orie O. Miller brought physician John Schmidt. Schmidt had intended to stay a year, but in 1943, his wife, Clara, a nurse, joined him, and they continued to work in Paraguay for many years. In 1940 the Society of Brothers (Hutterites) in England established a colony of 350 at Primavera in eastern Paraguay, and Vernon Schmidt and members of the Friesland Colony assisted this *Bruderhof* in constructing a hospital.

During the 1940s, MCC, joined by the Mennonite colonies, introduced a series of "thank you projects." MCC sponsored child-feeding programs and a hookworm control campaign among Paraguayan Indians near Friesland Colony. Deeply grateful to the Paraguayan government for accepting the refugees, MCC also built a leper colony for Paraguayans.

Beginning in 1944, MCC sought to develop a road to the isolated Chaco settlements. From 1954 to 1956, Vernon Buller, with an MCC bulldozer, improved the road between the narrow gauge railway and the Chaco colonies. In 1955 the U.S. government began funding the construction of a 250-mile graded road linking Asuncion with the colony center of Filadelfia. MCCer Harry Harder directed young MCC and Paraguayan Mennonite workers in building this lifeline to wider South American and world markets. During the next decade the Paraguayans extended this Trans-Chaco Highway beyond the colonies 250 miles to the northwest.

Thus, the Mennonite colonies and the neighboring Indian groups emerged as a field ripe for development. North American mission boards sent Mennonite Brethren and General Conference Mennonite pastors to Paraguay to minister to spiritual needs. One effect of some of these pastoral visits from North America was a strengthening of the walls of separation between conference groups.

The "Mennonite commonwealth" which arose in the thirties, although analogous to Russian Mennonite models, developed unique communal and centralized patterns. Each colony developed a traditional church and community system that centered around the *Oberschulze*, the powerful secular leader who worked together with a council of village leaders. The cooperative, the colony's major economic institution, served not only as a marketing outlet but also as colony general store, provider of public utilities, builder of roads, processor of cotton and peanuts, and cheese manufacturer. The first cooperative in Fernheim modeled cooperative structures not only for other Mennonite colonies but also other Paraguayan communities.

Whereas in Russia czarist officials had intruded on the colonies at many levels, the Chaco colonies were almost completely free of Paraguayan national government interference. Rarely did the Chaco colonies look to the distant Asuncion government for help. In fact the Mennonite colonies acted in behalf of the national government in collecting taxes and conducting the ten-year census.

The autonomous Mennonite commonwealth became a dual society of local government (Oberschulze, council, and cooperative) and churches (Mennonite Brethren, Alliance, and General Conference Mennonite) functioning with mutual tensions and yet reinforcing one another. MCC administrators visiting Paraguay usually made a round of visits to the Oberschulzen and church leaders to negotiate understandings for joint programming.

Meanwhile, in Europe, a militant National Socialist movement was on the rise, attracting many German-speaking people both within and beyond German borders. A resurgent pride in

German *Kultur* (culture) and German *Volk* (race) influenced many Mennonite emigrants from Europe to sympathize with the German *Reich*. They remembered with gratitude that in 1929 Germany had accepted them when doors to Canada, the United States, and other countries had been closed. In Paraguay, these loyalties led some colonists to form paramilitary German groups. After Paraguayan authorities banished two ardent pro-Nazi colony leaders from the Chaco, the issue receded. Some tensions lingered, however, between pro-Nazi and neutral factions and between some colonists and MCC.

In 1945, at the end of World War II, Mennonite Central Committee again faced the difficult task of relocating refugees. In the last months of the war thirty-five thousand Mennonites left the Soviet Union with retreating German troops. Many died during flight and most were captured and repatriated to slave labor camps in Siberia. Twelve thousand Mennonite refugees from Russia escaped repatriation and were found in all parts of the occupation zones in Germany, with several hundred in Holland.

Beginning in 1945, the United Nations took responsibility for caring for more than a million European refugees. In August 1945 MCC sent C. F. Klassen, a Canadian member of the MCC Executive Committee, to Europe for five months to tour the Allied occupation zones and negotiate with military authorities for the protection of Mennonite refugees. He met with hundreds of scattered refugees, many living in constant fear of repatriation. Klassen, who had been on the MCC staff in Moscow in the 1920s and had been an immigrant to Canada, brought hope to those living in poverty and peril in war-devastated Germany.

Most refugees wished to migrate to Canada, which was beginning to set up immigration procedures on a case-by-case basis. Meanwhile, these thousands of refugees in Europe, threatened with repatriation to the Soviet Union, felt that their lives were at great risk. Particularly vulnerable were the refugees slipping into Berlin, an island of safety in the Soviet Zone. In 1946, Peter and Elfrieda Dyck, MCC refugee directors, provided a community of refuge in the American sector of Berlin. By late 1946, the refugee colony, located only a few miles from the Soviet Sector, had grown to more than one thousand. Clearly, the refugees could not stay. MCC studied various possibilities. Might these displaced Mennonites go to Mexico, Brazil, Argentina, Uruguay, Paraguay?

In October 1946, the situation had become even more desperate and many refugees agreed to go to Paraguay, where colonists from previous migrations stood ready to assist them. The refugees were disappointed that they would not be permitted to enter Canada, but they looked forward to establishing new homes in a safe, stable community. As they prepared to travel to South America, several logistical hurdles remained. In order for the Russian Mennonite refugees to qualify for financial support from the Intergovernmental Committee on Refugees, they had to establish Dutch origin. American and European Mennonite historians attested to this, and the agency promised $160,000 in aid for the transport to Paraguay. Mennonite Central Committee coordinated the relocation effort in close cooperation with the United States government and officials overseas. Preparations entailed obtaining visas, reuniting families, and determining criteria for who might go and who must stay.

Years later, MCC leader William T. Snyder recalled phoning George L. Warren, a U.S. State Department official sympathetic to the Mennonite effort, with the victorious news that the first ship carrying Mennonites had left Bremerhaven, Germany. Warren responded: "You've done what none of the agencies have been able to do.... Your people had the nerve to take risks. You were also willing to put money on the line to move your people."

The refugees sailed first from Holland and then Germany in

four major voyages: 2,303 on the *Volendam*, which arrived in Buenos Aires in February of 1947, and subsequent transports on the *General Heinzelmann*, the *Charlton Monarch*, and again on the *Volendam*. By the end of 1948, nearly five thousand new settlers had arrived in Paraguay and formed two new colonies, Volendam in east Paraguay and Neuland in the Chaco.

MCC appointed experienced administrators—C. A. DeFehr, C. J. Dyck, and others—to purchase land, aid in settlement needs, and to provide linkage between colony leaders and North American organizations. Other Mennonite refugees from Russia and Germany made their way to Uruguay and Argentina. The Canadian option soon opened, and during the postwar migration more than seven thousand refugees went directly from Europe to Canada. After 1950, an estimated eight thousand Paraguayan Mennonites, assisted by Canadian relatives, left Paraguay for Canada. A significant contingent, known as the *Ruckwanderer*, returned to Germany. Had such an exodus not occurred, the present Mennonite population of thirteen thousand in Paraguay might have been tripled. In recent years some Chaco-born Mennonites from Canada have moved back to their native Paraguay.

Given the less than enthusiastic response of earlier immigrants to Paraguay, why did MCC in 1947 and 1948 choose to resettle thousands of German-speaking refugees in Paraguay? Again, the decision was made under duress and the options were limited. A deciding factor was the substantial MCC resettlement experience. By 1947, MCC had a major program of economic development underway in Paraguay, with no less than twenty-seven North American workers serving as agriculturists, health workers, teachers, and engineers. Another significant factor was the increasing stability of the existing colonies.

By 1951, MCC had spent approximately two million dollars in Paraguay in two decades. The refugee resettlement program had ended, and MCC began trimming the flow of resources to Paraguay as the Chaco economy improved. In the 1950s, MCC solicited from the U.S. government a million dollar loan for the colonies, a development that MCC administrator Edgar Stoesz points to as perhaps "the most significant thing MCC did to help the colonies ... economically." During the following years, MCC turned toward pressing needs in other areas of the world, applying its refugee assistance know-how in such places as Bangladesh, Bolivia, Afghanistan, Kampuchea, Vietnam, Zaire, and El Salvador.

MCC has received occasional criticism for its refugee aid programs. Some constituents have chided MCC for not giving more support to the colonists in the Chaco during their years of early struggle. Some have urged MCC to work more vigorously on behalf of Mennonites in the Soviet Union wishing to emigrate. Meanwhile, the MCC partnership with the Mennonite colonists in service to Paraguayan Indians has yielded new satisfactions. In recent years MCC has expanded its commitment to the more than ten million persons cited by the United Nations as refugees and displaced persons. In 1980 MCC reaffirmed its historic stance toward refugees,

> people who know no home but a tent, whose only food is an irregular ration, and whose future is uncertain and seemingly devoid of hope .... [A] solution to the refugee problem may well begin with us.

MCC's role in the two major migrations to Paraguay firmly established MCC's continuing mission of service and justice for refugees. Since 1975 MCC has assisted seven thousand refugees—most from Southeast Asia—to emigrate and to find homes in Canada and the United States. North American Mennonites who were once immigrants are sensitive to the needs of those who have fled from their homes. Similarly, the Mennonites in Paraguay long ago completed the transition from tenuous refugee status to stable community life. While still in the process of getting established in a new land, these colonists saw around them a nomadic native people and helped them to establish new agricultural settlements, bringing to full circle a program of assistance initiated by Mennonite Central Committee.

World War II and the Postwar Years

On September 1, 1939, twenty years after the end of the Great War, Germany invaded Poland. Within hours this war became worldwide in scope. It continued for six years until August 14, 1945, when the Japanese surrendered. Hitler, Mussolini, six million Jews, and thirty million others lay dead. Atomic bombs had obliterated the Japanese cities of Hiroshima and Nagasaki. It had been the most cruel and destructive war in history.

During World War II MCC administered sixty-two camps and units under Civilian Public Service, a program of alternative service for conscientious objectors (C.O.'s). In Canada a loose coalition of Mennonites, the predecessor of MCC Canada, provided liaison to the Canadian government for a similar program for approximately six thousand Mennonite C.O.'s.

In 1940, hampered by wartime restrictions, MCC initiated small service programs in France, Germany, and England. Late in the war MCC began programs in Egypt, India, and China. In 1943 MCC gathered sixty-five conscientious objectors for a summer of intensive training for overseas service. At the end of the war MCC launched relief efforts in war-ravaged Europe and China which dwarfed its programs of the 1920s in Russia.

Two case studies tell the story of World War II and its
aftermath. The first describes the alternative service programs
in Canada and the U.S., both of which brought divided
Mennonites together in a common task and prepared them
organizationally to launch a large relief program in Europe in
the late 1940s. The second tells of MCC's relief and
rehabilitation program in the four zones of defeated Germany.

Among many other programs from Europe which merit
study are these: the spin-off of auxiliary programs such as *Der
Mennonit,* Agape Verlag, Basel/Bienenberg Bible School, and
voluntary service; working with European peace groups in the
Puidoux peace conferences; providing a search service for
families of refugees from Russia; and the experience of one
thousand "Seagoing Cowboys" on boats carrying heifers and
horses to Europe.

4

Mennonites Go to War:
Alternative Service

*This thing is in our blood for four hundred years
and you can't take it away from us like you'd
crack a piece of kindling over your knee.*
                                        —Jacob H. Janzen

Wars bring Mennonites together. Wars bring out the best, or sometimes the worst, in Mennonites. In World War II, Mennonites concerned about military service learned much about national politics. The war tested Mennonite Central Committee's capacity to gain the trust of varied constituent groups as well as its ability to mobilize personnel and finances. In the U.S., MCC administered an alternative service program for five thousand men. In Canada, Mennonites and other peace church groups did not administer an alternative service program. Official Canadian and U.S. responses to issues of conscientious objection differed greatly.

Canada declared war on Germany on September 10, 1939, twenty-seven months before the United States entered the war. On August 27, 1940, in reaction to the sweep of German armies across the Netherlands and Belgium, the Canadian government published the National War Services Regulations. Six weeks later, on October 10, 1940, the United States approved the Selective Service and Training Act (the Burke Wadsworth bill). The following two sections trace the wartime pilgrimages of Canadian peace groups and a U.S. conscientious-objection coalition.

The Canadian Pattern

By the end of World War I, Canadian Mennonites had been exempted from military service. In 1922-23, with the coming of additional immigrants from Russia, Mennonites asked for complete exemption. In 1935 David Toews, Mennonite leader from Saskatchewan, sought and obtained governmental affirmation of this right. In July 1939, J. Harold Sherk, representing several Ontario groups, met with a minister in the federal cabinet and reported afterward that "the MacKenzie King Government would take the necessary steps to insure for our people freedom of conscience." In July 1940, Ontario-based Mennonite and Amish Mennonite groups, together with the Brethren in Christ, Old Order Dunkers, and the Society of Friends, formed the Conference of Historic Peace Churches and appointed a committee of three to speak to officials in Ottawa. David Toews joined the committee. On September 5, 1940, this peace church delegation met with the Associate Deputy Minister of War, who declared that he would not "deal with every group separately" and outlined plans for "military noncombatant service."

In Western Canada, Mennonites were divided. Those who had immigrated in the 1870s, known as the *Kanadier*, hoped for the total exemption they had enjoyed during World War I. Those who had arrived in the 1920s, known as the *Russlaender*, had participated in forestry and medical corps service in czarist Russia and now pressed for alternative service. Efforts to bring these two groups together failed.

On October 16, 1940, the Ontario group submitted a plan entitled "Canadian Fellowship Service," which proposed agricultural, forestry, and land reclamation work in lieu of military service. On October 22, a group of Russlaender Mennonites submitted a similar alternative service plan. Three weeks later, a joint East-West delegation of eight met with the two deputy ministers of National War Services, who showed no enthusiasm for the proposals. The deputies responded that "no provision should be made for conscientious objectors." They proposed noncombatant service under military control, promising that the men would not be required to wear uniforms. The following day the delegation submitted an amplified proposal for alternative service, signed by all eight. One delegate remained after the meeting to express a personal interest to the deputy ministers in medical corps service under military supervision. On November 22, the peace church delegates again met with the deputy ministers, who prodded them to accept a medical corps option. They refused. One official tried intimidation: "What will you do if we shoot you?" Jacob H. Janzen, who had experienced the revolution in Russia, replied:

> Listen, Major General, I want to tell you something. You can't scare us like that. I've looked down too many rifle barrels in my time to be scared in that way. This thing is in our blood for four hundred years and you can't take it away from us like you'd crack a piece of kindling over your knee. I was before a firing squad twice. We believe in this.

The delegation decided to bypass the deputies, and approached the Minister, the Honourable James G. Gardiner.

The Minister received them warmly. The delegates explained, "While it is true that some ... would be prepared ... to undertake ambulance work under military supervision, we feel that the large number of our men are strongly averse to undertaking any form of service under military authority." Gardiner responded, "There are one hundred and one things you fellows can do without fighting; we'll see that you get them." On December 24, 1940, the Canadian government amended the National War Services Regulations to provide for alternative service. The government agreed to provide room and board, and to pay each man fifty cents a day. The regulations permitted the peace churches to appoint religious advisers.

In July 1941, the first camp opened eighty-three miles northwest of Sault Sainte Marie, Ontario. The Department of Highways employed the men to work on the Trans-Canada Highway. In 1942, forestry camps opened in British Columbia; by 1943, seventeen camps were engaged in forestry protection and two in national park projects. The Department of Mines and Resources supervised five camps in Alberta, two in Saskatchewan, two in Ontario, and one in Manitoba. A camp in Saskatchewan was engaged in highway construction. On May 1, 1943, the Alternative Service System was transferred from military control to the Ministry of Labour, a civilian agency. Thereafter, most Canadian conscientious objectors served on farms and in factories. By June 1944, all but seven camps were closed.

By March 31, 1944, 8,932 men had been classified as conscientious objectors (C.O.'s) and were given a "postponement of military service." Approximately 63 percent of these were Mennonites, 20 percent Doukhobors, 10 percent Plymouth Brethren, Christadelphians, and Pentecostals, and 3 percent were Jehovah's Witnesses. On August 15, 1946, all C.O.'s returned to civilian life.

During the World War II experience, Mennonites and other peace-related groups in Canada never established a central organization for coordinating their responses to conscription issues. This contrasted with the arrangement in the United States. In 1944, upon his return from a third trip to Canada, Paul Comly French, executive secretary of the United States National Service Board for Religious Objectors (NSBRO), reported: "This program is more satisfactory to individuals . . . than the American system, but I have grave doubts as to whether it contributes as effectively to the total pacifist witness against war as the American system of men operating in groups."

The Civilian Public Service Program in the United States

World War I had resulted in unhappy experiences for conscientious objectors in the United States. Large numbers were drafted into the Army, where they were pressured into doing noncombatant service. Many who refused were court-martialed and imprisoned. In 1940, when Congress was considering draft legislation, the historic peace churches—Brethren, Friends, and Mennonites—and other groups urged that Congress provide for an alternative service program that would be sensitive to the rights of conscientious objectors. Officials who drafted the Selective Service and Training Act of 1940 (the Burke Wadsworth bill) broadened the definition of conscientious objection to include all "those by reason of religious training and belief" who could not participate in war. Under the new law, registrants who were denied C.O. status by their local draft boards could appeal.

Rather than being inducted into the military, C.O.'s were assigned to do "work of national importance under civilian direction." During the next six and a half years, twelve thousand men were assigned to Civilian Public Service camps. Of these, 4,665 (38 percent) were Mennonites. Following the Mennonites in number were Brethren, Friends, Methodists, and members of more than eighty other sects and denominations.

Members of the historic peace churches—spurred by the problems pacifists had encountered during World War I—had met occasionally in the intervening years to consider a united approach to conscription. In 1935 at Newton, Kansas, a group of Brethren, Friends, and Mennonites had adopted a "Plan of Unified Action in Case the United States Is Involved in War," which called for alternative civilian service for C.O.'s. Various delegations went to Washington to present the C.O. cause. From these cooperative efforts emerged the National Service Board for Religious Objectors (NSBRO), which represented the peace churches and other denominations. Officials of the Selective Service System, fearful that "misunderstandings and confusion" might result from agreements with different groups, had urged that "one central representative body be formed through which all matters could be cleared by Selective Service."

The Brethren, Friends, and Mennonites, with no clear picture of what lay ahead, agreed to divide equally the costs of the NSBRO. A board of seven was formed, with representatives chosen by the Methodists, Disciples of Christ, American Friends Service Committee (AFSC), Brethren Service Committee (BSC), Mennonite Central Committee, Federal Council of Churches, and the Fellowship of Reconciliation. M. R. Zigler of the BSC was elected chairman; Orie O. Miller of MCC, vice-chairman; Paul Furnas of the AFSC, treasurer; and Paul Comly French, executive secretary.

In May 1941, the first Mennonite CPS camp opened in the facilities of a former Civilian Conservation Corps camp near Grottoes, Virginia. CPS men worked with the Soil Conservation Service (SCS), and eventually, Mennonite Central Committee operated eleven base camps linked to the agency. In addition, MCC administered six camps with work under the direction of the U.S. Forest Service, four with the National Park Service, two with the Bureau of Reclamation, and one with the Farm Security Administration.

Beginning in 1943, many CPS men transferred from base camps to various special projects. By August 1945, 550 men were in dairy work; by December 1945, more than 1,500 men in twenty-six units were serving institutions for the mentally ill and mentally retarded. Other men entered projects of hookworm control with the Public Health Service and served in "guinea pig" projects of the Office of Scientific Research and Development. In 1943 Selective Service granted the Friends, Brethren, and Mennonites permission to send CPS men to West China to work with the British Friends in relief medical, and development projects. After the first eight men were sent, Congressional action canceled the program. The AFSC, BSC, and MCC also opened service units in Puerto Rico for community development.

Men in CPS base camps were not paid for their work; those in special projects received a fifteen-dollar allowance per month. Mennonite churches contributed more than three million dollars to operate the CPS program. In 1941, church members were asked to contribute fifty cents per member for CPS support. By 1946, when the program ended, the suggested quotas for each Mennonite church member had totaled $21.45. Approximately one half of the Mennonite men drafted during World War II served in CPS.

The CPS program operated under dual administration. Selective Service furnished "general administrative and policy supervision and inspection" and covered transportation costs to the camps. NSBRO, supported by commitments from the three historic peace churches, agreed to finance and supervise other aspects of the program, including day-to-day camp operations. This agreement was renewed from time to time. In the last months of the program, some church groups, concerned that the contract made them party to the enforcement of conscription, withdrew.

During the migration efforts of the 1920s, Canadian Mennonites had been schooled in the ways of national politics. In the U.S., World War II provided Mennonites with a crash course in politics. Before the 1940s, few Mennonites had worked in Washington; now twenty worked for NSBRO. Never had so many Mennonites written to officials or traveled regularly to nation's capital. Mennonite eyes were focused on Washington.

Melvin Gingerich, in his book *Service for Peace* (1949), and William Janzen, in his dissertation "The Limits of Liberty in Canada: The Experience of the Mennonites, Hutterites, and Doukhobors" (1981), have described Mennonite involvement in World War II alternative service programs. A primary source with insight into the political education of American Mennonites during the war is the thousand-page diary of NSBRO's executive secretary, Paul Comly French. French, a member of the Society of Friends and author of *We Won't Murder* (1940), had given crucial testimony on conscription in Washington, D.C. From 1936-39, he had headed the Federal Writers Project in Pennsylvania. The first president of the Newspaper Guild of Philadelphia, French worked for the *Philadelphia Record*. His diary, which records events from July 10, 1940, to December 31, 1946, is now housed in the Swarthmore College Peace Collection, Swarthmore, Pennsylvania. The following description of MCC's involvement in conscientious-objection issues in wartime Washington is derived from French's diary.

NSBRO was a fragile coalition. Each peace group protected its particular identity and had its own set of expectations. The Brethren and Mennonites, who between them represented 50 percent of the C.O.'s in CPS, wanted some collaboration within NSBRO, but not too close a collaboration, since both the BSC and MCC wished to give a distinctive stamp to their respective programs. Charles Boss of the Methodists and James Crain of the Disciples favored close cooperation. The Fellowship of Reconciliation (FOR) and the Federal Council of Churches sent mixed signals on collaboration. Throughout the war a debate smoldered within FOR as to whether it should withdraw from NSBRO, signifying its protest against conscription. The American Friends Service Committee, which had done more than any other group to secure provision for alternative service for C.O.'s and had expected to administer the program, found itself a minority voice within NSBRO. The AFSC, and its executive secretary Clarence Pickett in particular, often disagreed on issues with NSBRO administrator French.

NSBRO held together through six years of crises because the C.O. community had a common foe—the war effort—and constituted a minority voice, with few highly placed friends in Washington to promote its concerns. No viable alternative plan emerged which had a chance of gaining congressional and presidential approval. Conscientious objectors were stuck until the war's end with an imperfect machine with which NSBRO, the church agencies and Selective Service kept tinkering.

Although the NSBRO staff found some Selective Service staff to be persistently antagonistic, the wartime collaboration of peace churches and military leaders held together in part because General Lewis B. Hershey wanted it to. Hershey, who presided over the drafting of fourteen million men, gave disproportionate time to the twelve thousand C.O.'s. He and his staff kept an open door to French and his colleagues. Hershey frequently met with peace church groups and even spent a day with Amish leaders on a Lancaster County, Pennsylvania, farm. He saw himself as defending a civil rights cause threatened by nationalistic congressional and veterans groups. Despite his cordiality, General Hershey thought that pacifists were mistaken and that they had contributed to the malaise leading to World War II.

The popularity of World War II enhanced the power of Selective Service. Although French had a host of friendly contacts in Congress, the Washington press, and the bureaucracy, he observed that "we are not important to congressmen, and to most of them, we are a bothersome minority." No congressman in a district with a concentrated C.O. constituency would stick out his neck in behalf of C.O. concerns. The only congressmen who took political risks for C.O.'s appear to have been John Sparkman of Alabama and Paul Kilday of Texas, who had no C.O. constituencies, but who liked NSBRO's Paul Comly French and Claude Shotts.

French frequently expressed irritation with the political naïveté of his peace group colleagues, whom he thought overestimated the power of a few friendly contacts in Washington and underestimated the necessity of cultivating commitments from a core of Representatives and Senators if changes were to be made in alternative service regulations.

Ironically, the NSBRO and Selective Service saw eye to eye

on many issues. Both wanted more efficiency. Both encouraged a broadening of service options, although NSBRO and the church agencies sought these more ardently than did SSS. NSBRO, with the support of SSS, pressed for overseas programs, although the Starnes Amendment forbade overseas service for CPS men. Some issues provoked discord, however. In July 1943, Selective Service established the first government camp at Mancos, Colorado. NSBRO protested when the Selective Service threatened to use government camps for disciplinary purposes.

During World War II, word spread of the pool of reliable C.O. workers. In early 1942, the Federal Security Agency in Los Angeles asked for twenty men to help move alien Japanese to concentration camps. Several months later, Undersecretary of War Robert Patterson asked to assign one thousand CPS men to the War Department for railway maintenance in Montana and North Dakota. Senator Millard Tydings of Maryland called on General Hershey about "legislation to close the camps and hospital units and assign all men to farms." In 1945, three months before the detonation of the first nuclear device, General William Donovan of the Office of Strategic Services approached General Hershey for one hundred CPS men for a variety of research projects. Some of these requests were discussed with AFSC, BSC, and MCC officals, others were rejected immediately.

As the war continued, particularly from 1943 on, tension mounted between Selective Service and NSBRO. The peace church groups cited human rights problems, including Selective Service's harassment of Japanese-American and black conscientious objectors. Selective Service often invoked the threat of the hostile American Legion and Veterans of Foreign Wars while placing vexatious restrictions on CPS men.

The amiable Hershey floated above most of these conflicts. CPS workers experienced irritations primarily with Colonel Lewis F. Kosch and his staff. Kosch, who headed the Camp

Operations Section for the CPS program, was a spit-and-polish cavalry officer in charge of twelve thousand C.O.'s, some of whom would not make their beds or cut their hair. He registered much displeasure with the lack of order in certain CPS camps and the failure of certain church agencies to take charge. As time wore on, Kosch and his staff were increasingly prone, French perceived, to give orders arbitrarily while skipping the NSBRO consultative step.

Colonel Kosch announced on March 13, 1945, that camp leaders should be prepared to move four hundred men on two days' notice from East to West coasts. For several weeks he refused to divulge background information, but NSBRO pieced the story together: the Japanese had threatened to fire-bomb coastal forests. The first word had been that C.O.'s would be forced to work under army command. Although the danger faded, this experience ruptured peace church and government relations. During this and other crises, French and his staff were in daily contact with various service agency officials, including those of MCC in Akron, Pennsylvania.

As the war drew to a close, ideas emerged for a better alternative to Civilian Public Service. Kosch urged that Selective Service operate all camps as government camps. Others suggested that SSS remove itself from camp administration and leave all responsibility to NSBRO and the service agencies. The American Civil Liberties Union called for the NSBRO-SSS agreement to be replaced with individual work assignments. The Assistant Secretary of the Interior sought to transfer the CPS program from SSS to the Interior Department. Attorney General Francis Biddle proposed taking CPS out of the hands of SSS and placing it under a civilian board.

In 1946, President Harry Truman's secretary, David K. Niles, asked for French's recommendation. French urged an end to SSS control of alternative service and suggested replacing it with a system of carefully chosen individual work assignments. Niles reported that he would seek a favorable response from the President. This may have been the seed for the individualized 1-W service program that emerged in the 1950s.

Within weeks of their demobilization, some former CPS men embarked for Europe and Asia on MCC assignments. Mennonite Central Committee channeled its administrative structures and support systems into postwar ministries of relief reconstruction. The eyes of MCC shifted to the needs of war-ravaged Europe and Asia.

5

Amidst the Debris at War's End:

Germany

In those hunger years food was power;
apparently it was sometimes used to enhance
the political strength of the distributor.

During the spring of 1945, as Allied and Soviet forces were closing in for the final onslaught on Nazi Germany, MCC's staff laid plans to send relief to the German people. In the context of the times, such compassionate concern for Adolf Hitler's Germany seems incomprehensible. Hitler, Germany's dictator for twelve years and conqueror of Europe, epitomized monumental evil. Information about the horrors of Nazi concentration and death camps was reaching North America. The Third Reich appeared to be crumbling under the weight of its miscalculations.

Yet MCC and other North American relief agencies were poised to bring relief to an "enemy people." Mennonites, like others, found a way to distinguish between a leader's misdeeds and a people's forgivable loyalty to their leader. Meanwhile, as newspaper and radio journalists reported daily of saturation bombing of German cities, Mennonites wondered whether their distant kinsmen might be buried under the rubble.

As early as 1943, MCC Executive Secretary Orie O. Miller

wrote to the chairman of the newly formed American Council of Voluntary Agencies that MCC was looking forward to doing relief work in Germany. Although a long war may have been assumed, MCC records reveal no trace of anything but expectation of an eventual Allied victory. In May 1940, while the British were withdrawing defeated armies from a fallen France, MCC established its first continuing European base in Great Britain. MCC's program of emergency relief and welfare service in Britain involved twenty-four workers and continued until a year after the Allied victory in Europe.

In March 1945, six months after the liberation of Paris, MCC workers returned to France to open a large relief program centered on children's homes, material aid, and reconstruction teams. Eventually the program involved seventy workers. In July 1945, a month after the German capitulation, MCCers entered the Netherlands. Fifty-six MCC volunteers worked closely with the Dutch Mennonites in a nationwide relief program and in reconstruction work on Walcheren Island, which had been flooded by the retreating Germans. Upon completion in 1945 of refugee work in Egypt, MCC shifted workers to Italy to engage in relief services in cooperation with the Waldensians and other groups. A total of twenty-eight MCC volunteers served in Italy.

The "U.S. Trading with the Enemy Act" barred the door to relief work in Germany. The Allies set out to impose a hard peace by reducing Germany to a "pastoral state"—decentralizing, demilitarizing, deindustrializing, and democratizing the country. At the Potsdam Conference in June 1945 the victors stripped Germany of its breadbaskets to the east: Pomerania, Silesia, and West and East Prussia. Germany was split into four zones, each occupied by one of the four victorious powers: the United States, Britain, Soviet Union, and France. Allies gave orders to their occupation troops to strip factories of equipment for reparations pledged to the Soviet Union. The Allies also gave orders to expel German-speaking peoples from Eastern

Kiel
Lübeck
Bremerhaven
Hamburg
Espelkamp
Gronau
Berlin
Access road
Krefeld
East Germany
Bonn
Luxembourg
Frankfurt
Mainz
Czechoslovakia
Kaiserslautern
West Germany
Neustadt
Backnang
France
Stuttgart
München
Austria
Basel

Switzerland

MCC project locations
0   miles   100

Netherlands
Poland
East Germany
Belgium
France
West Germany
Austria
Switzerland
Italy

Europe and to ship them to the truncated Germany. Attempting to build a wall of separation between their troops and the defeated Germans, Allied leaders forbade "fraternization" with the Germans. The occupation forces, however, acknowledged a minimal commitment to stave off starvation, epidemics, and social unrest.

A starving Germany could embarrass the occupiers. Surveying the wasteland of defeated Germany, General Dwight D. Eisenhower, Supreme Commander of the Allied Forces, observed: "Germany is destroyed. . . . They face a problem of real starvation." He then asked a haunting question: "What are we going to do just to prevent on our part having a Buchenwald of our own?" MCC and other North American relief agencies wanted to help. They recalled Christ's command, "If your enemy is hungry, feed him; if he is thirsty, give him something to drink."

The first MCC representative to inspect Germany's needs was Executive Committee member C. F. Klassen, who arrived in late August 1945. Klassen, who twenty years earlier had worked in Moscow with MCC on relief and refugee tasks, served as a special commissioner to "assume responsibility for all displaced Mennonites in Europe" and to "provide for them until they can be settled in a permanent location." Eighteen weeks later he returned to North America to report on the "critical state of the refugees and the magnitude of the task." The Canadian Mennonite Board of Colonization agreed to be responsible for emigration to Canada, and MCC for emigration to the United States and Paraguay. Klassen, representing both the Canadian board and MCC, directed the European emigration program, which ultimately assisted twelve thousand Russian-born Mennonite refugees in the British and American zones, a few hundred in the French Zone, and several thousand displaced West Prussian Mennonites.

Throughout 1945, however, the U.S. State and War departments forbade relief aid to Germany. Finally, in December

1945, after repeated requests from the voluntary agencies, U.S. authorities permitted a team of seven to go to Germany to inspect the hunger problem. The American military authorities stated flatly that they would not deal with separate agencies. In 1943, the American Council of Voluntary Agencies for Foreign Service, of which MCC was a member, formed a Committee on Germany. On December 7, 1945, and January 14, 1946, the new committee created the Council of Relief Agencies Licensed for Operation in Germany (CRALOG). Eleven member organizations, including MCC, comprised CRALOG. On February 9, Robert Kreider, who had recently completed an assignment with Civilian Public Service, sailed for Europe as MCC's appointee to the first group of eight CRALOG representatives in the American Zone of Germany. Ten days later, on February 19, President Harry S. Truman authorized CRALOG as the sole channel for private aid to Germany.

Entering Germany on March 27, 1946, Kreider wrote of his first stop at Frankfurt:

> Never have I seen such complete destruction. In the center of the city we walked along narrow winding paths through mountains of rubble. I stepped into a shell of a department store where I saw almost no merchandise, only a few women looking through books of dress patterns. Buried in the rubble were doorways to basement shops and residences. The central railway station, the gutted skeleton of a roof still standing, was filled with thousands of drably dressed people with sacks and battered luggage: refugees, returned prisoners of war, the homeless, people on the move.

The CRALOG representatives viewed a shattered Germany. From 30 to 40 percent of the factories were destroyed. The industrial British and American zones were cut off from food-producing areas to the east. Soon the populations of these two zones soared from thirty-four million to forty-three million as expellees (*Fluchtlinge*) poured in from the east. An additional million and a half non-German displaced persons occupied requisitioned housing. These destitute millions pressed in upon a population with meager food reserves and an area that had lost 56 percent of its prewar dwellings. In the first post-war winter, 1945-46, the average daily caloric ration in the British Zone was reduced from 1,350 to 1,014. In December 1945 the ration in the U.S. Zone was set at 1,550 calories, highest of any of the zones, but less than half an American's daily average.

The first contingent of the CRALOG team that arrived in Berlin on March 28, 1946, introduced new problems for Military Government officials. The colonel who headed the Public Health and Welfare branch of the Military Government prepared orders attaching the eight CRALOG personnel to different military headquarters, with each to be subject to the call of military duty. The team balked at this infringement of their civilian status. Only after a review by a tribunal of three generals did the Military Government agree that the CRALOG team .was not subject to military duty. Further, they agreed that the team did not have to wear uniforms; thus, the CRALOG team was the first group in civilian dress stationed in the U.S. Zone. However, each CRALOG representative received a simulated officer's rating (major), used for housing requisitions, military railroad and airline travel, mess cards, clothing ration cards, currency control booklets, and Post Exchange (PX) and Army Post Office (APO) privileges. For a full month, the military and the CRALOG team negotiated these understandings. The U.S. occupation authorities, with an abundance of military bureaucrats, hovered over this early U.S. team more rigidly and patronizingly than did the French or British with later teams.

The eight CRALOG men were assigned to different offices in the American Zone. Kreider was first located in Wiesbaden, capital of the province of Greater Hesse; later he served in Berlin and Stuttgart. Soon after the team's arrival in April 1946 the first shipment of 7,535,000 pounds of flour, milk, vegetables, meats, and fats arrived at the port of Bremen. Relief supplies were shipped by rail from the Bremen warehouse to the warehouses of the designated receiving agencies. They were then distributed according to procedures outlined by the German umbrella organization *Zentralauschuss*... (Central Union of the Leading Agencies of Voluntary Welfare Activity for the Distribution of Gifts of Love from Overseas). The principal German distributing agencies were *Caritas Verband* (Catholic), *Evangelisches Hilfswerk* (Protestant), *Arbeiter Wohlfahrt* (labor), and the German Red Cross. MCC channeled its shipments to *Hilfswerk*, which used a network of parish committees to distribute relief supplies efficiently.

Never before had MCC shipped such a volume of aid as in this American Zone operation. Although widely praised for the generosity of its giving, MCC was not fully satisfied with its arrangements in the American Zone. In an area the size of Illinois, MCC was limited to one representative who was essentially an observer. Kreider could only encourage, not instruct, *Hilfswerk* in the preparation of reports and establishment of distribution guidelines. As he conducted spot checks, he wondered whether the recipients knew the source and spirit of the gifts. In those hunger years food was power; apparently it was sometimes used to enhance the political strength of the distributor. The Catholic and Lutheran sending agencies trusted their German counterparts with distribution decisions, but the Brethren, Friends, and Mennonite members of CRALOG sought a more active partnership. The latter three petitioned the American Military Government for permission to bring their own workers into the U.S. Zone for program development. The military denied this request.

In July 1946, CRALOG signed agreements with the British and French zonal authorities. In the same period, MCC submitted requests to the British and French for permission to conduct MCC child-feeding programs in the two zones. Both approved the requests, making provisions for initial teams of fifteen in the British Zone and ten in the French Zone. Meanwhile, in September 1946 in Stuttgart, Secretary of State James F. Byrnes announced the end of the purely punitive phase of the occupation. In October, Walter Eicher arrived from the U.S. to serve as CRALOG representative and to direct MCC work in the French Zone from headquarters at Neustadt a. d. Haardt, located in the Palatinate near a cluster of Mennonite communities. Also in October, Cornelius J. Dyck arrived to serve as CRALOG representative and MCC director for the British Zone. Two days before Christmas, seven MCC workers joined him at the new MCC center at Kiel in Schleswig-Holstein. Kreider coordinated the work in the three zones. Soon MCC adopted a new 3-2-1 formula on the allocation of shipments: three parts to the British Zone, two to the French Zone, and one part to the U.S. Zone. The British Zone was the most populous, urban, and needy. The French Zone, although small, was the poorest agriculturally and bore the burden of the French military living off the land. The U.S. Zone had the highest rations as well as an early start in relief receipts. A major factor in the shift of MCC shipments to the British and French zones was the receptivity of the British and French in admitting MCC teams.

In their history of CRALOG, *Transfigured Night,* Eileen Egan and Elizabeth Clark Reiss wrote of the Mennonite relief efforts:

> Already as the armies moved forward out of the south and sent in their missions and followed with supplies ... to liberated France, Holland and Belgium ... warehouses were filled, emptied, replenished. When the time came for work to begin in Germany, food, clothing and other supplies were on hand in the storerooms and volunteers were available.

In 1946, during nine months of operations CRALOG shipped ten million pounds of relief supplies; in 1948, twenty-six million pounds. In 1946 and 1947, among CRALOG contributors, MCC ranked first in the volume of shipments, in 1948, fourth. In 1947, four thousand of the 5,815 tons shipped overseas by MCC went to Germany. Egan and Reiss commented, "The record of Mennonite relief to Germany—all the while maintaining significant programs of assistance to war-stricken peoples in other countries on several continents—is a record that is incredible when one considers the size . . . of this church." During the first three years CRALOG as a whole shipped to Germany fifty-eight thousand tons of food, clothing, and other relief supplies. One German in three received some form of CRALOG assistance. A million children benefited from feeding programs utilizing CRALOG supplies.

The bitterly cold winter of 1946-1947 was known in Germany as the "Hunger Winter." In January 1947, with workers on the scene in the French and British zones, MCC staff rapidly initiated emergency programs patterned on MCC purpose and experience. Working within the context of CRALOG supply channels, MCC developed a network of program partnerships with German church agencies, city and provincial (*Land*) welfare agencies, military government, Mennonite church groups, and universities. By the end of 1947, one-third of the 137 MCC workers in Europe were serving in Germany.

On January 13, 1947, MCC launched a feeding program in Kiel for five thousand preschool-age children and a feeding program for three thousand sick, disabled, and aged persons. Similar programs were soon under way for four thousand children and one thousand old and feeble in Lubeck, and seven thousand children in Krefeld. In Kiel MCC fed 2,500 university students two meals a week. In the French Zone MCC opened child-feeding programs in ten smaller towns of the Palatinate. MCC also fed nine thousand children in the Saar, eight thousand in Ludwigshaven, and two thousand in Neustadt. By early summer in 1947, with substantial participation of German ageneices, MCC was regularly feeding 140,000 persons in Germany and many more indirectly through its CRALOG shipments to *Hilfswerk*.

Remembering MCC's feeding program in Russia twenty years before, many Mennonite refugees, some in dire need, anticipated instant assistance. But relief was slow in coming. Not until eighteen months after the war did the first CRALOG shipment arrive in the British Zone, where 80 percent of the Mennonite refugees were concentrated. In June 1946, *Hilfswerk* in the American Zone agreed to allocate five tons of MCC relief supplies each month to *Christenpflicht*, a Mennonite relief agency established in 1920 with headquarters in Ingolstadt, Bavaria. Led by the elderly, energetic Michael Horsch, *Christenpflicht* became a conduit of aid to Mennonite refugees in the American Zone. It established several child-feeding projects in Bavaria and administered a personalized package program to one thousand refugees in the Russian Zone.

Under the leadership of Cornelius Dyck and Ernst Crous, a Mennonite relief distribution system developed in the British Zone. The zone was divided into seven districts, each with a director. Through this Mennonite refugee network, MCC made monthly distributions reaching some six thousand persons. In the French Zone Mennonites had organized a relief committee to care for Mennonites and for neighbors in need. German Mennonite Richard Hertzler played a key role in developing a German Mennonite program of relief outreach to cities of the region. Walter Eicher and his staff met monthly with the Mennonite committee to review needs and distribute supplies.

With resourceful workers in all parts of Germany, MCC's program became increasingly diversified and creative. In Berlin, Lydia Lehman developed a parcel program for three hundred needy persons. In 1948, MCC opened its first neighborhood center (*Nachbarschaftsheim*) in Heilbronn, a city of sixty thousand in which one third of the people had been killed during a firebombing of the city four years earlier. MCC imported a pre-fabricated structure from Sweden and erected it in a clearing among the rubble. Under the direction of Marie and

Frank Wiens a broad community service program developed in cooperation with Heilbronn Mennonites.

During the summer of 1949 in the severely damaged Kreuzberg section of Berlin, MCC opened a neighborhood center under the leadership of Harold and Anne Buller. MCC established another center with activities for children, youth, and the elderly at Kaiserslautern in the French Zone. MCC headquarters at Kiel, Hamburg, Krefeld, Neustadt, and Frankfurt became centers of community activity focused on youth. In the British Zone, Erna Fast developed supplementary feeding programs for students at the universities of Hamburg, Goettingen, and Hannover. In the French Zone Paul Peachey introduced a student activity and assistance program at the University of Mainz.

In the summer of 1948, MCC, in cooperation with the Council of Mennonite and Affiliated Colleges, European Mennonites, and other groups, sponsored two international voluntary service projects, one at Hamburg and the other near Frankfurt. At the latter, volunteers renovated a medieval castle into a Protestant conference hostel. The following summer MCC sponsored similar international work camps at Stuttgart, Hannover, and Frankfurt. Approximately half of the workers at these camps were North Americans and half were Europeans, some from MCC's university programs. At Semback in the Palatinate six Americans and nine Germans built a Mennonite youth center.

At Espelkamp near Bielefeld in the British Zone, MCC joined *Evangelisches Hilfswerk* in transforming a former munitions factory into a community for refugees. This effort modeled a series of community-building projects that MCC later undertook with Pax volunteers. Encouraged by these experimental summer programs, MCC joined with German Mennonites and other groups in developing a year-round international voluntary service program. As a result of these experiences in youth work, MCC's Visitor Exchange (Trainee)

Program emerged. MCC staff also assisted the Council of Mennonite colleges in selecting German students for college study in North America.

In the late 1940s, only a few years after Germany and the Allies had been at war, MCC and German Mennonites were jointly sponsoring youth, church, and peace conferences. Never had so many North American Mennonite youth visited in German Mennonite homes and churches. But as this camaraderie developed, hostility intensified between East and West. Along every foot of the East Zone border, from the Baltic to the Danube, the Soviets were erecting barriers to prevent flight. In 1948 the Soviets imposed a blockade on all rail and automobile traffic to Berlin, an enclave deep in the Russian Zone. While MCC teams brought emergency food and clothing aid to residents in West Germany, another team of MCC workers, led by C. F. Klassen, gathered together refugees who had fled Soviet lands to the east. The MCC refugee team contracted for transportation and processed papers for those seeking homes in Canada, Paraguay, and Uruguay. Sensing that their fate hung on the great power struggles, Mennonite refugees from Russia watched anxiously the East-West tensions.

MCC explored possibilities of sending relief to the Russian Zone, which had reported great need. Although *Christenpflicht* systematically sent small food parcels to one thousand residents in the Russian Zone, MCC wished to do more. The International Red Cross offered itself as a channel for sending MCC relief to selected areas with occasional inspection trips. MCC, believing that the plan lacked little opportunity for interpretation, did not pursue it.

In the early 1950s West Germany—aided by monetary reform, unification of three of the zones, Allied help, and the will to rebuild, staged a sensational economic recovery and began to compete on the world market. MCC remained in the country with a diminished staff and focused on refugee housing and other projects in cooperation with the German Mennonites. The German experience illustrated for MCC the power of political and military factors in shaping the possibilities and limits of MCC action. In 1954 President Theodor Heuss of the new Federal Republic of Germany sent MCC and other agencies each a gift of fifty works of art to show gratitude (*Dankspende*) for postwar aid during the "years of our bitterest need." He declared, "These acts of brotherly love saved the lives of many Germans and helped the exhausted and the despairing to gather fresh courage."

Africa

As late as the mid-nineteenth century, Africa was for most people a great unexplored region, more a coastline than a continent. In the late nineteenth century, covetous European nations carved Africa into two dozen colonial parcels. Before 1956 there were only four independent countries in all of Africa: Ethiopia, Liberia, South Africa, and Egypt. Beginning with Ghana's independence in 1956, Africa gave birth to a score of new nation states. One African called it "the springtime of nations."

Mennonites planted churches in Africa early in the twentieth century: the Defenseless Mennonites, Central Conference Mennonites, and Mennonite Brethren in the Belgian Congo (Zaire); the Mennonite Brethren in Christ in Nigeria; the Brethren in Christ in Rhodesia (Zimbabwe); and in the 1930s, the Eastern Mennonite Board of Missions in East Africa.

MCC began its work in sub-Sahara Africa in the late 1950s just as a series of new nations were appearing on the African stage. MCC has been present in the most turbulent period of

Africa's history—a time when new governments have been impatient to expand educational systems, establish universities, build steel mills, launch airlines, and create armies and bureaucracies. Rival ideologies have continued to compete for the hearts and minds of the people of Africa.

Five case studies focus on critical issues: (1) experimenting with development strategies in Zaire; (2) providing teachers to staff African secondary schools in a period of explosive expansion; (3) serving on both sides of one of Africa's tragic civil wars; and (4) trying to be peacemakers on the edge of a racist and militarized African nation; (5) deciding whether or not to report politically motivated murders. We acknowledge with appreciation the work of Robert and Judy Zimmerman Herr in drafting the case study on the Transkei.

With MCC having served in twenty-two countries of Africa, many other topics invite study: emergency action in famine areas in Somalia, Mozambique, and Ethiopia; designing a holistic mission-MCC program in Botswana; doing development work on the southern rim of the Sahara; and adjusting a program in Ethiopia during the transition from monarchy to revolutionary government.

6

Helping Others to Help Themselves:
Zaire

*As time progressed, I began to realize that
COMAS was perceived by local Congolese as
belonging to someone other than themselves.*
— Fremont Regier

The biblical calling to help others is clear: feed the hungry, clothe the naked, shelter the destitute, bind up the wounded, befriend the despised. Helping, however, is an elusive art. Even with the best of intentions, helping can rob a recipient of self-respect and self-reliance. Critics charge that helping others may cause dependency, reflect condescending attitudes, and offer "Band-Aids" rather than surgery. Such talk, in turn, can rationalize laziness or insensitivity.

This study examines the challenges of helping villagers in Zaire during the 1960s and 1970s. It is based on a 1977 University of Wisconsin doctoral dissertation by Fremont Regier, in which he reviewed twelve years of personal experience in rural development work. While in Zaire, Regier and his wife, Sara, served under the auspices of the Congo Inland Mission (CIM) and Mennonite Central Committee.

Mennonite missionaries entered the Belgian Congo in 1912 to preach the gospel and to establish church communities with schools and hospitals. CIM personnel opened eight mission stations scattered over an area as large as West Virginia, with a population of four hundred thousand. These Congolese were of the Bapende, Bashilele, Baluba, Bawongo, Bena-Lulua, and Batshoko tribes. During the 1920s, Mennonite Brethren missionaries entered an area adjacent to the CIM mission field.

Soon after Congolese independence in 1960, Mennonite Central Committee sent short-term workers to assist in mission programs. Beginning in 1962, dozens of MCC teachers entered Protestant secondary schools throughout the country. In the early seventies, MCC personnel in the Congo (renamed Zaire in 1971) reached a peak of eighty-six volunteers. In 1971 CIM changed its name to Africa Inter Mennonite Mission (AIMM).

Zaire, which lies astride the equator, is approximately a third the size of the continental United States. In 1986 it had a population of thirty-two million. Rich in mineral resources—uranium, copper, cobalt, diamonds—it has long exported palm oil. In earlier years, farmers raised cotton under Belgian-imposed production quotas. Prior to 1908 the Congo remained under the domain of King Leopold II of Belgium, who cruelly exploited the Congolese. From 1908 until 1960 the Belgians ruled the Congo paternalistically. In 1960, as part of an Africa-wide surge of independence movements, the Congo freed itself from colonial control. Mennonite missionaries left the Congo during the civil chaos of 1960, although some returned late that year. From 1960 to 1967, tribal turmoil and guerrilla warfare wracked the country. Agricultural production plunged to its lowest level and since then has not recovered to pre-independence levels. Leader followed leader: Lumumba, Kasavubu, Tshombe, and Mobutu. In 1965 General Mobutu imposed military control over the entire Congo; he has since resisted all challenges to his rule. Presently, serious economic problems and political corruption plague Zaire.

The Nyanga district of the Mennonite mission field, where AIMM and MCC jointly sponsor rural development efforts, has a tropical climate. The area is covered with grassland sa-

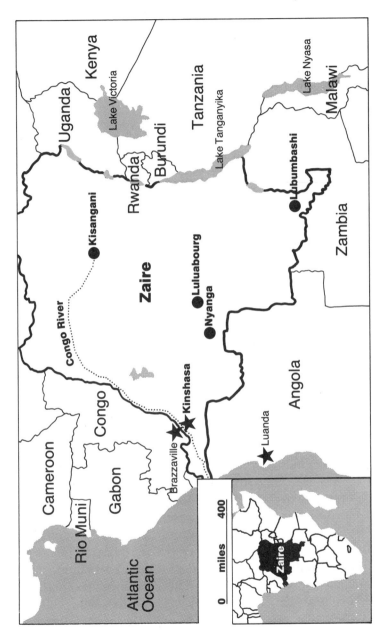

vanna, scrubby bushes and trees, and narrow strips of forest. The major food crops include corn, manioc, millet, peanuts, beans, sweet potatoes, bananas, pineapples, citrus fruits, and palm oil. Most of the marketed commodities are sold to local truckers for resale in the cities of Tshikapa, Kananga, and Ilebo. Consumer goods such as cloth, shoes, kerosene, bicycles, radios, tools, salt, sugar, and powdered milk return on the same trucks that haul produce to city markets. The unmaintained roads are wretched. The Bapende people traditionally raise goats, sheep, hogs, chickens, pigeons, and ducks. Caterpillars and flying ants provide a significant source of protein. Wild game and fish are a diminishing part of the local diet.

In 1965, the economy of the Nyanga district was in shambles. The new government, imitating earlier colonial rulers, imposed acreage production quotas, taxes, and fines. Farmers resented the government, which administered these rural policies with military brutality. At this low point in 1965, CIM, soon joined by MCC, established Congo Mennonite Agricultural Service (COMAS) to assist the Nyanga district in agricultural production. Fremont Regier, a specialist in animal nutrition and rural extension, served as program director until 1976. Arnold Harder, a specialist in agricultural education and community development, arrived in 1968 and with his wife, Grace, has remained with the program to the present. From 1965 to 1976 MCC provided thirty short-term volunteers, operating funds, and special project monies. The British agency OXFAM also contributed grants. At Kikwit in Kwilu province, the Mennonite Brethren and Mennonite Central Committee jointly sponsored the affiliated Protestant Agricultural Program (PAP).

Although in 1965 the Nyanga district faced dismal problems, development strategists throughout Africa were optimistic that the quality of rural life could be raised significantly. The 1960s were heralded as "the great decade of development." This was the era that celebrated the "Green Revolution" with new varieties of high-producing foodgrains, widely publicized World Bank programs, the explosive growth of the Peace Corps, the emergence of new governmental and voluntary agencies, and the establishment of university programs in international development. All this received a papal blessing when Pope John XXIII declared, "The new name for peace is development." COMAS was launched in a climate of optimism: surely, development experts could help third world peoples attain a better life.

Those designing COMAS were determined not to repeat the Belgian pattern of establishing agricultural schools that attracted students intent on fleeing rural villages for the cities. COMAS outlined broad goals for enriching the economic vitality, community stability, and spiritual life of the people of Nyanga district. COMAS extension agents planned to help individual farmers with a wide range of needs: fertilizer, machinery, disease control, insect control, weed control, animal breeding, and cooperative marketing. COMAS established a resource center at Nyanga with a farm, garage, and store. From the beginning, Regier asserted, "COMAS is dedicated to the village loincloth farmer."

Action centered around extension agents, usually a Congolese and an MCC volunteer, who went out on bicycles with bedrolls and a few tools and supplies to meet with farmers. Often the men of a village would gather to discuss common problems: credit, medical care, markets, tools, livestock. These talks invariably led to rabbits and poultry, and the COMAS agents suggested that those interested could gather and cut sticks, poles, bamboo, and vines. In six weeks the extension team would return to help anyone ready with materials to construct a henhouse or rabbit hutch. Then villagers with adequate preparations could qualify to purchase initial breeding stock at the COMAS center. The extension agents usually ate and lodged with the cooperating farmer.

In 1969, agents made sixty-five extension trips over eleven

different routes in Nyanga and other districts. Although in 1965 the Nyanga district had few rabbits, by 1970 approximately four thousand were being raised by more than 250 farmers. MCC worker Dean Linsenmeyer, who worked a 115-mile circuit with Ngenze Leonard, described one successful farmer:

> There are always some like Sha'Malanga in Kipoko village, for example, who has done such a tremendous job of going from the original three rabbits he bought from us in January to forty-seven rabbits in four months. He has rabbits to feed his family and visitors. He has helped numerous friends of his start their own rabbit projects, selling them rabbits and building hutches, each one just as neat and well-built as his own which Ngenze and I helped him build in December. Thinking of him giving an occasional rabbit to his struggling little church as his tithe gives me energy to push my poor old bike through this sand. . . .

At first, COMAS workers were not fully aware of how much the memory of harsh, demanding Belgian agricultural agents lingered in the minds of Zairian farmers. One Belgian agent, known as "The Lion," had induced farmers to grow cotton cash crops by "pushing people's teeth down their throats." COMAS, with its itinerating extension agents, however, worked at building relationships. One MCC volunteer who had the use of a pickup truck decided to use a bicycle instead because he wanted to be nearer to people, whom he valued over "how many hatching eggs we sell or how many rabbit hutches we build."

Although COMAS received wide praise as a model development program, director Regier perceived that "all was not well with the project and . . . local people did not feel ownership in it." This discussion came into sharper focus in early 1971 when AIMM transferred ownership of its mission property and responsibility for COMAS over to the Mennonite Church of Congo (EMC), later named Communante Menonite au Zaire (CMZ). COMAS became known as Service de Developpement Agricole (SEDA).

Policy problems began to surface. Church leaders, unsympathetic with SEDA's intention to serve village farmers, or more interested in personal gain, requested that they be given their own chickens and eggs for breeding and hatching. Church jealousy over the SEDA budget mounted. Pilfering by some of SEDA's own workers reflected a lack of identification with the program's purpose. Some farmers began increasing their rabbit stock, apparently to impress extension agents, while their children suffered from malnutrition. Regier sensed that many farmers were "raising rabbits because we had suggested it. . . ."

Regier, who had developed the program from 1965 to 1971 with little supervision but with the strong affirmation of CIM and MCC, became convinced that COMAS had been a "top-down" rather than a "bottom-up" program: "As time progressed, I began to realize that COMAS was perceived by local Congolese as belonging to someone other than themselves, that is, the foreign church . . . or the project director." Meanwhile, development theorists were beginning to express disillusionment with well-funded projects that pressed for expanded production. A new emphasis focused on the human component of development: care for persons, dignity of the villager, faith in human nature, partnership, reciprocity. Beginning in 1972, the persons associated with SEDA spoke a new language of development.

In 1972, Regier returned from a year's study leave, intent on learning whether the Zairians really wanted SEDA to continue. Church leaders, staff, and farmers all affirmed that they wanted the program; yet each group seemed to lack a sense of ownership. In 1972, SEDA introduced many changes in an effort to win their hearts and minds. But after more than fifty years of Belgian colonial and missionary "top-down" administration, it was difficult to reverse course. The first and most important step was a one-week seminar in October 1972 for forty-four church leaders interested in SEDA. One who attended captured the mood: "We never knew what SEDA was. Now we know and are going to tell our people at home."

Soon thereafter, SEDA staff launched a series of community extension programs. These took on a celebrative flavor as teams composed of a SEDA extension agent, an evangelist, a teacher from the Nyanga women's organization, a bookseller, a public health nurse, and youth folk singers joined together in leading weekend village seminars. One participant commented, "Now SEDA is really getting into the work of the church." In late 1973, the Nyanga church council decided to call the programs *Monyo Ohie Ohie Kudi Agasue* (New Life for All). Pastors handled the scheduling. From 1973 to 1976, twenty-seven seminars attracted an average of 1,783 participants per seminar.

SEDA shifted its emphasis from individualized itineration to a group approach with a variety of themes: literacy, Bible study, music, livestock farming, vegetable raising, soybean production, and mechanics. The director and the Zairian assitant director initiated in-service training sessions for staff members one morning per week to better acquaint them with SEDA policies and to discuss their questions and suggestions. SEDA staff participated in celebrative events such as preparing a float for a community parade and staging the annual Christmas pageant in church. In 1973, the church general assembly chose a Zairian staff member, Ngulubi Mazemba, to serve as assistant director.

The staff began experimenting with a new "silent approach" for extension visits. As before, agents visited villages, but this time they mainly listened to problems. Only when asked did they respond to questions on topics ranging from sewing machine parts to marketing produce. The recurring themes of these discussions were self-esteem, self-sufficiency, use of community resources, and assessment of needs in the context of the local church. SEDA staff emphasized stewardship of God's creation and using the Bible as a resource for community living. Out of such discussions in Nyanga ten men started a marketing cooperative which has survived and grown.

The general secretary of the church began to speak of "our SEDA." However, the task of correcting rumors and misinformation remained. The expectation of some local leaders that SEDA would become a money-making operation for the church persisted. Tribal rivalries surfaced in the selection of a Zairian assistant director. Some leaders criticized SEDA for concentrating too much on the Nyanga area and not spreading out enough to other districts. Church leaders continued to doubt whether AIMM, MCC, and the SEDA director would eventually relinquish their authority. In 1975, Ngulubi Mazemba was appointed to the SEDA directorship. Regier recalled: "Nyanga church leaders participated enthusiastically in the big celebration at the center when Ngulubi and I traded offices. . . . When in the fall of 1975 Ngulubi and I traveled to North America on a bridge-building mission . . . people finally accepted the fact that I was sincere in wanting him to have that post."

Perhaps the most significant indication of a new appreciation of SEDA came when the Nyanga church ordained six couples to serve as deacons and lay pastors. Of these, three of the men were members of SEDA's staff. Moreover, in 1974 SEDA was threatened by a national government takeover of foreign-related enterprises.

During a governmental inquiry, staff members declared: "Of course SEDA is in our hands. Of course it belongs to the Mennonite Church of Zaire." SEDA workers sometimes chanted, "SEDA *oye!* SEDA *oye!*" (Hail SEDA!).

With the shift from one-to-one extension visits to more group activities, much of the rabbit production declined. Yet those who attended to proper husbandry and nutrition found ready markets. A lingering dependency, however, continued among many farmers. Some commented, "Push us, encourage us, visit us, order us around, tell us what to do, and we'll do it."

Despite the opportunity for more autonomy, Zairian farmers and church leaders hesitated.

Members of a new marketing cooperative, however, were aggressive in raising rabbits and chickens and seeking to improve their farm operations. The cooperative built up cash reserves from undistributed dividends and initiated a farm loan program. After building their own office, they instructed their manager to learn bookkeeping and reporting techniques from SEDA's staff.

The Nyanga women's group emerged as a particularly vigorous development force. The women met regularly to study nutrition, sewing, child care, soapmaking, literacy, and the Bible. The local church provided a meeting room and AIMM worker Sara Regier acted as a behind-the-scenes organizer. One of the women, sent to a soybean seminar in Kananga, returned an enthusiastic and effective teacher in the women's program. It was this women's group, called "Maison Diaconale," that provided a trained leader for women's instruction on the New Life for All team.

In 1976, when Fremont Regier returned to North America, he and his SEDA colleagues concluded that in five years much progress had been made to foster a new sense of ownership by church leaders, staff members, and farmers. From his study of earlier development efforts in the Nyanga district, Regier was aware that SEDA initiatives had been held in check by Zairian attitudes toward foreign experts and missionaries. AIMM-MCC workers had arrived with power, money, and technical resources that were both wanted and disliked. Said one North American observer: "Church officials resented that which they could not control. Yet when it came time to give responsibility to Zairians whom they could control, they hesitated, [preferring] responsibility to remain in the hands of the missionaries they could trust. They were caught in the dilemma of not being able to live with missionaries and not being able to live without them."

Since 1976, SEDA has continued as a model of development, with visitors and trainees coming from a distance and praising the program. Development workers have combined hope and trust in the initiatives of the people and a modest assessment of their own significance in the process. They have come to accept backsliding as an occupational hazard and stick-to-itiveness as a cardinal virtue in development. Under the leadership of Arnold Harder, and, for a time, Ngulubi Mazemba, the program has continued to train extension workers and has moved into the areas of cattle raising, fish farming, farm produce marketing, and road maintenance. Some program leaders have faltered and fallen, but new leaders have emerged to carry on. One farmer reflects:

> Maturity doesn't come in one day.... SEDA is like Sh'a Yone [Frank Enns, the pioneer missionary who developed Nyanga station] in the old days. He worked and built. We never thought he would get old or leave—now he is gone but his work lasts on.... The church has no way to support itself. We farmers can help. After a few years people will see that we are serious.

7

Westerners Teach in African Schools:

Teachers Abroad Program

Most TAP teachers are intrigued by the opportunity of living in radically different cultures.

MCC service is impelled by forces that push and forces that pull. In the fifteen years following World War II, hundreds of American conscientious objectors met their alternative service obligations through Mennonite Central Committee's overseas Pax program: in Germany and Austria building refugee housing, in Macedonia and Zaire as agriculturists, and in other areas in unskilled and semiskilled work. Pax, however, offered few overseas service opportunities for women and men with advanced training. By 1960, Mennonite college graduates who wanted to use their professional skills in service abroad began to *push* for places to serve. Young Mennonite teachers, in particular, prepared for service but found few opportunities to go overseas. Their motivation reflected a tide of idealism analogous to the enthusiastic response to President John F. Kennedy's newly created Peace Corps.

MCC felt a *pull* for innovative programming from the independent countries of Africa. In 1960 and 1961, nineteen new nations emerged in Africa, all of which were straining to compress a century of development into a decade. Many African schoolteachers took part in the movement and assumed top government positions after independence, leading some to call it a "revolution by schoolmasters." Among national objectives, the nations gave highest priority to education. "When we win our independence," declared the educational chairman of the United National Independence Party in Northern Rhodesia, "we shall devote one half of our national income to education."

In the early 1960s, discussion in newly independent African countries centered on the Ashby Commission report, *Investment in Education*, which called for the newly independent Nigeria to give higher education top priority. An UNESCO-sponsored meeting of African Ministers of Education urged a massive expansion of secondary schools and teacher training colleges. Leaders of the new countries of Africa asserted a desperate need for college-trained persons to build the nation. A few years earlier, during the mid-fifties, only fourteen Northern Nigerians out of a population of twenty million had held college degrees. When independence came to the Congo (Zaire) on June 30, 1960, only fourteen Congolese were reported to be college graduates. One national Minister of Education lamented: "Not a week passes that I do not lose a teacher. Most are lured away to government positions." He added, "Seventy percent of our national cabinet are former secondary school teachers."

North American missionaries in Africa reported the need for teachers. Columbia University's Teachers College launched a highly publicized Teachers for East Africa Program. The Hershey Foundation developed a similar program for cocoa-producing countries of West Africa. The Peace Corps announced plans to send teachers to Africa. Protestant mission executives with years of experience in Africa—George Carpenter, Emory Ross, and Theodore L. Tucker—encouraged MCC to send teachers to Africa. For eight years, MCC had placed a total of one hundred teacher volunteers in the schools of the United Church of Canada in remote villages and coves along the Newfoundland and Labrador coasts. It had been a satisfying experience. In 1961 MCC appointed Robert Kreider, MCC Executive Committee member and academic dean of Bluffton College, to develop a self-supporting teacher-placement program in Africa.

Kreider sought counsel from mission, education, and government officials in New York City, Washington, London, and Geneva. He visited MCC teachers in Newfoundland. On a two-month tour of Africa he investigated educational needs and receptivity to a teacher-placement program. He wrote: "I was impressed by the hunger for education. I saw it in the desire to roll back the level of illiteracy which in the countries of Sub-Sahara Africa ranges from 60 to 98 percent. . . . I saw it at a middle school in Kasai Province in the Congo, where students, finding dormitories filled to capacity, came and built their own thatched-roofed huts to assure themselves of a place in the student body."

Kreider discovered that 80 to 90 percent of the schools in Sub-Sahara Africa were church-related. National Christian council leaders and public officials in Africa strongly encouraged MCC to place teachers in Africa. At its 1962 annual meeting, MCC approved plans for a Teachers Abroad Program (TAP). During the first year, 1962-63, twenty-three teachers served in four areas: Kenya in East Africa, the Congo (Zaire) in Central Africa, Northern Rhodesia (later Zambia) and Nyasaland (later Malawi) in South Central Africa, and Northern Nigeria in West Africa. MCC teachers appointed to the Congo first studied French for a year in Belgium or France. The first MCC TAP appointees taught in Presbyterian, Methodist, Friends, Anglican, and Baptist secondary schools and in teacher training colleges. In subsequent years, some volunteers taught in Mennonite and Brethren in Christ sponsored schools. Early in the TAP experience, MCC made a commitment to work with the churches in Africa. MCC has relied on African Christian councils for advice as to where MCC personnel can best be used. MCC has tended to place its teachers in church-sponsored schools in isolated areas that have difficulty procuring teachers.

Salary grants paid by the governments to church schools covered part of the TAP expenses. MCC pooled this income in a common TAP treasury; the funds paid for transportation, room and board, personal allowance, medical expenses, and vacations. MCC covered administrative and orientation costs with the aid of contributions.

At first, MCC planned for a program that would be needed for five, or at the most, ten years until the new countries could generate enough teachers to meet national needs. During the first ten years the number of TAP placements grew annually until 1971, when 215 persons taught in Africa. The number of teacher placements dropped from 126 in 1975 to thirty-five in 1986, while the total number of MCC workers in Africa during that period averaged two hundred. Today, African host countries for MCC teachers include Burkina Faso, Kenya, Lesotho, Nigeria, Swaziland, Uganda, Zaire, Zambia, and Zimbabwe.

MCC introduced the "TAP idea," born in Newfoundland, to its programs in Bolivia in 1969 and Jamaica in 1970. Over a period of eighteen years, 1969 to 1986, MCC invested a total of 477 teacher-service years in Bolivia and Jamaica, while in Africa for a period of twenty-five years, TAP teachers contributed 2,380 years of teaching. As the number of teachers placed by MCC in Africa decreased, the use of the category "Teachers Abroad Program" or "TAP" receded.

Teachers in Africa do not experience a simple success story of teaching only highly motivated students. Not all African students are eager and diligent. Textbooks often arrive late, if at all. Teachers struggle constantly with shortages of paper, chalk, laboratory supplies, and other materials. For many students, English or French is not the mother tongue; the teacher must use a second language acquired imperfectly by students in primary school. Often, teachers are asked to teach courses for which they have had little or no preparation. Some endure repeated attacks of malaria, dysentery, and other tropical ailments. Most are uncomfortable with a rigid educational system inherited from colonial rule, in which teachers are expected to drill students to memorize facts which will help them to pass nationally prepared and graded examinations. Often they are disappointed to learn that able graduates with formal secondary education are not able to find jobs.

Idealistic TAP teachers are sometimes frustrated with the knowledge that as short-term guests in a different culture, they have a meager chance of changing established educational patterns. Some encounter nationalist backlash: "White teacher, go home." In isolated mission schools, some have to live with fellow teachers whose behavior and values perplex and irritate; there is no escape. Some teachers become aware that they bring with them to Africa their own unique set of imperfections.

And yet, TAP teachers are intrigued by the opportunity of living in a radically different culture. The baffling educational system evokes endless discussion. Inquiring and responsive students are a constant delight. Many teachers become friends of Africans who live close to the soil, forest, and tribe. For most teachers this is a first experience of living with missionaries at a "mission station." Newcomers may ask embarrassing questions, but in time they learn to listen and observe. A Mennonite teacher tells of living with incongruities: "In Zaire I teach French refugees from Portuguese-speaking Angola in a Methodist school with a Canadian Baptist as headmaster."

Many teachers find the three years of withdrawal from American life and values a time to reflect on vocational goals and life purposes. Stimulated by the Africa teaching experience, dozens of TAP alumni have pursued master's and doctoral studies in language, African history and culture, tropical agriculture, and international development. They have sensed the exhilaration of being with a people during the first generation of their new nationhood: so much to do, so many problems to solve. They observe African leaders trimming their inflated expectations and settling down to the long task of national development. Some teachers find significant roles in the life of African churches. Teaching in Africa has offered opportunities for encounters between idealism and institutional realities.

The TAP teacher comes as an outsider, "an expatriate." For thousands of years Africans have had an effective educational system. Education in traditional African society centered on daily life and the initiation camp. In community settings, children and young people learned from their elders the skills of farming, hunting, and village living. In initiation camps, young men and women learned the history, lore, and secrets of a society which prepared them for adulthood. This was education without formal schools.

With the coming of colonial governments and missions, Western-style schools began to train a selected few Africans in European subjects: reading, writing, arithmetic, and hygiene. With this training Africans could become skilled servants, colonial clerks, and white-collar administrators. Although studies conducted in the 1920s and 1950s urged more holistic African educational systems, these European-style schools with a European curriculum persisted into the years of independence. African students were required to memorize the rivers of the British Isles, the kings of France, British weights and measures. The African leaders of independence—Felix Houphouet-Boigny of the Ivory Coast, Sekou Toure of Guinea, Tom Mboya of Kenya, Julius Nyerere of Tanzania, and others—criticized this elite schooling for the few. But since most educational officials in the new African countries were trained in this way, the European school system continued with only slight modifications. The system focused on state examinations as the means to obtaining a school diploma, the key to jobs, and upward mobility.

During the 1970s, critics from Africa and Latin America declared that Western-style schools were not producing the desired results in developing societies. Two provocative educators in Latin America—Ivan Illich in Cuernavaca, Mexico, and Paulo Freier in Recife, Brazil—criticized systems in which the pupil is "schooled to confuse teaching with learning, grade advancement with education, a diploma with competence, and fluency with the ability to say something new." Mennonite Central Committee's Nancy Heisey, in her 1977 pamphlet monograph, *Integrating Education and Development*, reviewed the Latin Americans' critique of "packaged instruction with certification" and their revolutionary alternatives. They emphasized the possibilities of nonformal education: the community as a resource, the student as a self-reliant learner, the role of dialogue based on reciprocity and respect, and the principle of "conscientization" (learning how the system works and moving toward political action to change it). These alternative theories were, of course, the work of outsiders; many Africans were seeking a uniquely African system.

Nancy Heisey, who served as a TAP teacher in Zaire and later administered MCC programs in Africa, outlined ways in which expatriate teachers can rise above entrapment by the structures. In the classroom, teachers can "contribute to their students' development of a sense of self-worth as well as piquing their intellectual curiosity and encouraging them to see themselves as contributors to solutions of community problems." The teacher can "encourage the students to investigate their culture and examine it realistically and positively." This can involve studying community water resources or the nutritional value of traditional foods, collecting old tales and proverbs, helping with adult literacy, observing traditional designs in African crafts. Although expatriate teachers cannot be active agents of change in African educational structures, Heisey encouraged teachers to suggest changes and, with care, to voice criticisms.

From the beginning of TAP, MCC staff wondered whether the new African countries were wise in placing so much emphasis on secondary schools and universities. Periodically, TAP evaluations have urged that African leaders and MCC should turn their attention to nonformal or village education. Programs outside the classroom may not lead to diplomas and certificates, but they do focus on the needs of women as the primary farmers; the needs of families in child care, health, and household arts; the needs of men for remunerative trades; the needs of pastors in biblical study and pastoral care; the needs of school dropouts for on-the-job instruction. In recent years, MCC has shifted from placing teachers in established schools to placing them in community development programs. In less formal settings, MCC teachers are more likely to listen, to observe, and to value the folk wisdom rooted in the African experience. Such programs are rarely funded by African governments; this trend, thus, requires of MCC heavier financial support.

In the Teachers Abroad Program in Africa, MCC has been less a manager than a facilitator and servant of others. Some observers urge MCC to operate its own educational programs as a means of modeling desirable alternatives. Others encourage MCC to help others carry out their programs. Perhaps MCC ought to do both.

> Eight hundred MCC teachers have gone to Africa to teach, and eight hundred have returned from three or more years as students of African culture. One TAP volunteer reflected: "I went to Africa to tell Africans what they needed. I returned, Africans having taught me what I needed."

8

Serving on Both Sides:

Biafra

When thousands of people are dying, MCC
ought not focus only on the theoretical questions.
                                        —Atlee Beechy

Biafra, the short-lived secessionist rival of Nigeria, is one of
the contested areas in which MCC has placed relief workers
amid extreme human suffering. From 1967 to early 1970, a
bloody civil war raged in Nigeria's southeast corner, where
members of the Ibo tribe, declaring their new government
"The Republic of Biafra," sought independence from Africa's
most populous nation. After nearly three years of fighting, the
federal military government defeated the rebels. But the cost
was high. By the end of the war some two million Biafran civilians were dead, many of them children who had succumbed
to a slow death of starvation. Three and a half million survivors—impoverished and displaced—were compressed into
the tiny, landlocked region.

Roots of Nigeria's civil war are found in the nineteenth-
century carving up of Africa by European colonial powers. Nigeria, independent of Great Britain since 1960, had within its
boundaries numerous tribes which held tribal loyalty above the
new national allegiance. Three powerful and competitive tribal

groups separated by the mighty Niger River—the Ibo of the east, the Hausa of the north, and the Yoruba of the west—dominated the country during the tenuous early years of Nigerian independence. The predominantly Catholic Ibos, highly educated and assertive in business, politics, and professional life, chafed under Nigeria's military and government rulers. In January 1966 Ibo military officers, seeking to ward off an alliance between Nigeria's north and west tribal leaders, staged a coup and assassinated Nigeria's prime minister and other high officials.

Within the new military hierarchy two leaders rose to power. One, Yakubu Gowan, belonged to a minority tribe in the north. The other, Chukwuemeka Odumegwu Ojukwu, was an Ibo. In the northern city of Kano, where MCC sponsored North American volunteers through its Teachers Abroad Program (TAP), anti-Ibo tensions heightened. In this Muslim-dominated northern city lived thousands of Christian Ibos who years earlier had left their native southeast. By the mid-sixties these Ibos comprised an upper-class minority in Kano and other northern cities. The able, educated, assertive Ibos—leaders in government and the professions—evoked resentment from their northern and western neighbors. In the summer and fall of 1966, anti-Ibo violence erupted. A military countercoup, followed by the massacre of thirty thousand Ibos, forced nearly two million of these people back to their ancestral area.

Nationalist leader General Gowan decided to balance Nigerian power by partitioning the country into twelve small states. The Ibos, however, resisted Gowan's plan, in which they stood to lose eastern coastal oil reserves and two major seaports. In May 1967, Ibo leader Ojukwu, caught at the losing end of this power struggle, announced a formal secession. He named the new Ibo nation after the "Bight of Biafra," a bay bordering the region's southeastern coast. Both military colonels built up their armies and launched a full-scale war. The Biafrans called it a "war of independence" and the Nigerians, "a rebellion."

In the remaining months of 1967, General Ojukwu invaded neutral provinces in the midwest and threatened to advance toward Nigeria's capital, Lagos. In return, federal troops seized Biafra's capital, Enugu. As the war escalated, more cities in northern, western, and southeastern Biafra collapsed: Nsukka, Onitsha, Bonny, and Calabar. By the spring of 1968, mass starvation set in as federal troops squeezed Biafra from all sides, down to an area one-third its original size. Munitions supplied by Great Britain and the Soviet Union aided the federal cause.

After federal forces took the Biafran shipping center of Port Harcourt, Biafra found itself cut off from the sea and from food supply lines. For the remainder of the war, weapons sent by France and food sent by relief agencies from around the world funneled into Biafra by air and landed on a seventy-five-foot wide airstrip at Uli. Joint Church Aid and Red Cross planes, carrying tons of relief rations stocked at the islands of São Tomë and Fernando Poo, provided a sustaining link between Biafra's seven million people and the outside world.

Mennonite aid to war sufferers originated with the presence of medical missionaries, placed by Mennonite Board of Missions, at Abiriba Joint Hospital in eastern Nigeria. Among the missionaries there when war broke out were Wallace and Evelyn Schellenberger. He was a doctor and she was a nurse. The couple returned to the United States in late 1968 exhausted from months of intense relief work in Abiriba. They carried a message of urgency to North American Mennonites about the intense human suffering in the African pocket of Biafra.

Mennonite Central Committee had begun its TAP program in Nigeria in 1963. Five years later MCC had more than forty workers in the country, mostly teachers but also Paxmen assigned to do agricultural development. In September 1968, MCC loaned two Mennonite nurses, Susie Miller and Barbara Souder, to the Christian Council of Nigeria (CCN). The two

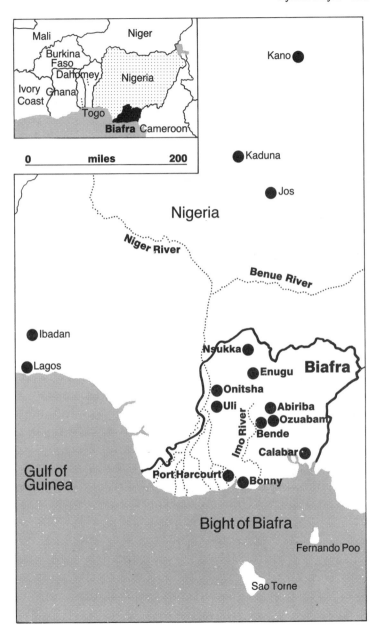

joined a CCN relief team at Enugu, the former Biafran capital city which had come under federal control.

Back in the United States, the Schellenbergers publicized the need for medical personnel on the Biafran side of the conflict, where kwashiorkor, or protein starvation, was killing as many as a thousand children in a single day. In response to the needs in eastern Nigeria the American Friends Service Committee and the Mennonite Central Committee formed Quaker-Mennonite service. In January 1969 MCC administrator Atlee Beechy accompanied the Schellenbergers and physician Linford Gehman to Abiriba to learn more about Biafra and to make recommendations for the new program. At the return of the missionary couple, many Biafrans greeted them joyfully: "Welcome. You must really care to come back at this difficult time." Another nurse, Martha Bender, joined the medical team two months later. A fifth member of the Quaker-Mennonite Service team was Jon Yager, who coordinated transportation and distribution of relief foods in cooperation with the World Council of Churches.

Working on "both sides" of the conflict was not a new experience for MCC, but it required logistical care and sensitive communication. The administration of relief aid had already erupted into a secondary battle among Generals Gowan and Ojukwu. The federal government objected to the airlifting of food to Biafra, since guns were also being flown in, but offered to provide food to civilians by road. Biafran officials rejected the offer, fearing that military troops would follow. Gowan's critics accused him of using starvation as a weapon over Biafra's faltering military stance; Ojukwu's critics accused *him* of politicizing the starvation of his people to gain international sympathy.

In 1969 Atlee Beechy noted:

> The power and meaning of tribal loyalties have seldom been fully understood by the West. . . . There is an atmosphere of

fear hanging over the people of Biafra. They believe they will all
be killed if the Nigerians take over.... Bitterness and hatred
... are deeply rooted and have been smoldering and breaking
out periodically for centuries.... The longer the war continues
the deeper the fracture becomes.

The Quaker-Mennonite presence in Biafra from 1969 to
1970 was part of an international relief effort. Three major organizations dominated relief operations: the International
Committee of the Red Cross, the Catholic relief agency
CARITAS, and many denominations doing relief work under
the umbrella of the World Council of Churches. All foreign organizations were obligated to relate to the Christian Council of
Nigeria.

The complexity of these relief agency relationships
concerned some in MCC. Clearly, Biafra was the scene of
intense human suffering, but some MCCers questioned
whether the assistance of international relief agencies simply
freed funds in Nigeria and Biafra for military supplies. Others
wondered whether MCC, if dependent on the directives of a
Nigeria-based relief agency, could still maintain its independent stance and serve victims of war regardless of their
political persuasion. MCC found the cooperative effort with
the American Friends Service Committee—a well-respected
agency accustomed to working independently—gratifying,
challenging, and sometimes frustrating. MCC veteran Atlee
Beechy, during the exploratory visit to Biafra early in 1969,
noted:

> The situation in Biafra is extremely complex and fluid. Changes
> can come very quickly. The pressures to support the national
> and military goals of Biafra are immense. The stark, harsh suffer-
> ing of the people break through at all points and present a
> human tragedy [with] dimensions we can only begin to
> comprehend.

Following are excerpts of letters written between January
and July 1969 to family and friends of the Quaker-Mennonite

service team. The doctors and nurses, who had to relocate several times, gave eyewitness accounts of events in the final grim year of war when Federal troops closed in on the Ibo people of Biafra.

From the Hospital at Abiriba

January 1 My responsibility is the male ward and half of children's ward. Most of the cases are war casualties, mostly gunshot wounds with compound fractures, many of which get infected.... The operating room is a mess.... It's almost impossible to maintain good aseptic technique all the time when there are so many abcesses to incise and drain and so many injuries to repair.

January 12 This area is quite safe. The airport, no. If the troops come we will know in advance and clear out, I guess.

February 9 Many [patients] are weakened by malnutrition and therefore more susceptible to bacillary dysentery, pneumonia, and meningitis, from which they die.... A grown man died on my ward the other night less than 24 hours after he was admitted. When they're extremely malnourished a full meal sometimes does them in, like it did this man. He came too late.

March 9 With an increase in patient load, our workdays are longer.... When one suddenly has to work furiously for a long stretch, even a 12-hour workday thereafter doesn't seem strenuous.

One of the hospital workers ... called the whole staff together yesterday to announce his intentions to get married next month. In the traditional manner the chiefs of the village sat around a table in the front of the room, and all the invited guests shared a feast of sorts—cut short by the scarcity of the food.... Many of the men here, young and old, can really conduct a church service with poise and confidence. They know the Bible well and they take religion seriously, especially now when they see themselves a little like David saw himself when he was surrounded by his enemies. They know that the Nigerian army is only 20 miles away and that the bomber may zoom down on them tomorrow.

March 29 We hear many rumors about the advancing army.... [Yesterday] there were several loud explosions and five minutes later two jets streaked north of the hospital going west, moving at top speed, empty and heading for home. I was relieved to watch them fade out of sight. When I walked back to the operating room, my patient, who already had his pre-operative medication, was nowhere in sight. He soon came walking in from his hideout under a palm tree in the bush.

March 30 The shelling is now close enough to shake the building and small arms fire can easily be heard. An Ilyushin bomber flew very low over the road several times this morning but dropped no bombs....

From Ozu Abam

April 3 [Last weekend] the Nigerians advanced very rapidly in a way we never expected. They came through some bush roads with heavy artillery and the Biafrans couldn't hold them back.... By Sunday they were within 5 miles of Abiriba and the shelling was so loud our house shook....

Sunday afternoon we started evacuating patients, staff, and equipment. We moved to Ohafia that night.... Monday a.m. Wally and I decided to try to get back into Abiriba to get a few more essential things. I can't explain how eerie it was driving back—we could tell the Biafrans were retreating.... *Thousands* of refugees were walking along the roadside.... [Tuesday] we decided we must evacuate again—off the main road and into the bush. We had about 40 patients we moved from Abiriba who were completely helpless with casts, etc. So we moved these poor people for the second time to Ozu Abam, where we're trying to set up a temporary hospital. Ozu Abam is really in the bush. . . . I think we've all aged 10 years over this.

From Umuahia

April 16 [in the bush] we were surrounded with Nigerians and so decided we'd better get to Umuahia and stay there a few days to see what would happen. We had to travel about 70 miles to get to Umuahia over bad roads. When we reached Umuahia—yesterday—all the "white people" had left the city and people were streaming out of the city in every possible direction. It was a pathetic sight—people carrying their only possessions on their head, children straggling along, crying of hunger and tired, cars were loaded down with people and possessions—no one knowing exactly where to go next. . . . The soldiers are tired of fighting and everyone is sick of war.

From Ihie

April 28 One hardly knows what to do, where to start. . . . We hold a clinic, give out a lot of vitamins and iron to dozens of children and adults with all the signs and symptoms of protein deficiency, when what they really need is milk, eggs, cornmeal, and stockfish but the supply at the feeding center is barely enough to provide two meals a week.

May 19 The hospital at Ozu Abam is perhaps the only civilian hospital functioning in the remaining part of Eastern Biafra. . . . It's discouraging, indeed sickening, to see the incidence of malnutrition soaring again in the Abiriba area, when two months ago we had actually almost wiped out kwashiorkor in that area.

Hungry soldiers, some of them carrying guns, at the various checkpoints along the roads constitute a disturbing influence to my peace of mind. Always in the corner of my mind, too, is the likelihood of getting stranded in the bush due to washouts or car trouble. I've changed 6 flat tires in the past month.

July 16 At a WCC meeting over two weeks ago we were warned to be very careful with facts and opinions in letters that we send out, not to say too much about the war or even to describe too vividly the signs of hunger that we see all around us. There's a fear that relief planes may be forced to land in Nigeria for inspection (so far it hasn't happened).

Planes are coming in at a rate of up to 12 Church Aid flights a night, enough to keep sick bays, hospitals, and orphanages from drying up, but not enough to prompt the Nigerians to interfere. It appears that in the talks between Nigeria and the relief agencies . . . food is equated with ammunition. . . . It's a pity that blame for prolongation of the war should be placed on those supplying the food rather than on the countries supplying arms.

On December 24, 1969, nearly a year after the Quaker-Mennonite team arrived in Biafra, remaining members Martha Bender and Linford Gehman left their clinic at the village of Ihie and crossed the Imo River to Obizi. The following morning, Christmas Day, federal troops blew up the bridge and invaded Ihie. Two weeks later, on January 9, 1970, Bender and Gehman evacuated by air to the island of São Tomé. On January 12, after rebel leader General Ojukwu and his family fled by plane, Biafra surrendered to Nigeria. An MCC relief worker on the Nigeria-controlled side recalled hearing news of cease-fire:

Our British colleagues from the Red Cross team at Uturu mission came roaring up our hill in the LandRover, to leap out and shout, "The war's over! Ojukwu's left! It's really over!" And we all stood speechless, that still Sunday afternoon, wondering what this news, if true, would mean for us at the Awgu Hospital and especially for the Nigerian people.

Starvation and the ravages of war persisted in the following months. Remarkably, the victorious federal government moved swiftly to feed and care for the people of Biafra. General Gowan called for a three-day period of prayer and asked Nigeria's fifty-three million people to accept the Ibos. In 1970 Mennonite Central Committee enlarged its Nigeria program, placing doctors, nurses, and relief administrators under the auspices of the Christian Council of Nigeria.

MCC administrators, looking back, acknowledge that working relationships with the Christian Council of Nigeria and other relief agencies—both during and after the war—were complicated by the fact that MCC workers served both sides. Atlee Beechy observed that the volunteers exhibited "courage, compassion, and commitment . . . a faith at work in raw, brutal, and harsh realities."

In the heat of civil war MCC administrators had wondered whether TAP persons in Northern Nigeria would be asked to leave because MCC was also assisting the rebel forces in Biafra. MCC attempted to be an apolitical presence in a politicized zone, yet the possibilities for "compromise" abounded. Personnel with AFSC carried messages between federal and Biafra territory. Was MCC's work on both sides of the lines seen as reconciling or treasonous? At what point should personnel in Biafra withdraw? In struggles for independence, whose is the just cause? Beechy concluded, "When thousands of people are dying, MCC ought not focus only on the theoretical questions. It was *right* for us to be there."

9

In the Shadow of Apartheid:

The Transkei

*Never can we allow the government to set the
terms of Christian fellowship. That's what
Pretoria has tried to do for a long time.*

The eyes of the black hotel clerk narrowed as we wrote our
address in the register. It was our first visit to Johannesburg for
a meeting at the South African Council of Churches office and
we were checking into a small hotel nearby for the night.
"Umtata, Transkei? Americans? What do you do there?" His
voice was full of suspicion. "Development consultant?" He
shook his head disapprovingly. "For whom—what government? You know you shouldn't be there."

"No, with the church, the Transkei Council of Churches.
We're here for a meeting at the SACC."

The change was immediate and the laugh warm and wel-
coming. "Oh, so you're one of Tutu's boys? Well, I hope you
have a good meeting. Give my regards to the bishop."

With whom we work is always important. It is perhaps especially important when we work in South Africa, racially divided
and internationally scorned. MCC has been working in the
Transkei, one of South Africa's black homelands, since 1978,
and our presence there has never ceased to be controversial.

117

How did we decide to go there? What does our presence there mean?

Background—South Africa

South Africa is a land of great beauty and great contrast. From tropical palm trees and sugarcane on its wet eastern coast to the arid Karroo, from the flat wheat lands of the high veld to the rugged peaks of the Drakensberg (Dragon-mountains), South Africa encompasses great variety and vast resources. There is variety, too, in its peoples. Most South Africans are black, members of several ethnic groupings. The most populous of these are the Zulu, Xhosa, Sotho, and Tswana peoples. There are also communities of Indians who were brought to South Africa by the British to work in the sugarcane fields. The "Coloured" people have as their background intermarriage between white settlers, Malay slaves, and native African peoples. With dark skins but a European culture they stand awkwardly between the blacks and whites. White people—descendants of settlers from as long ago as the 1640s—make up roughly one-fifth of South Africa's population. They are divided into two groups, the "English" and the "Afrikaners," the latter descendants of early Dutch settlers who speak a derivation of Dutch called "Afrikaans."

Throughout South Africa's history, various groups have been in conflict. Wars between the Zulus and other tribes caused migrations as far north as Malawi in the 1830s. Black inhabitants and white settlers fought many wars over land rights. The Anglo-Boer War, in which the British in 1903 defeated the Afrikaners and incorporated them into one country, is still remembered with great bitterness.

Currently, conflict in South Africa takes the form of racial division, symbolized by the word "apartheid." Apartheid, or separateness, is a political philosophy implemented by the Afrikaner-based National Party after it came to power in 1948, but the term is used more broadly to refer to any discriminatory

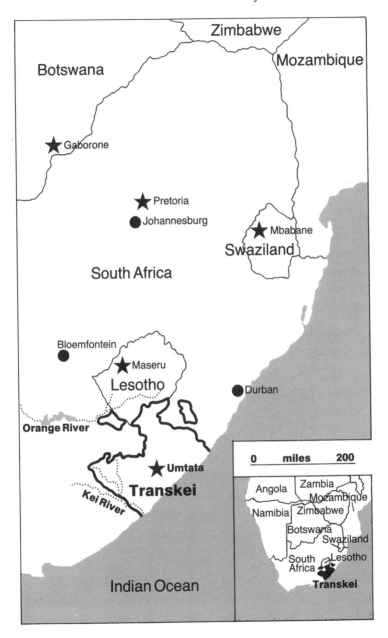

laws, including those passed before that date. The expressed goal of apartheid was segregation of the various groups that comprised South Africa, through separate living areas, separate public facilities, separate political structures, separate churches. The unspoken goal was white domination and retention of the vast wealth of South Africa.

Under apartheid, most of South Africa, including its best farmland and its reserves of mineral wealth, was preserved for the whites. Blacks were assigned to rural "homelands," largely barren areas which had already been native reserves. The crowded, impoverished homelands were to be the basis for black development. Some blacks would still be needed in white areas as laborers and would mine the gold and run the factories on which the economy depended. However, they would really belong in the homelands. This was the basis for influx-control laws and the migratory labor system. Blacks were to be in white areas only if they were employed there, and to prove this they had to carry a "pass" into which proof of their status was stamped. Families of workers were to remain in the homelands. These rural areas would eventually develop to the point that they could be given independence and function as completely separate countries.

Although the government moved more than three million (mostly black) people from their homes in an attempt to consolidate the separate areas, and although thousands were arrested each year for pass-law violations, the economic pull of jobs and the emotional pull of family ties drew blacks from homelands into the urban areas. Attempts at developing the overcrowded and poor homelands could not counter this move. More recently, the government has begun to backpedal, making some concessions that recognize the permanence of "urban blacks" in white South Africa. These concessions have been too limited to satisfy blacks, who have since early in this century fought to establish their right to be a part of the structure of a unified South Africa.

Thus, apartheid could not work, economically or politically. But the tragedy is that in some ways it *has* worked. Few whites know blacks in any roles other than those of servant, employee, or garage-station attendant. Even in the churches, with the exception of some prophets like Beyers Naude, whites are comfortable and silent. Many label the black Christians who speak out against injustices as "too political." Black frustration is heard rarely by whites or acknowledged as justified.

An eighteen-year-old from Johannesburg, visiting the Transkei, was shocked at the way people live: "I didn't know there was poverty like this in South Africa. And all these people—I've never seen so many blacks. In Jo'burg, it's easy to assume that whites are in the majority in South Africa."

Background—The Transkei

The drive south from Johannesburg takes one through miles of farmland: first, the rich, corn-producing high veld, with large fields reminiscent of North America's central plains, and later, the drier grazing areas dotted with sagebrush and sheep. The countryside is empty, with only the occasional farmhouse or small country town. Then one comes to the Orange River. On the other side of the river, there is no more grass. Rocky hills are dotted with small, round houses. Suddenly, people are everywhere: the women carrying their pails of water, the children with their tin-can toys. "Welcome," says the sign, "to the Republic of Transkei."

Not all of the Transkei's territory is as barren as that first sight. In good years, the rolling hills of grass which reach to the Indian Ocean support many cattle, although eroded gulleys testify to overgrazing. But everywhere are clusters of houses. The Transkei is full of people who have been forced out of the white towns, who can get no land outside the boundaries of these homelands. Most of the people here are the old, the young, and those who cannot get jobs "outside."

The Transkei is the home of the Xhosa, a proud and strong

people. The most southern of the Bantu peoples of South
Africa, they were the first to encounter white settlers moving
east from Cape Town in the early 1800s. The "Kaffir Wars" of
that time led to a stalemate. The Xhosa were granted land east
of the Kei River as a reserve which the settlers could not
penetrate. Their independent spirit led to resistance against
government interference as recently as the 1960s.

In 1963 the Transkei was granted self-governing status by
South Africa in preparation for becoming the first homeland to
be granted "independence" in 1976. The Transkei is governed
from the capital city of Umtata by a parliament, with a majority of members chiefs who owe their jobs and salary to the
government. The parliament is headed by the State President,
a Paramount Chief. The government, through the civil service
and paragovernmental organizations, is the largest employer in
the Transkei, and its budget comes predominantly from South
African "foreign aid." By far the majority of the Transkei's four
million people are rural subsistence farmers who depend for
their income and livelihood on cash earnings of family members working as migratory laborers in white areas of South
Africa. The wage earner, separated from his family for most of
his working life in the distant mines, returns home to his family
for only a few weeks a year.

It is difficult to estimate the extent to which the Transkei can
be considered independent. Its economy is based in South
Africa, but so is that of Lesotho to the north, which is internationally recognized. Organizations which are banned in South
Africa are also outlawed in the Transkei, and Transkeian security police work closely with police in South Africa. The
Transkei is very much a part of the larger system of oppression
and separation.

Because it functions as a part of the system of apartheid, the
Transkei has not been recognized as independent by the
international community. As a result, agencies and firms from
all over the world have generally refused to operate within its

boundaries, cutting the Transkei off from even the development help it might receive if it were an acknowledged part of South Africa. Reluctance on the part of the world community to open itself to the charge of supporting apartheid has led to the virtual isolation of this region.

Transkeians cannot speak freely about their attitudes toward "independence," since to oppose it openly would be considered treasonous. For some, independence is a source of pride, but many persons consciously speak of themselves as "South Africans." One man shows his Transkei passport, useless for travel anywhere beyond South Africa. "Not that I want it to be recognized," he hastens to explain. "What I want is to be legally considered what I am in fact—a South African from South Africa." With Transkei's puppet government, supported by South African money, it is difficult to conceive of "The Republic of Transkei" as anything other than a temporary arrangement.

The Debate—Can MCC Work in a Homeland?

What does it mean to work in a place like the Transkei? That there are human needs is obvious, but the root or structural causes of these needs are overwhelming. To get involved pitches one into the midst of a difficult dilemma. Will the good that MCC might do be outweighed by the negative attention a "foreign" presence brings? How can MCC maintain a focus on people and their needs when the political situation is so compromised? The testimony of an Umtata pastor helps to keep the discussion focused: "We are hurt by the ostracism of the world, especially by the churches. We didn't ask for this independence; it was thrust on us. It's as if we find ourselves on the cross. Please do not say, as did Jesus' tormentors, 'Save yourself.' Rather, come and suffer and agonize with us."

The "needs of people" remained a central focus during the long period of MCC discussions and consultations. But nothing is more complex than people, their needs, or how to be of help.

In a system of political injustice the oppression goes from top to bottom, and at times right through the church.

MCC first considered the possibility of placing personnel in the Transkei in 1976 after an agency representative met with a group of Protestant church leaders in South Africa. These leaders, facing the indignity of apartheid, wanted some help in their daily struggles. They expressed unhappiness with the tendency of Western observers to speak only of the large and abstract problems of injustice. They explained that if MCC consented to work in South Africa (the Transkei), MCC would find that the pressing daily needs of ordinary people would often take priority over lofty abstractions. Some in MCC wondered how a new program in this country might be free from government intervention. This concern led them to ask, "Does MCC sometimes not see clearly the forest for the trees?" Others in MCC replied, "Are not the trees actually people asking for help?"

The decision of whether or not to get involved was difficult. Some hesitated over MCC's involvement. They believed that the Transkei should not exist as an independent nation; the presence of MCC and assistance to the Transkei might make it stronger, part of the grand design of apartheid. Black people in South Africa were increasingly settling on the idea that they alone must be the creators of their liberation. MCC workers, usually white, might get in the way. Did MCC want to risk appearing to be "on the wrong side"?

Others, especially those living in this troublesome situation, reflected another point of view. Help can only build confidence, without which no change can come. The church in the Transkei asked for help. Should Mennonites refuse to aid a fellow Christian community because of a political situation over which they have little control? Surely MCC could say "yes" to certain people in the Transkei without saying "yes" to the government and its puppet relationship to South Africa.

Acknowledging that entry into the Transkei was a "calling"

for MCC was a slow process. Representatives of the Mennonite academic community were divided about MCC involvement but basically supportive. Mennonite workers in the South Africa region experienced a similar division, but after intense debate, most of them affirmed the new work. North American and European non-Mennonite church leaders, however, were almost unanimous in saying, "Stay out." Black American Mennonites also opposed MCC's entry. Individuals within South Africa, surveyed primarily through the South African Council of Churches, were divided. But the South Africa Council of Churches supported MCC after it decided to enter the Transkei.

Reflecting on the decision of MCC to enter the Transkei, one administrator has reflected recently that the consensus to enter the country was more deliberate than were some other decisions about entering new programs. He added, however: "History has made those deliberations into a much more significant and careful process than they actually were. In Transkei it was perhaps more important that appropriate personnel became available."

Program: Transkei Expansion

Ethical problems from everyday life in the Transkei posed questions for MCC. Initially, MCC was closely associated with the Transkei Council of Churches (TCC). Tim and Suzanne Lind arrived in July 1978 to begin a three-year assignment. Tim worked as a project consultant for the TCC and Suzanne concentrated on the issues surrounding the ongoing work of Mennonites in South Africa.

Late in 1979 the Linds' work was disrupted when the Transkei government issued banning orders for thirty-four organizations including the South African Council of Churches, of which the Transkei Council of Churches is a regional body. A reason for the attack on the TCC was that it had urged that the Transkei remain a "region" of South Africa and not an independent state. Although the banning was not without warning, it was a serious blow to the church community. In the uncertainty that followed, the Transkei Council of Churches decided to close its offices and continue only its most urgent program with skeleton staff. One TCC officer stated: "It was the Mennonites who made it possible for the Transkei Council of Churches to carry on while church leaders decided what steps to take next."

Negotiations with the government to have the ban lifted were fruitless. All doors seemed closed. With all conciliatory paths tested, TCC leaders decided to try the only remaining option: to open the TCC again and resume business as usual, stating simply that it was not the government's right to dictate the terms on which the church could operate. The government did not respond. At this writing the Transkei government has neither lifted the ban on the Transkei Council of Churches nor prevented it from doing its work as usual.

The TCC reestablished some of its programs and built up a new local staff. Although the Linds left in mid-1981, another MCC couple, David Neufeld and Maggie Andres, arrived later that year to work as community development workers in a rural area. In mid-1982 Robert and Judy Herr arrived. Robert worked part-time as a consultant for TCC program development, and both assumed responsibility for the growing MCC program activities in other parts of South Africa. Late in 1982, Larry Hills of Africa Inter-Mennonite Mission came to work in a TCC-sponsored Bible teaching program for African Independent Churches.

Over the years the contacts and relationships have grown slowly. MCC has cooperated with the Reformed Presbyterian Church, headquartered in Umtata, on visitor-exchange programs and on raising the issue of forced relocations in South Africa. Individual Mennonite workers have been involved in the South African Missiological Society, in a community worker support group, and in local university conferences and forums. Twice during these years drought relief schemes have drawn Mennonite workers into sensitive positions of negotiation between government and church.

There has been little reduction in tension between church and government. The unstated TCC position of no support for homeland structures has cast Mennonite workers in a suspicious light. On one occasion, this position led to a costly prison experience for a Transkei Council of Churches staff person. There have been many other occasions of uncertainty and of fear.

For local authorities, the Mennonite presence has been a mixed blessing. The proximity of international persons, so few in the Transkei, is valued. But MCC's work has consistently been to build up a local church organization that persists in ministering to *all* people, even those whom the authorities perceive as a threat. Mennonites are viewed by the Transkei government as questionable guests in this unique land.

Program: South Africa Expansion

Mennonite Central Committee's decision to work in the Transkei was a difficult one, and many of the issues first raised in 1976 remain. While MCCers working in the Transkei avoid sanctioning the "independent" status of the Transkei, it is because of this status that MCC has been able to have a South Africa program. Earlier attempts to place workers elsewhere in South Africa were frustrated. Mennonites working in the region are routinely denied visas to travel in the white areas of South Africa.

Even before MCC workers arrived in the Transkei, Mennonites were supportive of South Africans who objected to military conscription. When at first two, and then many more, young men whose churches were not peace churches chose jail rather than army service, MCC through its workers stood by them with personal and financial support. MCCers provided resources for the burgeoning conscientious-objector (C.O.)

movement which has become a significant force in South Africa to the extent that the government recognized the right to do alternative service. The South African C.O. movement and the campaign to end conscription are now strong enough to generate their own support and resources. But MCC was there at a crucial time. Perhaps this has contributed to the view of one of the top officials in the South African government that "Mennonites are considered very dangerous."

A second particular focus of MCC South Africa programming has been the issue of relocations, or forced removals. Beginning in 1980, MCC workers researched this issue, carrying on work started by the South African Council of Churches. Relocation research helped to sensitize the consciences of South Africans. As a result, the South African Council of Churches hired a fieldworker to deal with relocations and relocated communities. MCC now supports two SACC workers who assist communities wishing to resist removal. They also work with those who have been forcibly moved from their homes into designated homeland areas.

Throughout its involvement in South Africa, MCC has worked closely with the South African Council of Churches of which Archbishop Desmond Tutu and Beyers Naude have been recent executive secretaries. This ecumenical body is held in suspicion by the government because it speaks out on behalf of its church members, the majority of whom are black and are victims of apartheid laws.

MCC's work in the Transkei presents opportunities to understand and work with South African problems. MCC workers interact with people for whom migratory labor, influx control, detention without trial, and all of the indignities of apartheid are a way of life. In addition, the Transkei is a rural backwater, far from the centers of action and power. While anger and seething violence are not present in the Transkei in obvious ways, neither is there much vision for the work of reconciliation.

The Ongoing Dilemma

Prior to 1978 the dilemma as MCC understood it focused on the nature and implications of an MCC presence in a South African homeland. Today the discussion is rather one of how MCC can work there with integrity. MCC in the Transkei now has a history. MCCers have cultivated relationships and made commitments. The issues facing MCC workers are intense:

1. A decision to work only through church structures has allowed MCC to minimize contact with government homeland structures. However, should MCC consider placing personnel in other than church-based assignments?

2. MCC's work has been geared toward the rural areas of the Transkei, where victims of apartheid live on the bottom rung of the social ladder. Is it important to find other levels on which to work as well, to get closer to power centers? A heavy burden will continue to fall on the individuals responsible for dismantling apartheid and replacing it with new societal structures. Can and should MCC move closer to this process?

3. It is never easy to know whom to listen to when making decisions about involvement in South Africa. A pastor in the Transkei once told an MCC worker: "If I ever need to flee South Africa, and become a refugee in Lesotho or some other place, I would probably feel compelled to tell MCC to do the same. But as long as I am here, struggling in this context, I want you here working with me."

4. Currently, international attitudes are hardening on the issue of contact with South Africa. What does it mean for MCC to talk about program expansion when many demand a pullback?

5. Some leading members of the South African Christian community believe that as tensions rise, churches will be exploited in ways that do not enhance Christian fellowship. How do MCC workers, new to the country, find their way through these subtle but critical relationships?

In a discussion about whether MCC should be in the

Transkei, the General Secretary of the Reformed Presbyterian Church in South Africa stated, "For the Mennonites never to have come, or to go away for some political reason, would be to deny the universality of the church. Never can we allow the government to set the terms of Christian fellowship. That's what Pretoria has tried to do for a long time." This, in brief, has been the position of MCC, but the day-to-day steps are never an easy process. The way forward is as difficult today as was the initial decision to come to the Transkei.

10

Speaking Out:

Raids on Maseru and Gaborone

Often MCC workers are eyewitnesses to violent events reported at home on the evening news.

At 1:40 on the morning of June 14, 1985, Sara and Fremont Regier, codirectors of Mennonite Ministries (MM) in Botswana, woke abruptly to the sound of machine gun fire and bombs exploding close to their home in the capital city of Gaborone. They could hear shouting in Afrikaans, the language of Dutch South Africans, and countless rounds of ammunition directed at a house just down the street. A flash of light and flying debris accompanied the last explosion. After half an hour, when the sound of vehicles driving toward the border died away, Gaborone was shrouded in silence.

An hour of eerie quiet passed before Fremont and his teenage son, Nathan, ventured out to see how MM workers Henry and Naomi Unrau and their three young daughters had fared. In the small servants' quarters behind the bombed house, Henry, Fremont, and Nathan found the body of a young South African university student slumped in a corner. Shaken, they returned to their homes to sit out the night in darkness. Later an undetonated bomb covered by the rubble exploded, killing a man and injuring his wife.

In the morning, grim news reports and personal accounts confirmed what the Regiers and Unraus had already guessed: ten sites in Gaborone had been targets of the latest South African military raid, an attempt to destroy the African National Congress (ANC) as a political base a few miles from the South African border. Because the South African government had banned the ANC, a predominantly black political party opposing apartheid, many ANC members lived in Zambia, Botswana, and Lesotho. The raid left at least eleven South African refugees and Botswana citizens dead and more wounded.

The tragedy at Gaborone was reminiscent of the Maseru raid in 1982. South African commandos attacked twelve preselected sites in Lesotho's small capital early on the morning of December 9, killing at least forty-three people. Many of the victims were ANC-related refugees who had left South Africa because of the ban on their political party; twelve were innocent civilians of the Basotho tribe. There were three Mennonite mission and MCC families in Maseru at the time of the raid.

Incidents like these raise the issue of how personnel should react to military-political intrusion into their service programs. Often MCC workers are eyewitnesses to violent events reported at home on the evening news. In Botswana, where Mennonite Ministries is administered jointly by the Africa Inter-Mennonite Mission and Mennonite Central Committee, agency workers shared their neighbors' shock, sorrow, and anger in the face of the surprise attack and infringements of national sovereignty. They anticipated that North American government officials would receive falsified South African reports of the raid and that families and friends would read glossed-over news accounts of the massacre. They wondered: Are MCC workers responsible for sending accurate reports of politically charged events to MCC headquarters, to family and friends, to government officials, and to North American newspapers? Or do such responses contradict MCC's alleged nonpolitical presence or jeopardize the safety of personnel?

In the days after the raid on Gaborone, the South African press billed the attack as a great success. Sensational headlines like "ANC was ready to strike today . . . so the army struck first" and " 'No alternative' to raid" sought to convince readers of the necessity and the success of the attack. Foreign Minister Pik Botha reported that "Botswana had been given many warnings." A military leader explained that "this operation was not directed at the government of Botswana or its people—but at clearly identified militant ANC terrorists." Botswana's radio and press were careful to identify quickly and accurately the victims, some of whom were Botswana citizens. One Botswana headline read, "Vengeance: After Supper They Went to Bed— And They Never Knew What Hit Them. . . . "

What the newspapers failed to report, however, was that although South African officials claimed that their intelligence sources prevented the harming of innocent Botswana civilians, only four or five of the eleven people killed were actually on the army's target list. According to Botswana newspapers and firsthand information from Mennonite Ministries personnel, those few victims were hardly "trained terrorists." They were ANC refugees who protested the South African minority government through art, drama, music, and literature. The white South African student who was killed had been slated to graduate with the highest marks possible in math and physics. A pacifist, he had left South Africa to avoid military service. Others killed included a six-year-old child, a guest visiting a targeted couple, a Dutch citizen, and a young Botswana secretary. Of those who were South Africans, MM worker Jonathan P. Larson wrote to the Africa Inter-Mennonite Mission office, "It is difficult to understand why such people would be seen as a threat to the system of apartheid except perhaps in this regard, that they were fundamentally good and decent people who worked selflessly and who had left their country because they loved it too much to stay."

MCC has established guidelines for overseas workers facing national emergencies, although each crisis situation requires on-the-spot decision-making. MCC personnel are advised to keep in contact with local church members and other friends. They are required to remain in close contact with the country representative and the program administrator at MCC headquarters in Akron, Pennsylvania. MCCers are to use their own judgment in relating to the American and Canadian embassies. If the embassies initiate evacuation, it is up to the MCCers to decide whether or not to leave the country. However, personnel are advised that embassies sometimes use evacuation as political pressure rather than as an absolutely necessary safety precaution.

MCC and mission personnel did not feel threatened personally in either the Maseru or Gaborone raids, but they were careful to stay inside during the attacks and not to become visibly involved. In contrast to official reports issued by the attackers, workers wrote moving accounts from the perspective of the attacked. Sara and Fremont Regier notified the *Newton Kansan,* a local newspaper from their home community, that South Africa had killed and injured innocent people in the Gaborone raid. The letter appeared on the editorial page.

Three years earlier, following the Maseru incident, the MCC cosecretary for Africa, Nancy Heisey Longacre, wrote to U.S. Secretary of State George Shultz:

> In light of what we have learned from our field workers, I urge you to go beyond a statement of protest in order to assure that South Africa does not feel free to undertake similar attacks in the future. Our work with refugees in Botswana and Swaziland as well as in Lesotho makes us most concerned that similar violence not be directed at them and at the citizens who offer them a place of refuge.

Incidents like the Maseru and Gaborone massacres are not isolated events in Mennonite mission and MCC overseas fields.

Violent, politically charged crises persist in Africa and throughout the world. Restoring trust and stability in terrorized areas has become a significant task of church service workers abroad. Within weeks of the attack in Gaborone, a group of Quakers, Mennonites, and local citizens of Botswana initiated a "Buy a Brick" campaign to assist a Botswana widow whose home was destroyed. One goal of the widely supported building project was to bring various sectors of the Gaborone community together in the wake of the crisis.

As Mennonite service workers find themselves in areas where voiceless people are treated brutally, they ponder whether they should remain silent, not offending the authorities. Or, at some risk to the continuance of the program, should they speak out?

Asia

In the late 1890s, a generation before there was an MCC,
North American Mennonites responded to reports of famine in
India with shiploads of grain. Soon missionaries organized
congregations. By 1920 mission-planted communities grew to
include twenty thousand Mennonites in India, ten thousand in
China, and ten thousand in Indonesia, where Dutch
Mennonite missionaries had first arrived in 1854. At the end of
World War II, MCC entered Asia to serve in a series of crisis
areas. New mission programs opened in five Asian countries.
By 1986 as many as 125,000 Mennonites lived in eight
countries of Asia.

MCC has usually allocated one-third of its overseas budget
to Asia programs. The needs are immense: war destruction,
hunger, poverty, and homelessness. With more than three
billion people in Asia (60 percent of the world's population),
food and survival problems are critical. The emergence of great
new nations in modern history, such as India, Pakistan, and Indonesia, have led to chronic wars and the expulsion of millions
of refugees.

Asia is a continent of many world religions: Hinduism, Buddhism, Confucianism, Shintoism, Taoism, Islam, and others. MCC workers in Asia have the intriguing task of understanding radically different religious and cultural systems.

Here are four case studies from Asia: two on Vietnam, the battlefield of a modern "Thirty Years' War"; one on development work in Bangladesh, home of the poorest of the poor; and one on being servants and peacemakers amid the tangled political life of Kampuchea. In the latter, we have described more than in any other case study the political complexities that establish fences for MCC service and witness. We are grateful to Fred Kauffman for major work in preparing the case study on Kampuchea.

MCC's experience in Asia is rich in possibilities for other case studies: the orphan program in Korea and the painful task of designing a strategy of withdrawal, emergency relief operations in China at war's end and MCC's recent return through the inter-Mennonite China Educational Exchange program, the transfer of a medical program in Taiwan to a mission board, and the role of MCC SELFHELP in providing employment.

11

Working in a War Zone:

Vietnam

The business of MCC in the world is not purity.
The call of MCC is to be there . . . seeking the
way of peace, the way of the gospel in the midst
of war.

—Earl Martin

In 1954 Mennonite Central Committee became the first North American Protestant relief agency to enter Vietnam. Initially MCC assisted refugees from the north, distributing clothing, Christmas bundles, soap, and school supplies, as well as beef and surplus food staples from North America. Medical care quickly became another priority under the MCC program, which was established at the invitation of church leaders and the Saigon-based Republic of Vietnam (RVN). In the 1950s the United States government encouraged voluntary agencies to begin programs in Vietnam. Since the change of government in 1975, MCC programs of assistance to Vietnam have continued, albeit without MCC representatives living in the country.

The experience of Mennonite Central Committee in Vietnam poses many complex issues. Former MCC Vietnam director Luke S. Martin, who in 1977 authored a study of the MCC years in Vietnam, has suggested that MCC's service in that country falls into four distinct periods: 1954-59, when

MCC was shaping its involvement; 1960-65, when MCC worked closely with the Tin Lanh Church (Evangelical Church of Vietnam—ECVN); 1966-72, the period of Vietnam Christian Service (VNCS), an ecumenical partnership in which MCC took the leadership role; and 1973-75, when MCC again established an independent program. This study focuses on the years after 1966, when MCC struggled increasingly to maintain an identity separate from the U.S. military effort.

Prior to and during the war, U.S. policy makers characterized Vietnam as a domino in Marxist world conquest: as Vietnam goes communist, so will go the countries of Asia and Europe. A decade after the war ended, Henry Kissinger reflected that although the United States intervened in Vietnam under the premise that Hanoi represented "the cutting edge of Sino-Soviet global strategy ... in retrospect, we know that Hanoi was working for its own account." The former Secretary of State's concession that the war in Vietnam was essentially a local struggle contrasts sharply with the rationale of U.S. foreign policy and military action in the 1960s that Vietnam was the last line of defense to a world-conquering Soviet-Chinese alliance.

Many Americans believed that the U.S. was doing what needed to be done to stem the tide of communist aggression. This assumption had serious consequences for the MCC workers serving in Vietnam, since U.S. government and military personnel often assumed that MCCers were interested in reaching the same goals they were. The complexity of working in a contested area meant that for reasons of security and simple logistics, MCC workers had to make decisions about how closely they would work alongside U.S. officials and military personnel. Further compounding the difficulty of maintaining an identity based on Christian love, MCCers found that the Vietnamese themselves often confused them with the larger military effort. North American MCC workers resembled U.S. government and military personnel—looking

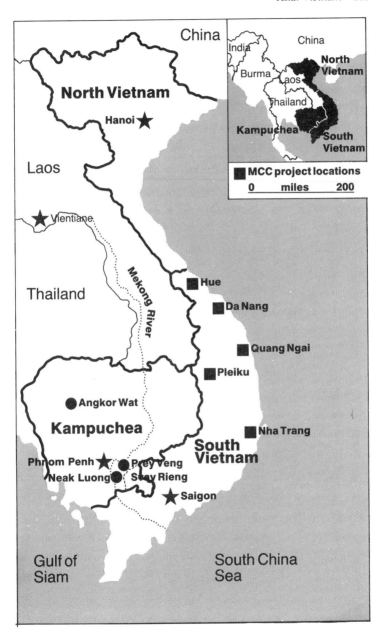

like counterparts, speaking English, and bringing aspects of Western culture to Southeast Asia. For these reasons it was difficult to explain the motivation of service which had brought the volunteers to Vietnam.

The problems of MCC workers who tried to make known their identity and keep the organization's integrity intact in the midst of chaotic conditions were many. Not only did MCCers have to relate in some way to U.S. military personnel and the U.S. government; they also had to define and redefine their relationship with the Vietnamese governments and try to express those ties adequately in day-to-day contacts with Vietnamese citizens. MCC also had a special relationship with the Tin Lanh Church, which had originated under the mission influence of the American-based Christian and Missionary Alliance (CMA) and was the only major Protestant church in South Vietnam. Mirroring the conservative, American nationalist, evangelical view of its parent church, the Tin Lanh Church largely supported the U.S. military effort.

Certainly, MCC's attempts to maintain a constancy in relation to each of these interests was not always successful. Evaluations of MCC workers since their departure from Vietnam have ranged from sharp criticism of MCC's policies to satisfaction. Some concluded, "Under the shadow of American military involvement and under the stress of cooperating with other U.S.-based relief agencies, MCC could not help but compromise its ethical standards." Yet others contended, "We did the best we could under extremely difficult conditions." David E. Leaman's study of the Vietnam Christian Service era, particularly the early years of 1966-69, identifies varied responses and consequent tensions among MCC workers over how best to espouse the philosophy of MCC while working in a combat zone. The anguish involved in day-to-day decisions and compromises led a few to question whether MCC ought to continue to serve in Vietnam.

Both MCC and Vietnam Christian Service (VNCS) administrators attempted to formulate policies which would give service workers realistic guidelines for how, under the duress of war, they might represent their agencies. One such set of guidelines was drawn up by MCC Asia Secretary Paul Longacre. While volunteers must "attempt to rise above political considerations and boundaries in service that is in the name of Christ," they must also recognize the impossibility of maintaining an apolitical stance, since Westerners in Vietnam represented particular political connotations.

At its conception in 1966, the ecumenical agency VNCS established complementary goals: to carry out a personalized yet impartial ministry of Christian service to persons in need, and to witness to the reconciling power of love in the face of fear, hate, and despair. VNCS policy dictated that assistance must be extended to individuals in need without regard to their political and social affiliations, but when aid was given to Republic of Vietnam (RVN) programs, VNCS must take special care to emphasize that the contribution came from the church rather than from the United States Agency for International Development (U.S. AID). Specifically prohibited for VNCSers was the giving of aid to the military, whether U.S., RVN, or the National Liberation Front (NLF).

These policies were not necessarily easy to implement. One MCC volunteer with VNCS, Doug Hostetter, was especially apprehensive because VNCS work was being embraced by American government officials. During his first year of service, he wrote:

> . . . I feel we are doing the same thing as the Military Civic Actions teams and U.S. AID, [which] are also serving people. . . . The VN and US military are definitely behind us in our program, evidenced by the $1,000.00 gift which the Air Force gave us for our Pleiku Hospital. I have had great cooperation from all the military and government men whom I have contacted. They often express that they feel that our work is very important in the winning of this war! . . . I feel that our message of peace and a God who is above nations and ideologies has been badly muddled.

Several months later, during an informal discussion, one of Hostetter's U.S. AID neighbors mentioned that some governmental workers and military personnel considered the presence of pacifists threatening. Hostetter wrote, "Most of them either have served their time or are serving their time and they look at us as 'draft dodgers.' " He concluded that they felt a kind of jealousy because the VNCSers around them were close to the Vietnamese people and did not live in fear. "Our houses are only 200 yards apart, and both the same distance from the V.C. territory, but [U.S. Aid personnel] have 12 guards, big lights, six-foot wall, sandbags, and barbed wire while our house is in the open, not even a fence around us." Finally, Hostetter acknowledged that VNCS did have a clearly different and independent stance from the military and hoped that this stance could be communicated in Vietnamese villages where VNCSers lived and worked.

MCC workers wrote candidly of distressing choices they were compelled to make. Some questions concerned the inappropriateness of cooperating with the Republic of Vietnam, which was intimately associated with the military. One visitor to VNCS units in 1967 felt that workers needed a stronger background in biblical and theological insights to "make the difficult decisions which they face."

The ethical dilemmas were nuts-and-bolts issues to the workers. For example, should they allow available medical personnel to assist in their work, even though those individuals were serving in the U.S. military? In Nhatrang, MCC worked alongside the Evangelical Church of Vietnam in operating two hospitals. Doctors were often in short supply. In the same city, U.S. doctors ran another hospital and volunteered assistance to the church-run hospital. MCC accepted the help of the military doctors but requested that they refrain from wearing their uniforms and from bringing firearms onto the hospital grounds. MCC also eased the shortage by transferring patients to U.S. medical facilities.

MCC had a difficult time knowing how closely to cooperate with the U.S. government. Some reliance on government civilian and military operations seemed inevitable. Unlike some church-related voluntary agencies, however, neither MCC nor VCNS accepted U.S. AID dollars to support their programs. MCC initially used Vietnamese communication systems but switched in 1965 to the U.S. Army Post Office because of the unreliability of the Vietnamese system. Although some workers questioned this shift, an MCC administrator later pointed out that the postal service differed from using PX privileges (used to some extent by MCC both in the 1940s in Germany and in Vietnam) in that "the postal service is necessary to the operation of the [MCC] program ... whereas PX might .... be more of an amenity for personnel." After MCC withdrew from VNCS on January 1, 1973, MCC used Vietnamese civilian communication systems once again.

A similar decision centered on transportation. Should MCCers choose to use the U.S. airline Air America—a civilian operation financed by the CIA—and available free of charge to voluntary agencies, or pay to use the Vietnamese airline? MCC opted to use the Vietnamese service, although ethical problems remained—the American government subsidized that operation as well via a grant to the Vietnamese government. More tangible was the difficulty MCCers faced when they learned that the airline gave them preference over Vietnamese travelers in boarding and taking seats.

William T. Snyder, who served as an executive administrator during many of the Vietnam years, reflected recently that military "assistance" was often offered to American volunteers and other Westerners when their security appeared to be at stake. He noted that often the MCCers were not threatened as gravely as those serving in the military:

> ... the identification we had in Hue with the local people in agriculture probably saved the lives of our people ... some of the

> Viet Cong sympathizers must have given the word that we were not unfriendly because the North Vietnamese troops that came in simply passed up the [MCC] house in Hue. I think we decided these things naturally. Most of it was decided on a local basis with local people.

Since MCC workers naturally had contacts with many local Vietnamese, the bonds of friendship and identification with the victims of war led many of the volunteers to seek to bring an end to the war. Some in the U.S. military viewed the lifestyle and projects of the MCC workers as a contribution to "pacification" which would win the hearts and minds of the Vietnamese for the U.S. and would ultimately shorten the war. Some MCC workers feared their presence in Vietnam supported U.S. military objectives, thereby prolonging the war. As the war escalated, many volunteers felt led to protest U.S. policies.

MCC and VNCS, however, concerned that their workers might be asked to leave the country, counseled against protestations in Vietnam. "Verbal witness . . . can cause misunderstandings [regarding] program, and restrictions on program," declared the VNCS advisory committee on peace concerns in 1967. The committee included representatives from Church World Service, Lutheran World Relief, and MCC. Pointing out that the agency was able to work in that country because it was a guest of the Vietnamese government, the committee recommended that VNCSers base their actions on *service*, with *witness* as a low priority. Furthermore, when volunteers had the opportunity to witness, they should not be "public and noisy" but should utilize private channels, preferably through their churches at home.

Not all VNCSers followed these guidelines, but personnel sponsored by the Eastern Mennonite Board of Missons and Charities were quicker to protest than were MCC personnel. Both Mennonite groups became more outspoken in their protests toward the end of the war. In the early 1970s, missionaries and MCC workers in Vietnam sent letters of protest to the U.S. president and members of Congress.

Some MCC and VNCS volunteers who stepped beyond the official guidelines in their protests did so because of a conviction that VNCS policy was simply too close to the U.S. military stance. Doug Hostetter was one who felt called to challenge the safe "limits" imposed from headquarters, for he could not ignore the injustice of "selective" aid:

> We are serving in areas under the control or partial control of the Vietnamese National Government. We have no people serving in VC controlled areas or North Vietnam. Thus while we are proudly proclaiming love and service to all people regardless of race, ideology, or nationality, in fact we are loving and serving only the people who by choice or default are living under the influence of the GVN.

One NLF representative invited an MCC worker to come to a village school in his territory to teach, but the Mennonite director of VCNS cautioned that too many risks were involved. Such openings to reach the other side were rare. In one province VNCS sponsored a literary project in which Vietnamese high school students taught in NLF areas; some patients slipped across the border from NLF territories for medical treatment. MCC and VNCS encouraged workers to identify as closely as possible with local Vietnamese, rather than with American personnel or Vietnamese government officials. MCCers were asked to serve where they could, not only in work but in all areas of life—identifying with Vietnamese by learning their language, eating their food, and living simply among the people. Some volunteers shared housing with Vietnamese families. They did not employ guards, and many did not make use of the U.S. military facilities—shopping centers, post offices, recreational areas, and snack bars—located in communities throughout South Vietnam. They tried to communicate impartiality by avoiding such expressions as "enemy" and "friendly."

Despite the daily process of living and working among the Vietnamese, some volunteers felt the overwhelming burden of being misunderstood—by both governments, by other Christian workers and missionaries, by Vietnamese churches and Vietnamese neighbors. James E. Metzler, who served in Vietnam under the Eastern Mennonite Board of Missions and Charities for five years, articulated the kind of pressure felt by workers in Vietnam:

> To most Vietnamese it was simply unbelievable that Americans would be sent to their land at such a time for any reason other than to support "the cause" in some way.... We gave bread in the name of Christ; they saw Americans with Saigon government permits handing out U.S. surplus goods for the interests of both governments.... Even evangelism [was] seen as supporting the cause, for few can imagine a Christian not being pro-Western! ... Some church leaders felt we ought not speak of "our government" or "our troops," which might be an important distinction for us. But for the Vietnamese, that was merely playing with words.

Alliances with churches in Vietnam were often as complex as working with government officials. As noted earlier, MCC worked closely with the ECVN, the main Protestant denomination in the country, particularly during the early and mid-1960s. MCC also maintained a close working relationship both with the Vietnam Mennonite Mission and with the Vietnamese Mennonite Church it founded. When MCC joined with two other voluntary organizations to form VNCS, contacts with Vietnamese Christian groups grew.

Some of these alliances were not particularly close because of support given to the war by the other Christian groups. American missionaries serving with the Christian and Missionary Alliance proved especially distressing to MCC and VNCS workers because they did not take seriously the peace position of Mennonites. VNCSers felt they had little in common with some of these Christians, but nevertheless were instructed by VNCS leadership to "continue efforts to bring moral and biblical truths to bear on [the] situation."

VNCS, like other service agencies, strove to place international volunteers in Vietnam. VNCS staff in Vietnam at different times included workers from Japan, India, the Philippines, Australia, Germany, Indonesia, the Netherlands, and Norway in addition to the United States and Canada. Moreover, a hundred or more Vietnamese were part of the VNCS staff each year, serving as nurses, social workers, teachers, interpreters, and administrative aides.

The international character of VNCS and MCC helped to diffuse the notion that they were simply two more American agencies "helping the cause." Yet VNCS in particular was a heterogeneous body with workers representing not only three separate voluntary organizations but individual viewpoints. A few volunteers caused headaches for their administrative superiors—some for being radically and vocally opposed to the war, others for not conforming to the VNCS standards of maintaining distance from the American military establishment in Vietnam. Some volunteers warned that VCNS was in danger of losing its moderate and flexible stance if it yielded to pressure by outspoken, critical workers. As a large organization, VCNS struggled to keep its "team" together.

A major philosophical breach arose within VNCS by 1968-69 as the war escalated and antiwar protests surged at home. At the heart of the controversy was whether VNCS could continue to proclaim itself impartial and apolitical when in fact the logistics and safety demands of the war led VNCS to serve only in areas under the RVN.

This dissension within VNCS found expression in a letter distributed by ten concerned workers, including four MCCers, in June of 1969. The letter, addressed to others within the organization, criticized the policies of VCNS, which asserted that no Christian/Western worker could be an apolitical force in chaotic Vietnam. The concerned workers called for recognition of the different philosophies present in the VNCS family regarding pacifism as well as various forms of nonviolent action.

The internal problems experienced by VNCS—perhaps

inevitable, given the diversity of viewpoints represented by both administrators and workers—led MCC in 1972 to withdraw from Vietnam Christian Service, with MCC once again responsible only for its own policies and program. Even after the relationship with Church World Service and Lutheran World Relief had ended, and MCC was again able to deal independently with the ethical decisions involved in serving in a contested area, different interpretations arose over how MCC could best do its work with integrity.

Some workers poured their energies into specific program assignments: medical aid, relief, literacy work, English teaching, aid to cooperatives, housing rehabilitation, agricultural assistance, and education. Others, like the Japanese volunteer Yoshihiro Ichikawa, described by longtime MCC worker Earl Martin in *Reaching the Other Side*, carved out a friendship role to Vietnamese villagers—drinking tea, talking, and finding humor and hope in the daily events of Vietnamese struggle.

Despite the case made by some that MCC ought to pull its workers out of Vietnam during the turbulent climax of the war, MCCers Ichikawa, Martin, Max Ediger, and James Klassen felt called to stay on after other Americans had fled. Martin came to believe that MCC belonged at the place of struggle: "The business of MCC in the world is *not* purity. The call of MCC is to be there in the most poignant and distressing situations, seeking the way of peace, the way of the gospel in the midst of war." In 1964 MCC worker Daniel Gerber disappeared; in 1971 Brethren worker Theodore Studebaker was killed; and in 1973 Quaker worker Richard Thompson lost his life.

Vietnam is not the only country where MCC has worked in or near a war zone. In MCC's first program in Russia in 1921, workers were caught between warring Red and White armies and were threatened by the presence of irregular brigand troops. One MCC worker, Clayton Kratz, lost his life in the crossfire of civil war. Concerns over "whose side are we aiding" did not emerge while workers gave full attention to the massive famine crisis. In other war zones MCC has been uneasy that its service might appear to be identified with one side more than another: in China during the challenge of communist troops to a faltering Nationalist government (late 1940s); in Algeria during the war for independence from France (1950s); in Nigeria during the rebellion of Biafra (1960s); in Zaire, where rival armies contended for control of areas independent of Belgian control (1950s and 1960s); in Cambodia and Lebanon, both plagued by a tangle of contending forces (1970s and 1980s); and in Ethiopia, where guerrilla forces control most areas of famine crisis (1980s).

In no war zone has MCC, or perhaps any relief agency, been able to provide equally balanced services to the people on the opposing sides. That which made Vietnam unique was that a major warring party was the United States, one of the home bases of MCC. Today MCC workers are experiencing tensions analagous to Vietnam in El Salvador, Guatemala, Honduras, and Nicaragua, where the United States is a powerful military presence. Difficult questions arise: Is MCC work propping up an oppressive government? Do the people understand that the MCC worker is not an agent of U.S. government? Is it possible for workers to be liberated from a military or colonial Western label? Is there some way to serve suffering people on all sides of a conflict?

In Vietnam, should MCC have withdrawn from "compromising situations" and made a clear, well-publicized statement of the reasons for withdrawal? Is it sufficient to develop the best possible program in a warring zone and not worry about the larger political implications? What are the dangers of rationalizing one's behavior when one is doing good? Do citizens need to apologize for being identified with their country? How can one be faithful when the issues and the choices are not clear?

12

Reaching the Other Side:

Vietnam After 1975

I have been astonished at the friendliness of the Vietnamese. The bitterness one would expect from people who suffered so enormously does not seem to be there.

—Louise Buhler

The spring of 1985 marked the tenth anniversary of the United States' withdrawal from Vietnam. For a few weeks major news sources focused on the war's impact on America: "Vietnam was America's longest, most debilitating war, and its memory still haunts the national psyche" (*Newsweek*). Vietnam received less attention: "An anxious, impoverished country, more than a little grim—the terrible random death of war has been replaced by the mean certainty of a police-state peace. Life may be better for most Vietnamese, but life is not good. Viet Nam is one of the poorest countries in the world...." (*Time*). While many turned brief attention to a part of the world which for ten years they had wished might be "out of sight/out of mind," Mennonite Central Committee continued its thirty-year-old program of aid to Vietnam.

The previous chapter examined MCC's presence in Vietnam prior to 1975. This chapter reviews the period since 1975, when the United States cut diplomatic relations to the socialist government of Vietnam. During these years MCC has sought to "keep the door open" to Vietnam by offering material aid and technical assistance.

In his book *Reaching the Other Side,* Earl Martin described the hurried evacuation of American personnel from the provincial town of Quang Ngai, where he and his family lived: "March 26, 1975—Just two days before flags like these would have spelled treason. Now they flew from every house. Even the horse carts and Hondas on the street were sporting Liberation flags.... The political universe had been turned on its head." Martin, together with MCC volunteers Yoshihiro Ichikawa, Max Ediger, and James Klassen continued living in Vietnam after April 1975. Klassen, in his memoir *Jimshoes in Vietnam,* has added additional insight to this story.

Reaching the other side is a theme which runs through MCC's experience in this anguished land. In the late sixties MCC began exploring the possibilities of aiding Vietnamese on the other side. MCC worker Peter Dyck met with representatives of the Democratic Republic of Vietnam (DRVN) and the National Liberation Front (NLF) in Paris and Algiers. Atlee Beechy, who had served as the first director of Vietnam Christian Service, followed up these contacts. Beechy traveled for five weeks during the summer of 1968, sometimes alone and sometimes with others, to meet representatives from the two organizations in Paris, Algiers, Prague, Stockholm, East Berlin, New Delhi, and Phnom Penh.

At each of these meetings MCC representatives introduced themselves as people seeking peace. They came with a document translated into French and Vietnamese entitled "A Brief Introduction to Mennonites and the Mennonite Central Committee," as well as individual Mennonite conference position papers on peace and war. All interviews were cordial. They centered around MCC's concern for Vietnamese on both sides of the conflict. The Vietnamese representatives invariably expressed appreciation for MCC's desire to help and then discussed what they felt was the major problem of the war, the sustained U.S. bombing. During one conversation a National Liberation Front representative said that his government was well disposed toward Quakers and Mennonites "because of your understanding of war." He added, "If there is no kind of bridge, how can there ever be normal relations?"

Although the Vietnamese representatives were interested in receiving aid from MCC, especially medicines and medical equipment, they said it was impossible to allow MCC personnel into the NLF and DRVN territory because of the insecurity of those areas. Despite MCC's success in initiating these discussions, only limited medical aid could be sent to the Vietnamese in NLF or Provisional Revolutionary Government (PRG) areas.

One result of the 1968 trip, however, was that MCC heard these representatives of "the other side" directly. Beechy concluded: "If and when peace comes, much help will be needed to rebuild the country. Individuals, groups, and governments will be welcome to help in the rebuilding as long as the assistance has no strings attached." Mennonites expanded these contacts during the early 1970s and by May 1975 MCC had contributed some $275,000 in relief material to civilians living in the DRVN and PRG areas of Vietnam.

Despite the increasing recognition in the MCC constituency that the agency had reason to serve on both sides of the conflict, some objected to what they saw as assistance to "the enemy." Some were concerned that sending relief to North Vietnam without accompanying personnel to monitor distribution and to personify MCC's motto, "In the Name of Christ," violated established MCC practice. Others argued that aid projected for the areas in question seemed excessive given the extreme needs in other parts of the world.

An MCC annual meeting in 1974 in Hillsboro, Kansas, centered on the debate. Mennonites who had earlier experienced life under communist rule in the Soviet Union testified at the meeting. Some recalled that MCC had on occasion sent relief to crisis areas where accompanying personnel could not enter. Others pointed out that some Protestant missionaries in Vietnam were closely allied with U.S. military interests. Two years later Atlee Beechy responded to a concern regarding MCC's policy toward Vietnam: "In a day in which we have very few bridges to the socialist and communist world, we need to take advantage of opportunities to establish relationships and to make a clear witness. . . . Some feel deeply that we should be doing as much as we can in view of U.S. involvement in the destruction."

Following the evacuation of Americans in 1975, MCC sent fifty tons of powdered milk and a shipment of clothing to Saigon (Ho Chi Minh City) for distribution by the Red Cross. In January 1976 MCC committed one million dollars in material aid for war reconstruction in Vietnam. Shipments included relief items such as canned meat, medicine, and soap. MCC sent developmental aid to Vietnam, including seeds, rototillers, and school supplies. The last MCC workers left Vietnam in 1976.

Today, many Vietnamese work on state farms and cooperatives. The government has sought to control most new industries although private enterprise continues in the South and "cottage industries" have sprung up in the North. Vietnam has attempted to unify the economies of the North and South, the latter formerly dependent on U.S. dollars and imported goods. The war inflated the population of Saigon (Ho Chi Minh City) and afterward many persons moved back to their villages. Some fled with the Americans. Others moved from overpopulated rural and urban areas to "new economic zones." At first, these massive relocation efforts failed because of poor housing and educational facilities, insufficient water, inadequate roads, and a lack of health facilities. Recently, however, the government has carried out its program of relocation on a smaller, more deliberate scale.

In 1975 the new Vietnamese government sought to industrialize the country and to collectivize agriculture in the South. Four years later, these ambitious plans brought the economy to near ruin. In 1980 the government introduced an incentive system which allowed farmers to sell surpluses on the free market. Food production rose dramatically. In 1985 the government increased salaries for state employees and abolished the subsidized food ration system, but inflation soon wiped out the benefits of economic reform.

MCC country representative Louise Buhler describes the plight of impoverished professionals:

> [The woman], . . . who occasionally accompanies me . . . has five years of education in the foreign language faculty of the University. . . . She speaks fluent French and English—her husband, a hydrologist, works in the Ministry of Water Resources—they live in a single room (20 square meters) apartment with their daughter and four other members of the extended family. . . . Their combined salaries are not sufficient to purchase adequate food (they rarely are able to afford fruit or meat) or adequate clothes. . . .
>
> Their dream: a room (10 square meters) for themselves, ... enough money to buy a bunch of bananas without calculating it into their budget, a warm jacket for their three-year-old daughter.

Vietnam was reunified in July 1976. The following year Vietnam was admitted to the United Nations. Vietnam's relations with China—historically problematic—have not improved, especially since the U.S. established diplomatic relations with the People's Republic of China. Relations with the United States have been nearly nonexistent. The United States has viewed Vietnam's occupation of Kampuchea since early 1979 as Marxist aggression. For the most part, political leaders have been trained in the North, which serves as the political center for both international contact and domestic affairs.

The present government began a reeducation program at the close of the war for some religious leaders and for those who had supported the previous Saigon government. For soldiers, this meant approximately three days of Marxist "political education." Reeducation has in some cases meant years of detention. Although grateful that there was no bloodbath, MCC has been concerned about human rights violations in this "reeducation" process. At the same time MCC has sought to maintain open communications and cordial relations with government leaders.

Despite a generation of war, Vietnam's population has grown from sixteen million in 1950 to sixty million in 1985. While Western observers have not seen evidence of widespread malnutrition or starvation, one word used to describe the Vietnamese is "lean." There is little food to spare. The South is the major source for the country's food supply. South Vietnam's wartime policy of moving people off the land so that they could be controlled more easily turned Vietnam from a rice-exporting country to a rice-importing country. During the war a million tons of grain was imported each year.

Since 1980 the Vietnamese have made agricultural production their top priority. MCC has assisted in agricultural development. An MCC delegation returning after a visit in 1977 reported on the critical shortages they observed but concluded: "The most important redeeming feature is that a minimum is available to all, and the government is working systematically to improve conditions aided by the determination and will of the people." One observer has described this as "stability in poverty."

Atlee Beechy reflected recently that "who defines one's enemy" is one of the critical issues posed in the Vietnamese experience. At the 1976 annual meeting of MCC when one million dollars were designated for Vietnam, some persons asked, "Why should we send so much to Vietnam when they're not even on the United Nations' most needy list?" In fact, that year the two Vietnams were not members of the U.N. and thus were not included in the tabulations of countries needing assistance.

Another problem facing MCC was the threatened U.S. State Department prohibition of MCC shipments to Vietnam under the Trading with the Enemy Act. MCC communicated its support to members of Congress who tried to prohibit an embargo on trade with Vietnam. Also during 1976, MCC encouraged its constituents to try to head off an embargo on trade with Vietnam and to support the normalization of relationships between the U.S. and Vietnam. MCC urged U.S. officials to provide major economic assistance through international agencies and to encourage private voluntary agencies to assist with reconstruction.

During their periodic trips to Vietnam MCC representatives have noted Vietnamese eagerness for open trade with the U.S., an interest in Western technology, and reluctance to rely so heavily on the Soviet Union. An MCC administrator who visited in 1984 observed, "Vietnamese genuinely like Americans. [But] U.S. [government policy] is driving Vietnam firmly into the Eastern Bloc nations. It would not need to be that way."

In 1978 U.S. relations with Vietnam became more tense because of Vietnam's invasion and occupation of Kampuchea. In May of 1981, the U.S. Department of Commerce denied an MCC application for a license to ship 250 tons of wheat to Vietnam. This surprising response followed nine previously approved applications. MCC stated to the U.S. government that MCC was simply helping those in need, including both Vietnamese and Kampucheans. Following the U.S. refusal to permit the wheat shipment, several members of Congress declared their support for MCC. The controversy coincided with cuts in aid to Vietnam from other nations under pressure from the U.S. administration, which hoped to force Vietnamese troops out of Kampuchea. In June 1981, following appeals by a dozen members of Congress, the Commerce Department reversed its decision and granted the license. MCC objected to the government's licensing procedures on shipments and particularly "the U.S. government's attempts to use food as a weapon. . . ."

While MCC has had difficulties in administering its program in Vietnam because of U.S. policies, other problems have arisen because of Vietnam's governmental policies. The major stumbling block to MCC program aid is Vietnam's refusal to allow expatriate voluntary agency persons to live inside the country. MCC's request for resident agency personnel has been turned down repeatedly, as have the requests of other U.S. agencies. MCC personnel visit the country periodically and check on projects; in recent years Louise Buhler has served as MCC's country representative. Assigned to Bangkok in neighboring Thailand, she has made two- to three-week trips every few months to followup material aid shipments and to determine the need for further projects. The Vietnamese have allowed her and other MCC representatives to visit areas which few North Americans have had the opportunity to visit. An MCC official comments, "Louise is probably more effective in program supervision from a Bangkok base than she would be as a restricted resident of Hanoi."

Buhler has traveled extensively in North, Central, and South Vietnam. She writes: "The visas [we] have received . . . are related to our ability to deliver much-needed and much-appreciated aid . . . [and to] the desire on the part of at least some Vietnamese to overcome their isolation." MCC delegations have been impressed that material aid to Vietnam is put to good use. Buhler reported in 1983 that the Vietnamese have "expressed deep appreciation not only for the items received but also for the friendship and the care that these gifts symbolize."

Two of the groups MCC has worked closely with in administering aid are VIETMY, a Hanoi-based committee that coordinates friendship and political contacts between American groups and the Vietnamese government, and AIDRECEP, the government committee that facilitates international aid. Although working through AIDRECEP has sometimes proved cumbersome, MCC has generally felt it to be helpful. Negotiations on projects are most often arranged with local leaders. A few projects such as MCC SELFHELP have been organized directly through export agencies and involve little bureaucracy.

MCC has continued to request that a representative be allowed to live in the country. In the meantime, MCC sends several delegations and consultants to Vietnam each year to plan for future programs and to exchange technical information on agriculture-related projects with the Vietnamese. MCC delegations traveling in the country have noted that the many levels of bureaucracy are "each striving for power." They noted that the style of communism of the Vietnamese is quite different from that of the Chinese and the Soviets and that Vietnamese officials have expressed disappointment with the sluggishness of the economy after ten years of rebuilding. They said that tensions exist between North and South (Southerners viewing Northerners as heavy-handed, bureaucratic, and old-fashioned, and Northerners viewing Southerners as lazy, undisciplined, and capitalistic).

MCC representatives find that certain subjects are not open for discussion. Yet they feel these visits help to heal the wounds of the war. One MCC visitor to Vietnam in 1982 reported:

> Aside from the necessary agenda items, we discussed a great variety of topics—economic situation in Vietnam, life of government workers, Vietnamese customs, Amerasian children, differences between the North and South, refugees, family planning, Buddhism, Christianity.... All in all, I certainly felt I was in the company of trusted friends."

Christians in Vietnam continue to meet but are in continual tension with the government, which has taken over their social service activities. Some Protestant pastors and Catholic priests have been arrested and accused of undermining the government. Periodically, MCC representatives meet Protestant leaders in the North, but find it more difficult to meet leaders in the South, where government officials are often unwilling to arrange meetings.

Because of the limitations posed by the two radically different governments, MCC's presence in Vietnam calls for flexibility. Those who have been to Vietnam express a renewed call to "keep the door open." As MCC chairman Elmer Neufeld commented after his spring 1983 trip, "There are obvious widespread continuing human needs in this small war-torn land.... When one sees the rather crude facilities overcrowded by sick and needy persons ... it doesn't seem appropriate to raise too many political questions about whether or not there should be a Christian response."

Questions for the MCC linger. Are the political policies and prohibitions of the U.S. or Canada binding on the binational MCC? Does our government define for us who are our enemies? How can MCC best give witness to Christian love in an authoritarian socialist state? Can MCC work on both sides in a conflict area to contribute to greater justice?

The wife of a U.S. Congressman remarked to an MCC administrator, "We need a listening post in Vietnam." With MCC's limited access to an isolated socialist country, what is MCC's responsibility in reporting what is seen and heard? Should MCC protest human rights abuses in Vietnam at the risk of disturbing friendly relations with the Vietnamese government? Should MCC press for meetings with church leaders, knowing that such pressure might jeopardize current projects?

Since 1984 MCC has provided medicine and medical equipment to several hospitals and primary health clinics, sponsored Vietnamese physicians and scientists attending professional conferences outside the country, helped to develop soybean varieties and uses and set up an extension station at the University of Can Tho, and assisted in developing irrigation networks and bee-raising. The Vietnamese sometimes refer to such efforts as "friendship projects." Buhler comments:

I have been astonished at the friendliness of the Vietnamese. The bitterness one would expect from people who suffered so enormously does not seem to be there. Rather, [they possess] a genuine attitude of "that was in our past; we want to look to the future."

A provincial official remarked to an MCC visitor after receiving aid to build a pumping station at Tan Xuoi: "Your material aid is important, but the spiritual assistance is equally important. The pumping station is situated at the crossroad of the three communes; it is a source of encouragement to the many people who pass by."

13

Focusing on Producing More Food:

Bangladesh

Bangladesh is a land reborn.
Freedom is in the air.
　　　　　　　—Maynard Shelly

On November 12, 1970, a massive cyclone hit East Pakistan, the country now known as Bangladesh. Accompanied by thirty-foot tidal waves that roared in from the Bay of Bengal, the storm killed some 500,000 persons. Millions of others were injured and left homeless. The small Asian country was devastated, yet the cyclone was only a prelude to the death and destruction to come.

Mennonite Central Committee, which in 1963 had assisted East Pakistani victims of another cyclone, returned to the country late in 1970 with material aid. Vernon Reimer, MCC director for neighboring India, was the first to arrive. Three Paxmen from Nepal joined him and assisted the East Pakistan Christian Council by distributing blankets, canned chicken, and equipment to flood victims.

Political turmoil erupted one month after the calamity. In December 1970, the Bengalis of East Pakistan won in the first democratic election ever held in their country. The Awami League, party of Sheikh Mujibur Rahman, won a majority of

seats in the East Pakistan Parliament. Nine months of civil warfare ensued.

On March 25, 1971, the West Pakistan army invaded the
eastern half of the country. The conflict resulted from a his-
toric, complex struggle between the Muslim rulers of West
Pakistan and the subject Muslim Bengalis of East Pakistan.
East Pakistan was separated by a thousand miles from West
Pakistan.

In 1947 both parts had become independent of India. Both
were Muslim countries and highly productive in agriculture.
Although East Pakistan was only one sixth the size of West
Pakistan, its population exceeded that of the West.

The terror—a bloodbath of murder, injury, and rape—lasted
from March through December of 1971. Three million people
died before the West Pakistani military government surrendered. In the meantime, a mass exodus of some nine million
West Pakistanis, some of them among the country's Hindu
minority, fled their homes to the neighboring Indian state of
West Bengal. The West Pakistani soldiers on their trail plun-
dered homes and burned villages. Some of the East Pakistanis
who remained, the volunteer "Freedom Fighters," tried to turn
back the West Pakistani military. The human costs were stag-
gering.

MCC Canada administrator John Wieler, who visited East
Pakistan in the summer of 1971, reported widespread
dysentery, pneumonia, cholera, tuberculosis, and malnutrition
among refugees. The government of India, under Indira
Gandhi's leadership, attempted to help millions of refugees.
India, however, was overburdened. Wieler spoke of the famine
yet to come in East Pakistan:

> Contributing factors are the after-effects of the November cy-
> clone, disruption of distribution and transportation systems, and
> the chaotic social conditions in many areas . . . . Seed distribution
> is a problem. There is a shortage of draft animals, many of which
> were drowned in the cyclone.

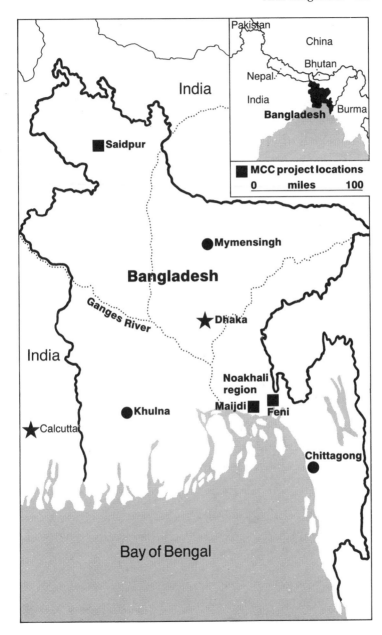

Wieler and MCC India's Vernon Reimer also met with a tiny community of Christians in the East Pakistan city of Dacca. On the basis of their exploratory visits, Wieler and Reimer recommended that MCC increase financial and personnel commitments to the East Pakistan region. Since the Indian goverment forbade foreign agencies to work near the border, MCC supported relief work through the Christian Agencies for Social Action and the Mennonite Christian Service Fellowship of India.

In October 1971, Griselda and Maynard Shelly of Newton, Kansas, arrived in Dacca as the first MCC country representatives in East Pakistan. They planned relief work in cooperation with other voluntary service organizations and gave moral support to the minority Christian community in Dacca. Together with MCC workers stationed in India, the Shellys coordinated material aid efforts. They kept North Americans apprised of the desperate plight of families in East Pakistan. After visiting the Garo aboriginal people in Mymensingh District, the Shellys told the stories of these converted Christians fleeing for the safety of India and then returning to their ravaged villages. "The bales of blankets and cartons of canned chicken in the storeroom of a church center," Maynard Shelly wrote, "will supply only a few of the neediest of these needy people."

MCC recognized that international politics were critical to rehabilitating the displaced Bengalis. John A. Lapp of the MCC Peace Section admonished North Americans: "We are a part of the political life of that country. Canadians and Pakistanis are part of the British Commonwealth. The United States has military bases there and supplies military and economic aid to Pakistan. These relationships involve obligations and power." Lapp asked American Mennonites to urge their government to cease giving military aid to Pakistan. Canadian and American governments, he believed, must pressure the Pakistani government to end the war.

By November 1971 MCC concentrated its material aid efforts among refugees in the border camps. MCC distributed tarpaulins for the emergency housing of some seventy-five thousand displaced persons and supplied fifty-five tons of rice and molasses, thirty thousand blankets purchased locally, thirteen thousand mats constructed by self-help producers, soap, and clothing. MCC also provided funds to a field hospital in Assam staffed by the Evangelical Fellowship of India.

On December 16, 1971, the East Pakistani guerrilla army and Indian troops defeated the West Pakistani forces. This cease-fire signified the emergence of Bangladesh as a new and independent nation. By late 1971, refugees in India had begun to trickle back, although they had little to return to. A tremendous problem for the new country was its absence of leadership and structures to cope with the influx of needy persons. India had been barely able to cope with the millions of refugees; how could a newly formed country without resources expect to care for its people? Until January 1972, Bangladesh leader Sheikh Mujibar Rahman remained in prison in West Pakistan. Thus, as one of the few voluntary agencies permitted to work in Bangladesh, MCC found itself placed in a void. Meanwhile, MCC's North American constituents—learning through television and the press of the Bangladesh plight—gave several million dollars for use in the stricken country.

In February 1972, Maynard Shelly reported: "Bangladesh is a land reborn. Freedom is in the air." Approximately half of the refugees had returned to their homeland. Food was arriving from around the world through the country's only open port at Chittagong. Eventually, nearly ten million Bengali refugees returned to their fields and villages.

Earlier efforts by the Shellys and Vernon Reimer—including explorations into fishery and rice projects—had been thwarted by the presence of the West Pakistan army. But even under a new government, rehabilitation promised to be very difficult. Nearly all of Bangladesh's citizens were extremely poor. The country was troubled by severe overpopulation and unemployment. After 1972, when the gates were opened wide to foreign voluntary agencies, approximately fifty agencies entered Bangladesh. The United Nations Relief Operation tried to coordinate a myriad of projects by holding weekly meetings of all the voluntary agencies. The agencies worked together closely to coordinate transportation and distribution of relief goods.

During 1972, MCC's first full year in Bangladesh, the agency committed approximately $900,000 to the country—at the time one of the largest annual relief commitments in MCC's history. MCC arranged with the Ministry of Relief and Rehabilitation to work with a rural cooperative in developing Sadhingram (Independence Village) in Noakhali District. MCC wanted to establish a model cyclone-proof village for two hundred families who had suffered during the 1970 cyclone. The plan involved construction of homes, latrines, a road, and tubewells for irrigation. The project also included agricultural assistance, with MCC providing tractors, fertilizer, and seed. MCC aimed to provide an example of long-range community development to "break the treadmill patterns that have kept the rural families of the subcontinent in perpetual poverty."

As new MCC personnel arrived, projects spanned housing construction, health care, and relief to the Bihari minority (Urdu-speaking Muslims huddled in miserable camps near Dacca and elsewhere).

It was in the field of agriculture, however, that MCC made perhaps its most significant contribution in Bangladesh. In one early agricultural project, MCCers transferred pullets and chicks from India to government poultry breeding farms which had been nearly destroyed during the war. Some persons close to the Bangladesh situation foresaw a large role for MCC requiring deep commitments of time and money. Some felt that what other agencies were doing—setting up quick, relief-oriented programs—would not have the kinds of lasting impact on the country that would contribute to its long-term recovery.

MCC opted very early for a long-range strategy to help

develop the nation's agricultural and human resources. MCC made its decision at the point of crisis, during a wave of outpouring of international concern. But MCC expected to find a continuing role of service for at least five years, and perhaps longer, after the world spotlight had shifted to other places and other crises.

The situation was unique: Bangladesh was a newly formed nation with a government unable to meet basic human needs but willing to tolerate and even support the actions of a foreign-directed service agency. MCC had worked at long-term development in other areas of the world, but often those efforts were frustrated by the restrictions placed by unstable or suspicious governments. The political apparatus in Bangladesh, however, was comparatively new, untried, and in search of bold new directions. Bangladesh's new constitution stated: "The State shall . . . bring about a radical transformation in the rural areas through the promotion of an agricultural revolution." In this setting MCC saw an opportunity to work on a large scale in agriculture and in social services.

While MCC administrators in North America placed a variety of technical experts in Bangladesh, they also sought broad leadership for the new program. In the spring of 1972, MCC assigned Leona and Arthur DeFehr of Winnipeg, Manitoba, as country directors. Art DeFehr, a furniture manufacturer, was a development-minded entrepreneur. An M.B.A. graduate of Harvard University, he was gifted in communicating and in looking at the "big picture." With additional workers and an increased budget, MCC was on its way to a forward-looking, experimental program in Bangladesh.

Agricultural development was the kingpin on which MCC's broad strategy rested. In 1972 the agency made a five-year commitment to working in Noakhali District, a delta region located in the southeast corner of Bangladesh between Chittagong and Dacca, which had been hit hard by the typhoon two years earlier. MCC selected Noakhali for several reasons. It had already been the site of storm relief MCC activity. Food production in the area was low. Substantial sections of land near the Sea of Bengal, the dry and salty char areas, supported the growth of only one rice crop each year. The hard-working Bengali farmers of the district had known a lifetime of repeated tragedies. Few nonagricultural jobs existed. Underemployment was a serious problem. The new government, short on trained leaders, could provide few officials to serve the populous area.

Noakhali District's high birthrate had led by 1972 to a population of three million (two thousand persons per square mile). Already before MCC arrived, farmers in the productive nonchar areas had begun to experiment with nontraditional patterns of agricultural production in a desperate attempt to produce more food. MCC workers believed that if they could make a significant impact on the food production on the Noakhali region, with its chronic and unique problems, the development program could become a model for agricultural regions elsewhere.

MCC's five-year program called for a budget of $250,000 per year for the first three years. Part of the money supported a staff of twenty workers and established programs in nutrition, rural health, and education. The major block of money financed the agricultural development program, including training, cooperative development, irrigation, seed purchases, and food-processing facilities.

MCC set one major goal: to upgrade the nutritional level of people in Noakhali District. MCC recognized that this would require working (1) with farmers to diversify farming and modify methods, (2) with village cooperatives to support widely targeted educational programs, and (3) with women of the region, the preparers of food. MCC recognized some large obstacles as well: lack of population control; a semifeudal land tenure system typified by absentee landlords; an insecure bureaucratic government; unpredictable rainfall and torrential summer storms; and cultural reliance on rice as the Bengali staple, a food low in protein and lacking many vitamins.

Nevertheless, in 1972 Mennonite Central Committee workers introduced diversified farming to the Noakhali region. Country Director DeFehr, Project Coordinator Ken Koehn, and a team including an agronomist, a crop scientist, a nutritionist, an extension worker, an agricultural engineer, a mechanic, a farm manager, and a poultry pathologist, prepared an intensive winter crop-diversification program. The team, centered at Maijdi in Noakhali district, chose six thousand acres in which to begin the innovative program. Local farmers planted on their land many crops including oilseeds such as soybeans, rapeseed, and sunflower; grains such as sorghum, maize, wheat, and barley; and forage crops such as alfalfa, clover, and sudan grass. Many of the seeds came from India, although MCC and cooperating foreign agencies also introduced Georgia peanuts and Dutch potatoes and onions. The team chose crops carefully after studying agricultural patterns and seeking foods that would complement nutritionally the traditional rice dishes.

Large-scale development, with which MCC hoped to impact the entire Noakhali region, called for several major changes: a reduction in rice acreage and consumption; a tremendous increase in acreage devoted to winter crops such as cereals, legumes, and oilseeds; and a shift in diet from rice-based consumption to a mixture of rice and vegetables.

MCC helped farmers plant several crops during the winter. Traditionally, Bangladesh farmers had not utilized the winter growing season, but MCC researchers found that with the right combination of crops, Noakhali District had three growing seasons comprising the entire year. Based on new cultivation patterns, a farmer might have, for example, rice in the spring, a second crop of rice in the summer, and potatoes during the winter *(boro)* season. DeFehr noted that "land is the most valuable resource in Bangladesh." Arguing for diversified crops and scientific methods, he voiced a broad hope:

> . . . given an approach where land, water, ploughing capacity,
> [and] people were all utilized in the most productive manner,
> there is no question that Bangladesh could feed its present
> seventy-five million people, and probably double that number.

MCC workers, pleased with the results of the 1972-73 winter
harvest, expanded plans for the remainder of the five-year
program. For each crop which MCC introduced, members of
the team worked as partners with local cooperatives to move
the crop through several stages: discussion and planning; research and limited testing; large-scale testing and demonstrations; limited distribution; seed production; and finally, large-
scale distribution. MCC staggered its use of the crops so that at
all times a certain number were at each stage in the developmental cycle.

MCC-directed support services bolstered the agricultural
program. By its second winter—1972-73—MCC placed
workers in education and extension work: literature distribution, training sessions and test plots, and women's training. The
agency sought close relations with villagers and farmers. One
year MCC held twenty planting demonstration days for
farmers to explain the new seeds and demonstrate techniques.
In addition, MCC planted ten major plots at key locations.
Here MCC agriculturists tested many varieties under different
conditions and encouraged farmers to view the results. MCC
hired five graduates of an agricultural college to care for the
plots and to do extension work with villagers. Finally, the team
invited twenty women leaders from five *thanas* (local areas) for
a two-week course in nutrition, hygiene, and gardening, and
then hired half the pupils to teach women in their own thanas
the art and science of gardening. An MCC nutritionist studied
Bengali cooking habits and designed an educational program
for women to introduce new vegetables and other foods into
their daily meal preparation.

As growing seasons passed, the dream of a productive Noakhali took on the shape of reality. DeFehr, after the experiences

of the first year, defended Noakhali as a good location for the MCC program. The political impact of development and productivity, he noted, was enormous. Noakhali, site of the char lands, had attracted government-wide attention and had become the focus of much cooperative activity. MCC, which had initially hoped to provide a model for development, was pleased at the government's embracing of the program.

Sometimes the MCC relationship to the government was direct—as when agriculturists delivered, in person, vegetable seed packets to the prime minister and secretary of agriculture to publicize a major effort for distributing seeds to all nineteen districts of Bangladesh. The government encouraged the Noakhali program and in 1975 awarded to MCC one of three gold medals for its contribution to agricultural development through research and experimentation.

Just as significant were the responses of lower levels of government. Local and regional officials found it easier to relate to MCC, operating on a five-year commitment, than to other agencies which came and went. MCC workers observed, "Now community leaders are beginning to call on us instead of the other way around."

The Bangladesh program was in many ways unusual. Rarely had MCC had opportunity to make such a large impact on a country or even on one part of a country. The Bangladesh story became one of involving many local persons in a program of national or "macro" proportions. The test plots and demonstrations impressed national and foreign observers.

The unique aspects of the Bangladesh program prompted some within MCC to ask whether it was justified in emphasizing quantity versus quality or program development versus human resources. Some critiqued the ambitious program as insensitive to the needs of the Bangladesh people. They felt that in few areas had MCC attempted to revolutionize the life of so many people as in seeking to change the farming patterns and diet of the Noakhali people. The critics pointed to a massive intrusion by MCC workers into the life of a society. DeFehr responded:

> [Our critics] advise starting with people and move to projects. True, but . . . . Bangladesh can't get to where it wants to go, starting from where it is! . . . . The introduction of scientific winter cultivation on a large scale in a short time will require some new starting points. We are trying to build those starting positions. Bangladesh will have to choose whether it wants to follow through.

MCC's agricultural program grew to include testing varieties of rice for a higher yield. MCC agriculturists described themselves as students of the Bengali people, culture, geographic area and limitations, cropping patterns, and weather conditions. They adjusted the program around these variables and pondered the relationship between emergency relief work and long-range development. They concluded that although the two strategies are often seen as antithetical, in Bangladesh relief work and development had gone hand in hand.

Through the 1970s and 1980s, MCC's other programs in Bangladesh expanded. While agriculture remained important, MCC volunteers moved into new areas of service work: maintaining more than five hundred tubewells for drinking water; distributing material aid; establishing feeding and educational programs at Bihari camps at Khulna, Dacca, and Saidpur; and managing a SELFHELP Crafts program for Bengali women. This program, named Jute Works, encouraged the development of jute handicrafts for export and enabled women to support themselves.

In 1985, fourteen years after MCC began its Bangladesh program, the country's population had doubled to a total of ninety-seven million. The number of MCC personnel was thirty-one, including fourteen in agricultural production. But the staff represented only a fraction of the MCC work being done in Bangladesh; in the same year, MCC employed 110 Bangladesh workers. MCC-directed food production, still based in Noakhali District, branched out to include poultry farming as well as fish, shrimp, and silkworm farming and fruit and spice tree cultivation. MCC workers were involved in cooking demonstrations and other opportunities through a new Job Creation Program. A recent thrust of MCC work in Bangladesh has been economic development, much of which has helped Bangladesh women. As one tours Bangladesh MCC-related enterprises today, one sees Bagdha Woodcrafts, Sunshine Spices, Banalata Sales Center, Shebanipur Handloom Factory, Shapla Garments, Mirpur Wheatstraw Centre, Action Bag of Saidpur, and Surjosnato, a coconut production center. MCC SELFHELP purchases in Bangladesh have risen from $2,315 in 1973 to $184,800 in 1985.

MCC personnel who were involved early in Bangladesh reflect on the uniqueness of the program. MCC has concentrated one of its largest and longest-sustained programs in a Muslim society with only a handful of Christians. In fifteen years of service in Bangladesh MCC has committed nearly nine million dollars in cash and four and a half million dollars in material aid. Much of its work has been accomplished outside of national church structures. Bangladesh was a new country which needed and wanted creative ideas. MCC administrators in Bangladesh planned a strategy which worked well as long as the government was dependent on the districts and thanas. Access to top officials came easily in these circumstances and MCC's lasting presence in the country resulted in cumulative relationships. One MCC administrator noted: "In Bangladesh there was always someone in government who knew MCC and was willing to do us a favor."

The year 1985 was a difficult one for Bangladesh, a country rocked again by a cyclone which hit the coast off the Bay of Bengal. Twenty thousand people died in the Noakhali region, the heart of MCC agricultural work. As in 1970, the storm prompted MCC to work with other agencies in providing emergency care and material aid. The recent storm is a grim reminder of the regularity with which tragedy strikes the small country. The doubling of population in a short time is a warning that in this tiny land food producers are racing to keep ahead of hungry newborn babies. Given the inability of the country to restrain its explosive growth, efforts to increase agricultural production become an unending struggle. Yet the Bangladesh story remains one of perseverance, survival, and hope.

14

Replanting the Killing Fields:

Kampuchea

When I am reborn, may I not be Khmer.

In the markets and along the roads of Kampuchea, old friends meet by chance after years of separation. Smiles fade as the familiar question arises: "How many of your family are still alive?" The friends listen attentively to each other's stories of survival during ten years of war and bloody revolution. What lies ahead for them in the future is unclear.

Kampuchea, formerly called Cambodia, is a country the size of Missouri located betweeen Vietnam and Thailand. It has a population of about seven million. In the 1960s Prince Sihanouk struggled to keep the kingdom of Cambodia out of the war raging in Vietnam. But in 1969 President Nixon ordered the secret bombing of Cambodia, marking the end of Cambodia's relative peace. The bombing spawned a brutal civil war beginning in 1970 with the ouster of Prince Sihanouk and ending in 1975 with the victory of the radical communist Khmer Rouge.

The Khmer Rouge triumph resulted in three and a half years of forced collective labor, starvation, and summary executions under the leadership of Pol Pot, who dreamed of creating a classless peasant society called "Democratic Kampuchea." One man's story during these years is recounted in the book and film *The Killing Fields*. Pol Pot, who hoped to regain territory lost to Vietnam hundreds of years earlier, also launched attacks on Vietnamese villages.

In response, Vietnam invaded Kampuchea in December 1978, driving the Khmer Rouge from power and setting up a pro-Vietnamese government. Free from Pol Pot's grip and fearing famine, hundreds of thousands of refugees left Kampuchea and poured into Thailand in 1979. Since then, Kampuchea has made a remarkable start toward recovery from the U.S. bombings, Pol Pot's devastating revolution, and guerrilla warfare.

In 1979 Mennonite Central Committee representatives first visited Kampuchea. For the next two years MCC worked through other agencies to help both Kampucheans inside the country and refugees along the Thai/Kampuchean border. In September 1981, MCC placed its first workers, Minh and Fred Kauffman, in Kampuchea and began shipping material aid to the country. MCC and four other North American-based aid agencies have continued working in Kampuchea while the U.S. and Canadian governments have maintained strong opposition to the pro-Vietnamese government there.

The MCC school kit program, designed as an act of people-to-people cooperation, became instead a symbol of bureaucratic callousness. In Kampuchea there had been a tremendous surge of interest in children's education soon after the country was freed from the Pol Pot regime which had halted all schooling. In 1981, MCC launched a campaign to collect eighty-six thousand school kits for primary school students in Svay Rieng Province. Each drawstring bag contained two notebooks, a pen, pencils, and a ruler. MCC hoped that the program would be a popular Christmas project among North American Sunday school classes.

In November 1981, MCC's program hit a snag. The U.S.

Department of Commerce denied MCC a license to ship the kits, citing the Trading with the Enemy Act. MCC Asia Secretary Albert Lobe appealed for a reversal of the decision, stating: "The Commerce Department decision is a serious infringement on our prerogatives and understanding of Christian compassion to people in need. We are opposed to the Commerce Department's attempt to determine for us whom we should help."

Lobe encouraged MCC constituents to write their members of Congress and news of the license denial reached the press. Major newspapers issued editorials and feature articles criticizing the government's decision. The editor of the *Minneapolis Tribune* wrote:

> The American government invokes transparent double standards.... The United States is now exporting large amounts of grain and other goods to the Soviet Union—whose invasion of Afganistan was brutal and wholly unjustified. But it forbids small gifts of pencils and notebooks that might, very indirectly, ease pressures on Vietnam—whose invasion of Cambodia, however much at odds with notions of sovereignty and proper international conduct, did stop the Khmer Rouge from butchering Cambodians.

Students at Linville Mennonite School in Paradise, Pennsylvania, who had assembled approximately one hundred kits, wrote letters to the President following a slide presentation on the Kampuchea school kit project. One second-grader wrote, "Dear President Reagan.... We have a boy in our group that came from Kampuchea. He told us about what happened to his father. And that was sad. The boy is a refugee from Kampuchea. Please let us send the kits. *Please*. From Matthew Howe." President Reagan's personal secretary phoned the school principal and said: "The president hopes that you will be able to send your school kits to Kampuchea."

In response to the unfavorable press coverage and a number of letters, the Department of Commerce reversed its earlier license denial. In March 1982, the first shipment of nine thousand school kits arrived in Phnom Penh, and MCC representatives distributed the kits to students in Svay Rieng Province. They reported, "We were keenly aware of the privilege of being the link between children in North America and the students in Svay Rieng, halfway around the world, who had known little but war and suffering during their lives."

A Ministry of Education official who witnessed the distribution remarked that the children found the kits to be "more personal than receiving identical supplies from a large stock." Students in Kampuchea received over 100,000 school kits prepared by Mennonites and Brethren in Christ, as well as by Lutherans and Canadian Baptists who joined in the effort. Lobe later observed that if the U.S. license had been denied, MCC as a binational organization could have assembled and shipped school kits from Canada.

The pupils in Kampuchea descend from a once-proud and powerful people whose kingdom extended to much of present-day Thailand, Laos, and southern Vietnam. Its kings built the world-famous Angkor Wat and hundreds of other stone temples to the gods of their Indian mentors and priests. From the 1300s through the late 1800s the Khmer kingdom lost cohesion and much of its territory to Siam (Thailand) on the west and Vietnam on the east. Had the French not colonized Indochina in the mid-1800s, the kingdom of Cambodia might have disappeared in the Thai-Vietnamese struggle for regional supremacy.

The kingdom of Cambodia regained its independence from the French in 1953 under the leadership of King Norodom Sihanouk, who two years later abdicated to enter more fully into the country's political life. Although conservative and autocratic in domestic policies, Prince Sihanouk fostered ties with communist China, North Vietnam, and the Soviet Union, as well as with the United States, France, and other Western countries as he pursued his goal of neutrality and nonalignment. The war in neighboring Vietnam, however, doomed his efforts.

Under pressure from China and foreseeing an American defeat, Sihanouk allowed the Vietnamese communists to use Cambodian territory for refuge and supply lines. President Nixon, within four months of his November 1968 election, ordered the secret bombing of suspected Vietnamese targets inside Cambodia without informing Congress or the Cambodian government. It marked the beginning of a tragic end for traditional Cambodian society.

As the secret bombings spread into Cambodia they stirred deep anger among rural villagers, who comprised 85 percent of the population. The March 1970 ouster of Prince Sihanouk by right-wing General Lon Nol further disrupted traditional village life. Many rural Cambodians sensed a loss of identity and security as the ancient Khmer monarchy crumbled, and they knew instinctively that the urban elite represented by General Lon Nol would bear no good for them. Then Prince Sihanouk, in exile in Peking, threw his lot in with his former enemies, the "Khmer Rouge" communist revolutionaries, and broadcast appeals for villagers to join him in the armed struggle against Lon Nol. Many responded to his call, and the small band of three thousand Khmer Rouge grew to seventy thousand guerrillas, including many young orphans whose parents had been killed in the bombings.

The civil war raged on from 1970 to 1975 with a new campaign of U.S. bombings reaching a peak in 1973 before Congress forced their suspension. Suffering enormous battlefield losses to the bombings and well-supplied army of General Lon Nol, the young guerrillas fought on with a determination borne of rage. By the end of the civil war, the U.S. had bombed virtually every village, 10 percent of the people had died, 30 percent were uprooted, two thirds of the draft animals had been killed, and food stocks were depleted.

In April 1975, within two hours of their victory, the Khmer

Rouge evacuated the residents of Phnom Penh. The Khmer Rouge broke the power of well-organized wealthy families by scattering them throughout the country. The newly named "Democratic Kampuchea" became one vast work site, a peasant state. Religion, Western education, banking, trade, and contacts with foreign countries were viewed as tools of the exploiters and were expected to perish at the hands of the revolutionary *Angkar* (organization).

The Khmer Rouge forced people into collectivized "villages" for the next three and a half years, often hundreds of miles from their homes. Many were separated from family members. Work was heavy and hours were long. The collective kitchens provided starvation rations, at first due to the shortages left by the war and later because rice was exported in exchange for military supplies.

The Khmer Rouge's paranoid concern with "enemies" increased, and in 1977 more ruthless guards purged the existing ones in many provinces. Punishment became more arbitrary, and some guards executed persons for the slightest misconduct. (In the north and east, where Pol Pot had failed to consolidate his power, there were fewer killings.) Although the number of deaths under the Khmer Rouge will never be known, estimates by Khmer scholars range from one half to one and a half million.

During the 1970-75 fight against Lon Nol, the Khmer Rouge was made up of several factions. Following their victory, the leader of the most radical faction, Pol Pot, took control by killing all challengers, including veteran revolutionaries from other factions. Pol Pot's drive to consolidate his power in 1977 led to the purge of persons suspected of opposition, especially former urban dwellers and the educated.

MCC workers have noted that despite the centuries-old history of the country, the historical reference point of many Kampucheans is the three-year Pol Pot era. In 1983, a man told MCC administrator Lobe:

I had four children during the Pol Pot time. My oldest son was very hungry; he went to get food from the camp kitchen and the Khmer Rouge soldiers caught him. They tortured him. He died. All four of my children and my wife died during those years. It was a good thing they died. The suffering was too much.

An integral part of Pol Pot's dream for Democratic Kampuchea was to regain territory lost to Vietnam three hundred years earlier. Although he had benefited greatly from the Vietnamese communists' help during the early years of the guerrilla fight against Lon Nol, Pol Pot considered the Vietnamese Kampuchea's primary enemy. He purged anyone he suspected of having pro-Vietnamese sentiments and began launching attacks across the border into Vietnam, burning villages and killing civilians. China, Pol Pot's main ally, provided arms and ammunition. Worried by the prospect of Vietnam becoming a regional power allied with the Soviet Union, China was reassured to see Pol Pot keeping Vietnam off balance.

In December 1978, having failed in attempts to negotiate with Pol Pot, Vietnam invaded Kampuchea. Within two weeks, on January 7, 1979, a pro-Vietnamese government arose in Phnom Penh. The new "People's Republic of Kampuchea," under the presidency of Heng Samrin, a former military commander in a Khmer Rouge faction opposed to Pol Pot, announced its goal as "advancing toward socialism" and emphasized the importance of solidarity with Vietnam.

In September 1979, following months of fighting in the countryside, the Khmer Rouge collapsed. Civilians on the verge of starvation fled to Thailand. The world shuddered at the spectacle of hundreds of thousands of exhausted and brutalized refugees along the Thai border. The United Nations spoke of "a million dead by Christmas." Television crews and journalists descended on the border to report in sordid detail the plight of the refugees.

From 1979 to 1981, a massive international relief effort

resulted in $286 million in U.N. and Red Cross aid to refugees along the Thai border. During the same period, U.N. and Red Cross relief aid inside Kampuchea totaled $366 million. Food, rice seed, agricultural tools, and vehicles were channeled through the new government. Some forty private aid agencies played a major role in the relief effort as well, especially along the border. To the distress of some supporters, MCC did not rush to join the agencies at the border.

MCCers had been in Thailand for several years prior to the refugee crisis and had established relationships with Thai service agencies. The MCCers observed how the rapid influx of large international organizations and multi-million dollar refugee budgets excluded Thai groups from responding to the crisis. They also saw that desperately poor Thai farmers were being displaced by refugees and Khmer rebel armies. MCC's refugee work focused on helping Kampucheans trace missing family members.

This approach was not favored by some strong MCC supporters in North America who wanted to launch a large relief program on the Thai border. One proposal called for a $5.5 million feeding program. Others observed that relief goods at the border often slipped into the hands of Khmer military factions jockeying for power. To this the advocates of massive aid insisted that some of the relief aid would nonetheless get to the needy. They charged, "While we argue about how to help, people are starving at the border."

From 1979 through early 1981, MCC worked both along the border, where relief action was well publicized and popular, and inside Kampuchea through the few agencies which had secured permission from the government. By early 1981, MCC personnel had visited Kampuchea four times. With forty relief agencies working on the border, MCC chose instead to focus its efforts inside Kampuchea, despite difficult political and logistical problems.

This decision countered conventional relief agency wisdom.

To work in Kampuchea meant that MCC would be closely associated with a new Marxist government suspicious of people from the West, especially those from the U.S. MCCers were quite isolated from the general population: they were confined to a hotel, could not visit people in their homes, and were chauffered around by a government driver. MCC projects could be done only through Kampuchean government agencies. Aid shipments were negotiated with departments of health, education, or agriculture. Goods were turned over to the departments and MCCers participated as monitors rather than as distributors.

In the face of these limitations, MCC decided to go ahead with a program in Kampuchea. Other agencies had proven it could be done. The Kampucheans appeared determined to rebuild and more than half of the 800,000 refugees had returned to their country. Soon after the Kauffmans arrived in Phnom Penh in September 1981, MCC shipped laundry soap for hospitals, canned beef for returning refugees, two trucks for the Kampuchean Red Cross, and carpentry tools for primary school construction. MCC repaired the hospital at Neak Luong, the town the U.S. bombed by mistake in 1973. (This hospital was the setting for the opening scene in the film *The Killing Fields*.) MCC also repaired two buildings at the Prey Veng provincial hospital.

In 1984 MCC added an international dimension to its program in Kampuchea. The first of two Indian Mennonite medical programs arrived from the Dhamtari Christian hospital in Madhya Pradesh to work at the Prey Veng Hospital. The program helped with surgery and provided support and encouragement to the hospital's staff and recently graduated doctors. MCC also supplied approximately four thousand dollars in medicines each month. In 1985 MCC began a program of child care and nutrition in Prey Veng in cooperation with UNICEF and World Vision.

MCCers learned of an acute shortage of soap in hospitals.

Kampuchea's small soap factories employed experienced soapmakers but lacked the necessary fats and oils. By 1986, MCC and the Ministry of Industry had set up three simple oil mills to produce coconut oil and rubber seed oil for use in soap-making. A Filipino friend of MCC helped to establish the coconut processing.

With abundant land but unpredictable rainfall, Kampuchea needs to manage the Mekong River's great water resources. MCC provided rice to pay Kampuchean workers who repaired irrigation and flood-control works through a program known as "Food-for-Work." MCC imported two types of manual irrigation pumps from Bangladesh for testing in Kampuchean conditions. In another irrigation project, the Cuban Council of Churches sent MCC a civil engineer to set up a center for producing concrete culverts. And MCC has plans to rebuild a five-thousand-acre irrigation project by 1989.

MCCers have found that implementing projects through the Kampuchean government has limitations. Political decisions can have a major impact on choosing projects. As a result of the Khmer Rouge debacle, few technical experts remain in the country. Bureaucratic delays can bring projects to a halt. The culvert production center lay idle for months due to difficulties in obtaining gravel. In spite of these delays, MCC projects have moved ahead and MCCers have established congenial relationships with the Kampucheans involved in these projects.

Particularly gratifying for MCC has been the opportunity to develop an international team: Indian medical personnel, a Cuban civil engineer, a Filipino consultant, and an American and Vietamese-American couple as codirectors. Despite real differences in expectations and cultural backgrounds, all rate the international team experience as positive and have encouraged further attempts of this kind.

In the wake of war and revolution, Kampuchea has made significant progress toward normalcy. The present Vietnamese-backed government has provided a degree of stability. Family life is again at the center of Kampuchean society. Children are cherished with an intensity born of experience with the frailty of life. Traditional family life, however, has been threatened by the death of so many men through war, the purges, and starvation. Women make up 70 percent of the adult population in many villages. There are now more primary students in school than at any time in Kampuchea's history, although the quality of education is irregular.

Agricultural production is hampered by the shortage of men and draft animals. Pol Pot's ambitious and poorly engineered irrigation network often provokes flooding, and the country faces a serious shortage of fertilizers and pesticides. But although production is still less than half than that of the best prewar years, Kampuchea is nearing self-sufficiency in rice production.

Kampuchea is a mix of revolutionary change and traditional ways. While the government strives to follow "the road to socialism," free markets dominate the exchange of goods—rice, fish, meat, vegetables, and basic necessities—as well as consumer goods smuggled in from Thailand. Buddhism is again an integral part of community life; however, monks are expected to promote government policies. Christians, less than one-tenth of one percent of the population, are suspected of being agents of the West and do not have permission to gather for worship.

The young government, made up primarily of people with no previous administrative experience, has developed a functioning bureaucracy but suffers from an extreme shortage of skilled administrators and technicians. This, plus the government's commitment to centralized planning, makes government programs cumbersome and inhibits personal initiative. Moreover, roads are badly deteriorated and telephone contact with the provinces is possible only a few hours a day.

Kampuchea's efforts to move ahead are blocked by outside power struggles over which the country has no control. The age-old conflict beteen China and Vietnam is the heart of the problem. Warm relations between these countries in the 1960s during the war against the U.S. deteriorated to open hostility by 1977 as Vietnam aligned itself with the Soviet Union. After Vietnam ousted China's ally, Pol Pot, the Chinese launched a month-long military attack on Vietnam to "teach Hanoi a lesson" and began rebuilding the Khmer Rouge as a guerrilla force along the Thai-Kampuchean border. China and Thailand struck a deal which permitted China to supply the Khmer Rouge over Thai territory in exchange for a promise to halt assistance to the Thai communist movement.

China is angry at the Vietnamese for establishing regional control over Laos and Kampuchea, countries traditionally within China's sphere of influence. Strategically, China fears military encirclement by the Soviet Union, which maintains 400,000 troops along the 4,700-mile common border and trains nuclear weapons on China. The Vietnam/Soviet alliance gives the Soviet Union access to air and naval bases in Vietnam.

In spite of widespread condemnation of Pol Pot's "Democratic Kampuchea," the U.S., China, and Thailand have led the movement to continue giving the deposed Pol Pot regime the Kampuchean seat in the United Nations General Assembly and to deny the pro-Vietnamese government this recognition. Democratic Kampuchea retained the Kampuchea seat from 1979 to 1981. At that time it became the Coalition Government of Democratic Kampuchea after Prince Sihanouk and a pro-Western group of Khmers joined with the Khmer Rouge in an uneasy alliance. All three parties are bitter enemies from the past but have formed the coalition under pressure from China to present a united front against the Vietnamese in Kampuchea.

This international power struggle leaves many Kampucheans feeling helpless. Enthusiasm for rebuilding has dwindled and people often speak of the future with pessimism. A mood of self-recrimination is present among the people. Some have wished aloud, "When I am reborn, may I not be Khmer." Three fears dominate the outlook of Kampucheans: fear of another major disruption due to war, fear of the return of the Khmer Rouge, and fear that the Vietnamese who liberated them from Pol Pot will stay indefinitely as the occupying power.

The superpowers have fought over tiny Kampuchea. The present Marxist government is maintained in power by 150,000 Vietnamese troops. It is today one of the poorest countries in the world but is blocked from receiving international aid available to other poor countries. The uniqueness of this situation poses a series of difficult questions for MCC:

1. Recalling the U.S. ban on school kits, when one's government says no, should one take no for an answer?

2. Given the historic MCC preference for personally supervised distribution of emergency relief supplies, are there situations when it is appropriate to turn over such materials to governments for distribution? How concerned should one be that some of the gifts are used by the government to serve its interests and maintain its power?

3. Some critics would say that MCC aid is supporting a Vietnamese occupation of Kampuchea. How should MCC answer this charge?

4. Can MCC serve in good conscience in a country where the Christian minority is not permitted to meet for worship?

5. Should MCC help those who were once Khmer Rouge murderers but are now destitute and harassed refugees?

Telling the Story

The MCC story is a composite of tens of thousands of stories. Whenever those who have worked with MCC gather, they share stories of their experiences. Some stories are dramatic, such as the midnight exodus of a trainload of a thousand refugees from Berlin. Some stories are humorous, such as embarrassing blunders in speaking a strange language. Some stories touch the heart, such as a family's gratitude for a house rebuilt after a hurricane. Mennonite Central Committee is sustained by the remembrance of and the retelling of stories.

The Bible emphasizes storytelling as "bringing all things to remembrance." The unique quality of biblical storytelling is its honesty. Jesus called on his followers to tell it like it is: "Let your yes be yes and your no, no." The biblical counsel to report simply and truthfully calls for a Christian organization to share information with integrity. This is not easy. Each of us listens and reads differently. What one wants to have emphasized, another wishes to be left unreported. One is reminded of the New Testament exhortation to "speak the truth in love." The gift of sharing information, therefore, is balanced by the gift of receiving, testing, and evaluating it.

Those interested in the work of MCC not only read news releases but also talk with persons who have served with MCC. Oral information enriches the written word. In this book of case studies, readers become aware that only a few of the stories have been told. The reader's own search for more information may lead to the best case studies of all.

The apostle Paul in 1 Corinthians offers this wisdom: "Now we see only puzzling reflections in a mirror, but then we shall see face to face. My knowledge now is partial; then it will be whole, like God's knowledge of me."

15

Reporting the MCC Experience:

Images and Posters

A veteran MCC worker and church leader writes of his childhood:

> Few books captivated my interest as much as *Feeding the Hungry: Russia Famine 1919-1925*. It told of how friends of our family had gone to faraway Russia and helped save from death thousands of people like the Klassens, Epps, and Schmidts who were then arriving as refugees in our community. More than a hundred photographs in the book—mass graves and corpses, emaciated children, feeding kitchens, scenes of destruction and poverty—etched themselves deeply into my consciousness. As long as I live I shall remember those haunting photographs.

The widely distributed *Feeding the Hungry*, written by P. C. Hiebert and Orie O. Miller, helped keep the MCC vision alive through the 1930s when MCC was less active. Much of the text of the book consists of reports from MCC workers in Russia, originally news releases sent from the early Scottdale, Pennsylvania, headquarters of MCC to editors of church papers. Thus, "Information Services" dates back to the beginning of Mennonite Central Committee.

The 1985 *MCC Workbook* reports that in twelve months Information Services, based at the Akron, Pennsylvania, headquarters, sent no less than 313 News Service articles to editors. News releases also flowed from the Winnipeg, Manitoba, offices of MCC Canada and from regional and provincial MCC offices. Of the Akron news releases 95 percent appeared in at least one publication and 64 percent appeared in at least four publications. In addition to news releases, MCC and MCC Canada publish a variety of periodicals and newsletters: *Jottings* (quarterly inserts for church bulletins), *Intercom* (newsletter for MCC workers and alumni), *MCC Contact, Dialogue on Disabilities, Conciliation Quarterly, Peace Section Newsletter, Word and Deed, SELFHELP WORLD, Washington Memo,* VORP's *Network Newsletter* and *Accord*, and others.

Although the News Service is the backbone of MCC's information distribution system, each year Information Services also publishes fliers, advertisements, posters, brochures, booklets, study packets, displays, and books. The late Doris Longacre's *More-with-Less Cookbook*, published by Herald Press, is MCC's all-time best-seller. One of the busiest areas at the Akron headquarters is the production room with its offset printing facilities capable of mass producing book-size publications and multicolor brochures.

The Chinese adage that "one picture is worth a thousand words" is reflected in Information Services' production and distribution of posters, 16mm films, filmstrips, slide sets, and videocassettes. The audiovisual staff report 2,841 bookings in one year from its catalog of films and audiovisual aids, such as *Famine in Ethiopia, Hear Us: Voices Out of Central America, Harvest Against Hunger,* and *Give Me Your Hand.* MCC photography crews have gone to Africa, Bolivia, Bangladesh, Central America, and Thailand to film documentaries. MCC receives many requests for videocassettes, suggesting an emerging media interest.

The most discussed communication medium of MCC is the

pictorial advertising that Information Services places each month in church periodicals. MCC ads, produced systematically since 1973, have led to the printing of selected ads as fliers or as posters for bulletin boards. Ten of the best of these ad-posters are reproduced in this chapter. One might ask: Do the image and caption in the poster convey honestly and persuasively an essential theme of the MCC experience? What kinds of images communicate the MCC spirit?

The MCC story is told orally, in print, and in photograph. The most authentic way in which information is shared is through MCC workers, who return to describe their experiences, show their slides, and answer questions. There are few Mennonite and Brethren in Christ congregations that do not have members who have served with MCC. These MCC alumni are among the best sources of MCC information.

MCC leaders acknowledge that some of the most powerful stimuli for constituent giving come from outside MCC information channels. On the evening television news one may see on-the-scene reports of hunger in Somalia refugee camps, dead bodies in the "killing fields" of Kampuchea, devastated villages in the wake of a hurricane in Haiti, or the rubble of civil war in Lebanon. Often these reports of suffering reach the eyes of MCC constituents more quickly than do the news releases from Winnipeg or Akron. Invariably, gifts and inquiries flow to MCC headquarters after extensive televised coverage of a world crisis. Supporters of MCC have come to assume that their service agency will be well informed on the need and alert to responsibilities to respond.

In orienting volunteers to the work of Information Services the department provides each worker with a twenty-one-page booklet, *Reporting and Photogathering*, which describes its work and the volunteer's role in news gathering. It offers tips on writing news and feature articles that will be acceptable to editors. This includes a checklist covering testing for truth and balance, the importance of direct quotations and active verbs, and concern that the article is readable. The booklet ends with the counsel, "Give us the raw material of experience; we can polish it." Information Services solicits natural, close-up photographs with three basic elements, "the local person, the MCCer, and the project in which both are involved."

Information Services speaks of itself as providing "a link between MCC and its constituency":

> Many constituents have little information about MCC. Many also have little contact with people in developing countries or the poor in North America and may have only minimal understanding of the issues. . . . It is easy for them to perceive MCC's efforts at "education" as . . . criticism of the North American constituency. Our goal is to share information about MCC work, to generate goodwill and support toward MCC, and to share more clearly the concerns of MCC and MCCers, so that our constituency can understand and identify with those concerns.

Although MCC's constituency is diverse, MCC administrators ask questions of themselves, for example, What would Ezra and Mary Miller in Metamora think?

A question which MCC Information Service staff may ask frequently is this, What will the editors of church periodicals and hometown newspapers use? Editors vary in their criteria for accepting articles. Some editors tend to print the less controversial articles (such as activities of Mennonite Disaster Service) in preference to the more controversial (for example, peace-related) articles. Some editors seem to prefer articles on overseas topics to ones on domestic topics.

The Akron staff exercises care in how it reports events which will be picked up by national intelligence-gathering agencies. For example, an article on work with refugees fleeing the Republic of South Africa or an article on a government's diversion and mismanagement of famine aid may threaten the status of a partner agency.

Information Services is aware, as one former director of the department stated, that sometimes the "telling-it-like-it-is directness" of some writers "knocks heads with . . . the quiet-in-the-land, avoid-conflict carefulness" of others. As another former director commented, "Sometimes honesty means reporting bad news or problems." Examples of this could be the pilfering of funds by a trusted national, relief shipments rotting on the docks near a famine area due to political infighting, or heralded development programs which falter and fail. One may ask, Do constituents expect the Akron and Winnipeg staffs to maintain in their reporting an invariably positive image?

Questions arise when MCC workers see issues differently from Ottawa or Washington officials. Should workers with field experience at variance with government interpretations voice their concerns? Should dissenting eyewitness reports be distributed to the press? MCC is sometimes perplexed by calls from constituents for more balanced reporting. What is "balanced" reporting—that which is compatible with Pentagon explanations? Or do MCC field reports offer a "balance" to the news releases from government sources? This issue arises, for example, during reporting on human rights violations in Israel, El Salvador, or Paraguay, three countries that are on friendly terms with the United States and Canada. Can MCC, which represents Christians with alternative perspectives on issues of war and injustice, be expected to submit reports that are different from those of the secular media?

When the mass media publicizes an international disaster, MCC must decide whether it will quickly join the chorus of those presenting their programs. Other Mennonite church agencies may fear that MCC as a visible famine relief agency is draining funds from equally important but less dramatic programs. Hence, MCC must be careful in preparing advertisements that have a fund-raising appeal. Ads can be threatening competition to other good but less publicized causes.

What is the MCC image and who controls it? With news of MCC activities coming from many sources—both Akron and Winnipeg, regional and provincial offices, and hundreds of

Old MCC Symbol   Current MCC Symbol

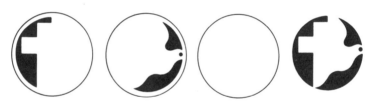

**Elements of the MCC symbol—"motivation": Christ; "action": compassion; "simplicity":
Mennonite heritage; "round form": global service.**

returning workers—centralized control of information and
image seems impossible. Many shape the image, but does
anyone control it?

We all live by symbols. MCC has had two consciously
designed emblems or symbols. The first was designed in the
early 1940s during World War II by Goshen, Indiana, artist
Arthur Sprunger, who integrated six motifs: the cross, a dove,
heads of wheat, clasped hands, a globe, and the name "Mennonite Central Committee." In 1968 another artist, Kenneth
Hiebert, was commissioned to design a new symbol. In the discussion leading to the new design, many themes in the MCC

experience emerged: living in tents, working in areas of tension, modeling servanthood, in the name of Christ, meeting human need—stability, pioneering, reconciliation, international perspectives, intercultural sensitivity, and more.

The artist describes the genesis of the idea:

> I saw the problem as bringing the message of the emblem into a concentrated, simplified, and active form, with the goal that it also have an enduring quality.... By simplifying the form radically it would be useful in many kinds of applications and in any size or color.... This basic form is the visualization of the slogan "In the Name of Christ"—the pouring of compassion from the cross, the hard form of the cross yielding to the fluid form of the dove....

This poses the question, What other visual images communicate authentically the MCC story?

Recognizing the power of visual images, pictorial advertisements have been published in the church papers over the years. Reprinted as fliers and posters, they have appeared on family, school, and church bulletin boards. Ten of these are shown on the pages that follow. Each evokes discussion: What feeling is created? What response is invited? Is it authentic? How does a picture communicate beyond words? Are the words essential to the picture? Beyond these are larger questions: How best can MCC tell its story? Are there new ways in which the story should be told?

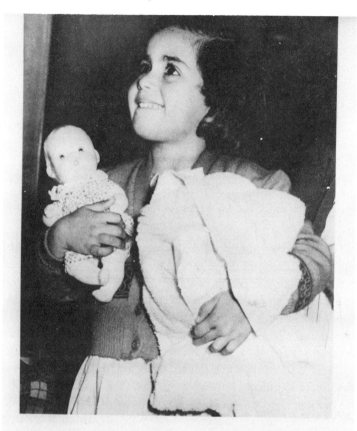

Christmas Bundles! "Every man shall give as he is able, according to the blessing of the Lord your God which he has given you." Deut. 16:17. Bundles for Christmas, 1963, should be in by July 1. This beaming Jordanian girl demonstrates the joy which these gifts bring to underprivileged children.

1. Christmas bundles!   Poster of the month, 1963

Editor: Larry Kehler

One of the earlier posters, artist and photographer not known. This is a classic relief-promotion poster with a more explicit explanation of the picture than might be used today.

2. . . . but through love.   Poster of the month, 1971

Editor: Don Ziegler
Artist: Stan Miller

Christ, the great teacher, teaches us to rise above our self-created complexity and confusion and to turn to him and see the way, the truth, and the life. . . . If art parallels life, and I believe it does, then the simple act of designing a poster is parallel to a simple action in life. . . . I would like to think that this poster reflects a softness, a gentleness, a simplicity, to which all people can relate.—Stan Miller

3. Many gifts, one spirit.

Annual report poster, 1973

Editor: Don Ziegler
Artist Ken Hiebert

In 1973 salt did not have the onus it has today, with changing dietary preferences. The theme was born out of an interaction among Bill Snyder (MCC Executive Secretary), Don Ziegler (Information Services Director), and me as designer. Bill was always anxious to state the big concept for MCC . . . somewhere at the leading edge of graphic communication—daring, involving, risk-taking like MCC itself—delivered in such a way as to bring the constituency along in a growing process.

The salt poster gets its impact from taking a humble version of a humble tool and transforming it, by its sheer monumentality, into a symbol at once vast and powerful. The association with the MCC mark is such as to link the action with the motivation—in the name of Christ. The salt poster is in the permanent collection of the *Gewerbemuseum Basel* in Switzerland.—Ken Hiebert

4. It's a sin to build a nuclear weapon.   Poster, about 1977

Editor: Sarah Eby Ebersole
Staff person: John Stoner
Artist: Kathy Bartel

I conceived the idea of doing this poster after reading an article with this title in *Sojourners,* February 1977, by Richard McSorley and reprinted from the *U.S. Catholic.* McSorley's article was clearly on the cutting edge of the times. More than six thousand copies of the poster have been published in two printings. . . . I remember a letter from a man who displayed the poster on the wall of his cabin in a nuclear submarine. . . . I suspect that the poster made as much of a contribution to changing people's minds as did a book on the subject. — John Stoner

I tried several designs, settling on the final choice with John Stoner's aid. He felt that the remains of a charred landscape was "realistic," that there would be an earth left, though devastated. It was printed in flat black, then varnished to show the landscape. — Kathy Bartel

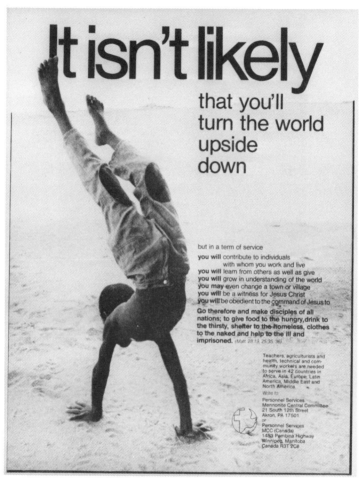

5. It isn't likely.   Monthly ad, 1980

Editor: Kristina Mast Burnett
Artist: Judith Rempel Smucker

The idea came from the Personnel Department which wants humble workers who are sincerely motivated, not ones who want to leave their mark in the world. The headline grew out of the photo. I wanted to take the edge off the message, make it playful, energetic, eye-catching. The boy on his hands has nothing to do with the copy but the strong visual attracts attention to the age-old theme that service is a radical action even if we don't see visible results. — Judith Rempel Smucker

6. Sharing, it's part of being . . . .   Poster, 1982

Editor: Gerald Schlabach
Artist: Jim King

We had this lovely photo of the Haitian father feeding his child. . . . Was there some way to communicate that rich, white North Americans do not have a monopoly on sharing? My experience living in a squatters' community in Guatemala as a short-term MCCer after the earthquake was that the poor are really much more generous than the rich. If they can do something to help one of their own in need, they will often give their last bit of money or dip into their meager savings. I don't want to romanticize the poor but perhaps do want to demythologize our own generosity. . . . The approach was to be more positive, subtle and warm: showing a nonwhite, non-North-American doing the giving for a change, ... [to] find a slogan that would suggest the universality of giving.—Gerald Schlabach

7. Hunger still haunts.

Poster, 1983

Staff person: Jocele Meyer
Artist: Judith Rempel Smucker

There had been a lot of media publicity just prior to this poster about starvation in the Horn of Africa. We needed to take an overworked theme and communicate its continuing urgency to a glazed audience.

People see so much that their senses become dulled. We wanted an approach that was subtle yet insistent: good intentions and a sympathetic attitude are not enough. This photograph maintains the dignity of a hungry child. The purpose is not a shock tactic in the mode of distended bellies. The poster simply reminds people that hunger is always with us. . . . The words are placed in a stalking manner. The girl's figure, printed in brown, becomes like a ghost—haunting.—Judith Rempel Smucker

8. A modest proposal for peace.   Poster, 1984

Staff person: John Stoner
Artist: Jim King

The idea for this poster grew out of a telephone conversation with Dale Brown, Bethany Theological Seminary, in which Dale mentioned the way M. R. Ziegler used to go to World Council of Churches meetings, listen to the long discussions about Christian unity, and then say something like this: "Couldn't we take a small step first and simply agree that as Christians we will not kill each other?" Dale said there would be a sort of embarrassed silence for a few moments and then the discussion would continue on different lines. —John Stoner

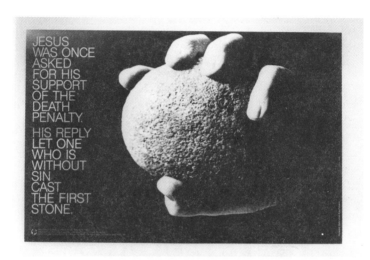

9. Jesus was once asked for his support of the death penalty.   Poster, 1983

Editor: Howard Zehr and Joel Kauffmann
Photographer: Howard Zehr

I decided to do a poster on the death penalty and asked Joel Kauffmann to work on it with me. We liked the idea of something biblical. We tried to be as true to the biblical passage as possible, but wanted to link it to the death penalty and to use contemporary and nonsexist language. We refined it word by word. . . .

We decided on a photograph because we wanted it to feel realistic, perhaps a bit threatening. We also considered whether the hands should be black or white, but since white support for the death penalty is stronger than black (and since blacks are more often the victim of it) we decided on white. We gathered a group of volunteers and photographed groups of hands. When we looked at the proof sheets, however, we selected a single hand.

The response to this poster has been gratifying. Several people have reported that their position on the death penalty has been changed as a result of the poster. In Montgomery, Alabama, the state anti-death penalty coalition and churches went together and paid to have a new version of this enlarged to almost billboard size, then to have them put on the sides of city buses as advertising. . . . —Howard Zehr

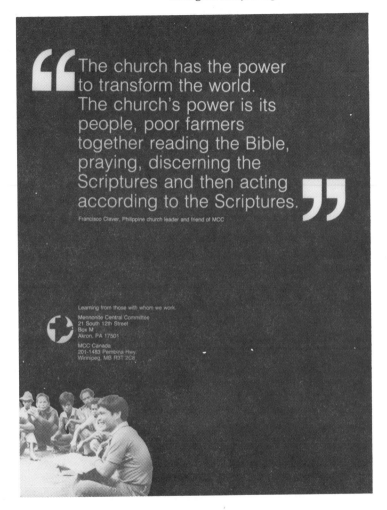

10. The church has the power . . . . .   Monthly ad, 1985

Editor: Kristina Mast Burnett
Artist: Scott Jost

This ad represents a developing attitude of MCC work as a process of mutual sharing . . . trying to be sensitive to those with whom we work. . . . By soliciting quotes we were not in complete control of the outcome and could learn about things in ways we had not thought of before. —Scott Jost

The Mediterranean

Instanbul (formerly called Constantinople) served as the staging base for MCC's efforts in 1920 to send relief to famine areas in the Soviet Union. Since World War II, MCC has served around the rim of the Mediterranean, first in Egypt, then in Italy, Greece, Turkey, Lebanon, Israel, Jordan, Yugoslavia, Morocco, and Algeria. Today programs remain in Lebanon, Egypt, and the West Bank area occupied by Israel.

The Mediterranean, where Muslim, Hebrew, Greek Orthodox, Coptic, and Roman Catholic meet, is a fascinating arena of competing world religions. Bishop Irineos of Crete once said, "Here is the area from whence have come the great ideas of the world." Beyond the Mediterranean to the east are concentrated the richest of oil fields. In Lebanon and Israel, along the narrow coastline of the Mediterranean's eastern edge, are focused ancient hostilities that imperil the peace of the world.

Here are three case studies, the first set on the island of Crete, with a charming Orthodox bishop and his people in a program of agricultural development. Case studies on Lebanon and the West Bank describe the quest for peace and justice in oppressive and violent environments. In seeking to understand the issues involved in MCC's presence, one becomes aware of the antiquity of the Middle East, the depth of religious loyalties and animosities, the great power struggles for control, the hospitality of the people, and the beauty of these lands of desert, coast, and vineyard.

We thank Martha Wenger for her contributions on the West Bank study and Mary Sprunger for hers on the Lebanon study. Other topics might also have opened windows to understanding the MCC experience in this region in times past: fraternal relations with Evangelicals and Coptics in Egypt, carrying on the work during Algeria's war of independence with France, and strategies of withdrawal after twenty years of service in Jordan.

In the thirteenth century a Catholic scholar, Ramon Lull, traveled to all parts of the Mediterranean telling of his vision for the peoples of that inland sea, "He who loves not, lives not." He reasoned:

> I see many knights going to the Holy Land beyond the seas and thinking they can acquire it by force of arms; but in the end all are destroyed before they attain that which they think to have. Whence it seems to me that the conquest of the Holy Land ought not be attempted except in the way in which Jesus Christ and his apostles acquired it in the first place, namely by love and prayers and the pouring out of treasure and blood.

16

Working with Our Friend, the Bishop:

Crete

The Crete program, which combined the
bishop's dream with MCC's cows, chickens, and
young workers, was unlike any program [MCC]
had administered.

One of the most unusual programs in MCC's history was its agricultural development work in Crete, the largest island of Greece. In 1961, MCC workers entered Crete to establish a technical training school. Several years later Bishop Irineos, who lived in Kastelli and served as the Metropolitan of Kissamos and Selinos districts in western Crete, invited MCC to come to the island again, this time to develop a model for farmers in the region. MCC agreed, and planned an agricultural program designed to be MCC-supported for eight years, from 1965 to 1973, with local Greeks to assume responsibility at the end of the period.

Just east of Kastelli is Kolymbari, today the site of the MCC-initiated farm known as the Agricultural Development Center (ADC). During the sixties and early seventies, most workers arriving in Crete were sponsored by MCC's Pax program, in which young conscientious objectors worked in developing countries.

In ancient times Crete was a center of Minoan culture, from

which the tradition survives of King Minos of Crete, the first sea power. In time the Cretans developed patterns of commercial life and military education much like that of Sparta. Persons were classified as full citizens (the Dorians), underprivileged citizens (Achaeans), serfs (Minoans), and slaves. Rome and Constantinople ruled Crete for nine hundred years. Paul and Titus visited the island. During the Middle Ages, Crete came under the control of exiled Arabs, and later, under the control of the Venetians and Byzantines. Ottoman rulers (Turks) took control of the island in 1669, and Cretan rebellions continued until Crete's independence in 1898 and its annexation to Greece in 1908. In 1941 the Germans invaded and occupied the island until its liberation in 1945.

The area of Crete is 3,217 square miles. Most of its topography is mountainous, although the northern coast of the island offers a more gentle, sloping landscape with a greater concentration of arable land. In the early 1960s, when MCC began its program in western Crete, about 70 percent of Crete's 483,000 inhabitants depended on agriculture—chiefly olive, wine, and citrus fruit—and livestock—cattle, sheep, and goats. Cretan farmers enjoyed an ideal climate and reasonably fertile soil. But by the 1960s, limited arable land and primitive technology had resulted in a depressed economy. Young people left Crete for better economic opportunities. Poverty was widespread, especially in rural areas and villages. Few farmers had ever seen a tractor.

MCC first established a model farm in Macedonia, Greece, to demonstrate farming techniques to rural Greeks. The Paxmen initiated livestock management, importation of breeding stock, sprinkler systems, and soil conservation. Women entered the MCC program to teach home economics classes with lessons in nutrition, sewing, child care, first aid, and hygiene. Pax workers introduced methods of canning food and began commercial canneries to provide new employment. When MCC ended its involvement on mainland Greece in 1966, it turned responsibility for its programs over to the government's Agricultural Services, which used Greek leadership to continue the farm in Macedonia.

In 1960 MCC learned of Bishop Irineos through a theologian and sociologist, Alexander Papaderos. Studying in Mainz, Germany, Papaderos, became acquainted with Peter Dyck, MCC's director in Europe. The Greek scholar suggested that together the Orthodox Church and MCC establish an agricultural school, operate a girls' school, and establish a "department for ecumenical encounters." Papaderos argued persuasively the need for MCC intervention in Crete:

> Many villages exhibit even yet evidences of the total destruction of the last war.... People have little enthusiasm for the work.... Out of this situation grows a destructive power of prejudices and spiritual weakness which spoils the otherwise noble, reputation-conscious, and exceptionally hospitable souls....

Not all of the ideas proposed by Papaderos materialized, but from 1961 to 1964, MCCers in Crete worked to establish a technical school for students twelve to eighteen years of age. A German MCC volunteer, Klaus Froese, and two Americans, Richard Kauffman and Orpha Zimmerly, initiated the project. In 1964 the government transferred responsibility for the school to the bishop. The stage was set for a more expansive program of cooperation between Bishop Irineos and MCC.

The bishop was interested in working with Mennonite Central Committee because he believed that Mennonites would be tolerant and low-key in their work among Orthodox society. Papaderos also felt that the Greeks would work alongside Mennonites despite the islanders' apprehension that these Protestant Christians might proselytize. In 1962 MCC worker Richard Kauffman reported to Peter Dyck:

> The bishop, being broad-minded and realizing the importance of church unity, has decided that the best way for his people to

learn to know and accept other Christians is to have several Protestants living here with them. This gives us a challenge, different from any we had quite expected. We can only pray that our lives are good enough for this task.

The bishop's invitation to MCC resulted in an agricultural development program that aimed to provide food for nearly one thousand students in the diocese. Second, an educational center would be located at the farm. The program began in February 1965 with the arrival of former Macedonia workers Roger Beck and Bill Nice. Louise and Virgil Claassen became program directors. During MCC's involvement with the farm, as many as twelve Mennonite Central Committee workers served together at one time. Volunteers invested most of their efforts in the livestock and extension programs of the Agricultural Development Center.

The MCCers soon discovered that insufficient land was available for the ADC, in spite of early promises by the bishop for as many as 125 acres. In reality, the farm was made up of tiny plots which were not contiguous and which barely amounted to fifteen acres. This, coupled with a lack of capital and problems in retaining Greek workers at the farm, provided the MCC team with ongoing frustrations. The experience of working with the bishop himself was one of the difficulties— and joys—reported by workers in Crete. His personal appeal and buoyant spirit are highlighted in this 1963 report from Peter Dyck:

> Obviously we need a lot more money than what is budgeted by us and needless to say the bishop is as good as broke. He is by no means broke in enthusiasm and faith that God will supply. . . . During our discussion in the monastery. . . . I pointed out that a great deal more—and especially money, would be needed to make the project a going concern since there were no buildings on the land, no other machines, etc., to which he replied that we had a great God who could certainly supply all things; then with a twinkle in his eye, which even though we were sitting by candlelight, we could not help but see, he added, "And I think God will provide all else we need through the Mennonites."

By 1968 the goals of the program had expanded to include a food production center to supply food for the bishop's schools and hostels, a demonstration center for modern farm practices, and a distribution center for improved breeds of livestock, poultry, feed, and seeds. MCC also wanted to train farm youth and provide short courses for farmers.

By 1972, MCCers at the Agricultural Development Center and local Greeks agreed that MCC had done well in meeting these goals. MCC had emphasized the educational and extension aspects of the center and asserted that the center ought to be left in the hands of the Greeks after seven years of training. The bishop believed that the projects begun with the assistance of MCC workers would instill hope among his Orthodox parishioners. Papaderos, who had since returned to Greece, commented at the conclusion of MCC's involvement: "The project was a signal that the church feels responsibility for the problems of the people. This has special meaning for us, for we have been accused of being very conservative. A project like ADC shows that the church does look forward."

The agricultural projects begun by the MCC team included a swine-breeding program, (MCC brought two hogs to Crete from northern Greece and later imported others from the United States), a dairy project to provide milk, poultry management, an artificial-insemination program for sheep, a rabbit-breeding project, beekeeping, and a feed mill. By 1972 MCC concluded that the most significant and successful efforts had been the swine, poultry, sheep, and feed mill projects. MCCers also built greenhouses and initiated vegetable production at the ADC. The ADC did not attempt to influence the three dominant agricultural activities in Crete—olive, wine, and citrus production. But it did help to diversify the agriculture of western Crete. In his 1972 report on the MCC experience in Crete, Paul Longacre concluded that the ADC had taught local farmers the importance of systematic care and feeding of livestock. Largely because of the bishop's influence and concern for promoting the farm, officials and farmers throughout western Crete recognized the agricultural contributions of MCC. Longacre noted that most villagers and farm families had visited ADC:

> In 1967 Virgil Claassen estimated that 5,000 persons visited ADC. Dave Gerber characterized many of the visitors as "zoo visitors." They came to see the "exotic animals" from abroad and the new types of farm buildings and practices. Bishop Irineos encouraged the "zoo visitors" to come and MCC to keep many interesting animals at the center to attract visitors. In the past few years ADC has maintained a steady flow of serious visitors. . . .

More difficult to evaluate was the influence of the MCCers on the spiritual life of the community they served. Both Papaderos and the bishop advocated ecumenical friendship and exchange of ideas as the means to quicken spiritual vitality among their people. Some MCC personnel worked explicitly at sharing expressions of faith. Loretta and Roy Kaufman joined a team sponsored by the World Council of Churches in the city of Iraklion. In 1971 another volunteer worked with theologians at the Orthodox Academy of Crete. MCC workers at Kolymbari distributed Bibles but were asked to stop within a year. A Bible study class led by Louise Claassen ceased meeting as a result of government pressure. Orthodox Church leaders, skeptical of the Mennonites' motives, also discouraged such activities.

These responses reinforced the view among some in MCC that "the mission concept just does not exist in the Orthodox Church, and what we in Protestantism and in the West call missions, the Greek Orthodox Church always calls proselytism." Some MCCers concluded that the best contributions they could make were in the day-to-day relationships with people at the ADC and in the villages. One MCC country director cited the Greek word *leitourgia*, meaning the integration of work and worship, as a symbol of these relationships.

Father Irineos Athanasiadis, who later became the Metropolitan of Kydonia and Apokorons, worked closely through the sixties with the MCC team as assistant to the bishop. In 1970 Father Irineos came to the U.S. for study at the Associated Mennonite Biblical Seminaries. He commented that the MCC workers had had a limited but valuable impact on the Orthodox Church:

> Total identification was not possible because we came from different theological understandings. From the Orthodox Church's point of view, bread, wine, and water, and the liturgy were most important.... But the farm really helped in the betterment of the people. You helped enrich the Orthodox Christians' lives....

MCC volunteers, despite ambivalent feelings about the contributions they were able to make spiritually during their service in Crete, maintained that the exchange of traditions had enriched their own understandings of Christianity. Loretta Kaufman commented on her newfound appreciation for the Orthodox liturgy and services. Kaufman noted that the birth of her daughter in Crete had provided an occasion to discuss believer's baptism with local friends, who acknowledged respect for her and her husband's wishes not to baptize the infant.

The relationship between Bishop Irineos and MCC was one of give-and-take, although in many instances MCC volunteers chafed a bit under the "cooperative" structure of this unique service assignment. MCC was reminded constantly that the Crete program, which combined the bishop's dream with MCC's cows, chickens, and young workers, was unlike any program it had administered. Moreover, projects initiated by the MCC team would have to be transferred to Greek leadership. This called for appropriate of timing in phasing out the program.

Bishop Irineos was an extraordinary churchman loved by his people. His intense personal interest in the school and farm prompted MCC administrators to wonder if they should attempt to build a program more independently from him. Yet they hesitated to draw back from the relationship because he made possible warm interaction between the Greek community and the development workers. In the first months, MCC workers realized that they would be more effective if they could free themselves from being the bishop's personal and privileged "guests." They enjoyed being in his presence, however, and did not miss opportunities to travel with him during his visits to outlying villages. MCC administrators who learned to know him described him as a man with deep faith in God's providence, a "sensitive, polite, and very intelligent person who is also somewhat of a schemer . . . ." One observer noted: "Kolymbari is a most blessed area because of the bishop. He has sound objectives and people know it. His concept is to go to the people rather than to have the people come to the church."

In 1973, after eight years in Crete, MCC turned the management of the ADC over to a Greek director. But when Bishop Irineos was transferred abruptly to Germany, MCCers remained in Crete as advisors to the new director. Fern and David Gerber, who had helped the ADC to mature, coordinated aspects of the leadership change, spending many hours with the farm's new Greek director. Naomi and William Stoesz held the advisory role from 1972 to 1974, followed by Mildred and Harold Nigh from 1974 to 1977, when MCC withdrew from Crete.

The dramatic story of Irineos' withdrawal, and return in 1980, cast MCC into a national struggle for human rights. Irineos' Greek supporters asserted that he had been appointed archbishop of Germany because of his opposition to the junta government that had risen to power in 1967. The bishop opposed the junta's infringement of individual rights and its seizing of political prisoners. After his "promotion" to Germany, he continued to preach resistance to the junta. In a 1974 speech from Bonn entitled "Is the Church's Witness Silent?" he put that resistance into Orthodox language: "Let us lift up the standard of God. Let us raise and let us confess the icon of man." Taken in its context, the speech was an electrifying freedom statement. Greek scholar Papaderos credited MCC with giving the bishop a high enough profile to enable him to resist the junta effectively.

In 1980, six years after the fall of the junta, Bishop Irineos returned to Crete to assist in the installation of a new bishop for his old diocese. However, his people wanted him, not the new bishop, and a group of citizens kidnapped Bishop Irineos and told both government and church that they would release him only if he were made their bishop again. The government had a political debt to Irineos for his opposition to the junta, so it concurred. But the Orthodox Synod of Crete dragged its feet until extremists walled up the church doors and threatened to kill one priest a week if their demand was not met. And so, in March 1981, Irineos returned to his office, an office virtually empty, since the bishop's popular support was not matched by ecclesiastical support.

Since his return, the bishop's job has not been easy. In the 1960s he and MCC rode the crest of an economy that had nowhere to go but up. Bishop Irineos was a wonder worker who brought a school, a farm, a bank, and industry to his area. In the 1980s the magic has been less potent. Yet he has persisted with his institutions of mercy, and the Agricultural Development Center continues. In fact, the bishop's original dream, that the farm would provide food cost-free to his hostels (a dream deemed impractical by MCC two decades ago), has now become a reality.

Since 1984 the Agricultural Development Center has had a new Greek director, a semiretired businessman who is making the farm viable. Harold Nigh, country director from 1974 to 1977, has visited the bishop and ADC several times in the past decade and has arranged for shipments of repair parts, replacement livestock, and hatching eggs from Ontario, Canada. In 1985 the ADC director visited Mennonite farms in Ontario and took a short course in artificial insemination for hogs.

A change in ADC philosophy evolved during the mid-1970s to an emphasis on using local feedstuffs such as olive leaves, residual waters, and pomace instead of using exlusively imported feeds and Western methods of growing forage. The farm's present director has adopted this idea and is experimenting with feeding cows the green grape stalks from the local winepress. As a result, reports Nigh, ADC has become a center for alternative approaches to food production.

MCC came to Crete at the invitation of the bishop to assist for a limited time in an agricultural development program and left Crete after reaching its minimal objectives. MCC's contribution may be measured less in agricultural productivity than in the warm relationships between volunteers and the Orthodox people of Crete. Perhaps the significance of MCC's presence for a decade at Kolymbari will be in the continued visits of MCC personnel to Crete and exchange visits of friends to North America. The Agricultural Development Center no longer has the "spit and polish" it had in the sixties when low-cost Pax labor was available. But it continues to fulfill its original agricultural mandate and remains a point of continued contact between Mennonites and Orthodox Christians.

17

Hearing Their Cries:

West Bank

When "Z" cried out for them to stop in the name of God, one man replied, "You have no God."

Palestinian spring in 1976 was no silent blooming of beauty on hillsides. It was an explosion. The anger, frustration, and resentment that had accumulated steadily over nine years of military occupation by Israel could no longer be suppressed. Half a million Palestinian Arabs in the West Bank of Jordan proclaimed to the world their hatred of nine years of Israeli military occupation and their determination to control their own destiny.

The Mennonite Central Committee unit in Jerusalem had faced turbulent times before. In 1948 the Zionist dream of a homeland in Palestine was realized through the birth of the state of Israel. War erupted between the Arabs and the Israelis. MCC entered Jordan in 1950 to meet the needs of refugees made homeless by the 1948 conflict. In 1956 the Egyptian government nationalized the Suez Canal Company, leading Israeli, British, and French forces to invade Egypt. The Suez crisis contributed to subsequent tensions between Palestinians and Israelis. In June 1967 these tensions escalated into full-scale war. Israel's army swept over the neighboring Arab lands during six days, occupying an area three times her original size. As a result, more than a million Palestinian Arabs in the West Bank and the Gaza Strip came under Israeli military occupation.

After the war MCC reassessed its position and decided to continue its work in the West Bank. Then, in October 1973, a fourth war commenced. This time the Arab armies posed a threat to Israel's seeming invincibility. Israel's armies turned back the attack and held on to their occupied territories, but there was no repeat of the victory of 1967.

New self-confidence and hope began to build among the Palestinian Arabs in the aftermath of the war. In November 1974, Yassir Arafat, chairman of the Palestinian Liberation Organization (PLO), triumphantly addressed the General Assembly of the United Nations. The PLO's leap from defeated obscurity to international recognition was confirmed in December 1975 and January 1976 when the U.N. Security Council invited the PLO to participate in debates and decision-making. West Bank Palestinians responded to these victories with new hope for change. Yet several local events in the West Bank threatened the Palestinians, making them more aware of the burdens of military occupation.

Two events heightened tension between the occupied Arabs and the Israeli army. First, in November 1975, a group of extreme nationalist Israelis (the Gush Emunim) asserted themselves in Sebastia, the site of ancient Samaria. They were determined to establish a Jewish settlement in the West Bank in defiance of official Israeli policy and international understandings. The Israeli government, reluctant to move against the settlers who were supported by the powerful National Religious Party, asked the settlers to move to a nearby army camp to await a government decision.

The second provocation was a lower court ruling in January 1976 which authorized public prayer in Jerusalem on the

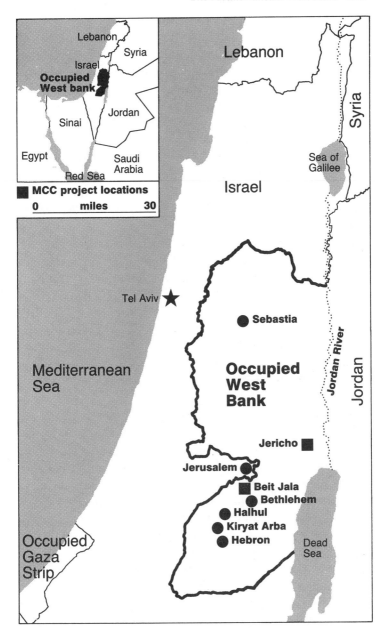

ancient site of the Jewish temple, now a Muslim shrine, the Al-Aksa Mosque. This ruling ran counter to an earlier decision by the Supreme Court of Israel that Jews could visit the area but could not hold prayer services there. Muslims were outraged at the new decision which they felt threatened the sanctity of their holy place. At the end of March, the Supreme Court over-ruled the lower court decision.

Demonstrations sparked by these provocations soon mount-ed to a major Arab protest against the occupation. Students poured out of West Bank schools to demonstrate and marched down streets to the stirring rhythm of PLO chants. Merchants went on strike in support of the students and in defiance of the occupation authorities. Israeli soldiers attacked the demonstra-tors with riot clubs and tear gas and fired shots into the air. The violence escalated as demonstrations spread into the West Bank hills north of Jerusalem and into East (Arab) Jerusalem.

The conservative Muslim town of Hebron (Al-Khalil, "the beloved of God"), which normally avoided political confronta-tion, became involved in the conflict. Hebron, the ancient city of Abraham, is holy both to Jews who revere the patriarch as the founder of Judaism and to Muslims who honor him as the first believer in one God.

Because of its historical and religious significance, Hebron was a prime target for the Gush Emunim, the religious na-tionalists who were attempting to settle in Sebastia. In 1968 a small group had established a settlement at Hebron in defiance of official Israeli policy. Eventually the nationalists obtained government approval for their "village." Additional land was then expropriated from Arab landowners to allow the settle-ment to expand. The presence of these zealous Jewish na-tionalists at the settlement, named Kiryat Arba, irritated the equally devout Muslim Hebronites. For a time animosity was veiled between residents of this armed Jewish island and the unarmed, occupied West Bank Palestinians. But when the wave of Palestinian demonstrations against the occupation reached Hebron, hostility broke out between the parties.

On March 20, 1976, a Palestinian agriculturist for MCC set out to work on a project at Hebron. He had nearly reached Hebron when he passed the village of Halhul, eerily silent under the complete house arrest imposed by the Israeli army as punishment for the villagers' earlier demonstrations. He was surprised to see a woman and her son walking along the road toward Hebron. Picking them up, he asked how they had managed to leave Halhul with the curfew still in effect. They showed him their permit to visit Hebron Hospital. The woman's husband and another son had been injured the previous night by a group of Israeli soldiers demanding entrance to the family's home. When they complied the soldiers burst into the room, beat them with clubs, smashed family pictures and took one thousand Israeli pounds (about $130).

The assailants forced the father and two sons outside at gunpoint to the main road of Halhul, where nine others from the neighborhood had also been gathered by soldiers. For two hours they were forced to stand with their arms in the air. Finally they were released and an officer, alarmed by the extent of their injuries, sent the father and one son to Hebron Hospital.

The MCC worker continued on to Hebron. He arrived upon a chaotic scene. Roads were strewn with stones and black smoke poured from old burning tires set afire in protest. Soldiers in armored troop carriers chased demonstrators down the streets while demonstrators hurled stones in return. Hebron, a conservative Arab community, was thus reluctantly drawn into confrontation with the occupation army. Israeli officials imposed a curfew for the next three days.

Later that day in Jerusalem, MCC worker LeRoy Friesen learned that an article describing the Israelis' use of dogs to attack Hebronites had been censored from the East Jerusalem Arabic newspaper, *Il Fajar* (The Dawn), by Israeli authorities. Friesen and the Palestinian agriculturist decided to travel to

Hebron to try to verify the censored report.

That evening the MCC unit—two American couples, a Palestinian couple, and an American student—gathered in the Friesens' home in an Arab Muslim neighborhood of East Jerusalem. Friesen related the grim scene just witnessed of military occupation. He noted that the Palestinians, often reluctant to talk about such hardships to outsiders, had been so abused that they were willing to talk despite the threat of reprisals. Since the army had the authority to bar the press from "sensitive areas," no reporters had yet reached the region. Even without that restriction, relatively few international reporters tried to get their stories firsthand from West Bank Palestinians. Most journalists simply relied on Israeli sources.

Hebron residents had told Friesen of being awakened in the night and beaten by soldiers for no reason other than Palestinian identity. Each person who related an incident mentioned others who had experienced similar mistreatment.

The story of "Z" from Hebron was particularly disturbing. "Z" had been sitting in front of his brother's shop when a group of Jewish civilians from Kiryat Arba approached and forced him and another man into the back of a van. A third man, the victim of a beating, was already being held in the vehicle. The Israelis told "Z" that they were going to the Military Governor's office, but instead they drove up the hill toward Kiryat Arba.

There, under the direction of a rabbi from the settlement, the men were forced to strip and give up their identity cards. Fearing for his safety, "Z" showed his abductors a newspaper clipping he carried with his identity booklet. The clipping described how his grandfather had saved the lives of sixty-eight Jews during the 1929 riots by hiding them in his home. Unmoved, the rabbi responded by cursing "Z."

Another man grabbed "Z" with one hand and held a dog on a chain with the other. He said: "If you threw stones today, tell us and you can go home. If you lie, the dog, will know." When

"Z" told him that he hadn't thrown stones, the man released the dog which then bit "Z" on the arm. Another man said, "We want to live in peace with you; tell us who threw the stones." Again "Z" refused, and the dog bit his fingers. "Z" screamed, but his captors beat him on the back and on the leg with a club.

"Z" and the other two Arab men were then forced into an underground shelter. Their captors lined them up against a wall and beat their naked bodies with the dog's chain. When "Z" cried out for them to stop in the name of God, one man replied, "You have no God."

Finally the Arabs were ordered to get dressed in two minutes. Unable to comply, they were beaten again. The Kiryat Arba men put them back into the van and took them to the Israeli Military Governor's office, where they turned the prisoners over to the occupation authorities. As they left, "Z" shouted that he would get revenge. The Kiryat Arba men turned back but the army captain intervened, saying, "You have done enough to him today." "Z" received treatment in the Israeli military clinic and later received anti-rabies treatment at Hebron Hospital.

"Z" 's experience was not an isolated incident. Arab doctors at the hospital estimated that at least a hundred persons were treated for fractures, head wounds, and cuts following clashes with army personnel. Eight were treated for dog bites. "Z" 's experience was unique in that his captors had been a group of civilian vigilantes—the harassment of others in Hebron and in the neighboring villages of Halhul and Beit Jala had been at the hands of Israeli soldiers.

After Friesen recounted these incidents at the MCC meeting, unit members discussed how they might respond. They were aware that volunteers from some foreign agencies might say: "We have no right to interfere in the internal affairs of this nation. We will do our relief and development work and keep quiet about injustices we see."

Although MCC's initial involvement in the Middle East had been in the form of relief distribution of food, clothing, and blankets to Arab refugees, the emphasis had shifted gradually over the following twenty-five years toward more long-term programs. MCC started vocational training programs, a school in Jericho, sewing centers, and summer camps. MCC workers opened a needlework program for refugee women and a high school for Palestinian boys in the village of Beit Jala near Bethlehem. In the 1970s MCC initiated an agricultural development program. After the 1967 war half of MCC's operations were in areas occupied by Israel.

New concerns about the application of peace and justice principles took shape when the Friesens began a full-time "peace-maker" assignment in Jerusalem. Over the course of four years they felt increasingly that they should act as advocates for oppressed persons. They continued to hope that the two sides would move toward lasting reconciliation.

An MCC document outlining objectives and priorities for personnel in West Bank gave evidence of MCC's commitment:

> —To affirm, throughout activities and programs, the integrity of both the Israeli and Palestinian peoples, in the latter case particularly as such integrity is challenged by the occupation of the West Bank.

> —To administer programs which reflect the best long-term interests of an unoccupied West Bank.

Given this justification for MCC presence in the West Bank, the MCC unit faced the question of whether to address the human rights violations. Realizing that they were the only outsiders who knew of "Z" 's story, the volunteers felt they could not remain silent. The mistreatment of "Z" was only one of many incidents of abuse of Palestinians that had come to their attention during the spring of 1976. In past weeks they had learned of other brutal encounters: killings, torture, and vandalism. The MCCers knew that the actions against "Z" by the

Kiryat Arba settlers might be explained as the excesses of extremists who were, at times, an embarrassment even to the Israeli government. However, they found the scope and pattern of abuse by Israeli soldiers more difficult to explain and agreed that the MCC voice had to be raised in some way.

The unit members knew the risks if they chose to take a public stand against the actions of the occupation army. The government might close MCC projects in the West Bank. Thus the volunteers hesitated to make a decision without consulting the MCC headquarters in Akron, Pennsylvania. They felt it unwise to communicate such sensitive information over the telephone. They also questioned whether the Akron staff could grasp the immediacy of the situation without a detailed explanation.

There were also personal risks to consider. What would happen to "Z" if his story was published? What about the two Palestinian workers associated with MCC? They did not want to leave their home on the West Bank. Moreover, several Americans, who had invested five years in service and Arabic studies, might be asked to leave.

The emerging consensus seemed to be that the volunteers could not go public with the incident because of high risks to MCC and the possibility that no meaningful change would result. The MCCers were drawn to a more indirect approach: communicating quietly with a few key persons who could exert influence in the right places to bring about change. These persons were international reporters and prominent Israeli journalists who were open to Palestinian perspectives. Despite their hope that these persons might be willing to help, the unit members recognized the limits imposed on journalists in reporting human rights violations. Because restrictions on the movement of the press in the West Bank could be increased, they decided to present "Z" 's story and contextual information to two members of Knesset, the Israeli Parliament.

Several weeks passed before a response came. On May 6, the

editor of a dovish Hebrew periodical, *Emda,* asked to meet with Friesen. At the same time, an article attributed to Friesen appeared in a Hebrew daily, *Davar.* It focused on military and civilian mistreatment of Palestinians and mentioned that complaints had been registered with the Israeli Ministers of Defense and Police.

The *Emda* editor explained that the two Knesset members had shared Friesen's reports with him and that the three, concerned, had decided to bring the incidents to the attention of the Ministers of Defense and Police. In addition, they had decided to print the story about "Z" 's treatment in the next issue of *Emda,* which was to appear in a few days. The editor said he had tried to contact Friesen earlier for his consent, but decided to go ahead when he was unable to reach him.

Friesen was dismayed that some of his material had been published without consent. Since the issue of *Emda* was already printed, he decided to allow it to be distributed, provided that any mention of MCC would be blacked out. He explained to the editor that he saw MCC's position as highly vulnerable and that publication of his reports had gone far beyond the original goal of raising the awareness of a few individuals.

Within the next few weeks a third newspaper, *Ma'ariv,* also published an article referring to Friesen by name. In subsequent conversations with two members of the international press, he learned that they too had received copies of his reports.

In spite of the widespread distribution of Friesen's material, he was not contacted by either Israeli government officials or the Israeli press after May 7, 1976. The government conducted no public investigation of the events in Hebron. MCC continued its operations in the West Bank and MCC workers continued to observe violations of Palestinian rights. In 1980 an MCC worker testified before a congressional committee in Washington, D.C., on Israeli withdrawal of water rights to Palestinians and the rapid expansion of militarized Israeli settlements on the West Bank. As a result, Israeli government officials denied a visa for the worker to return.

In 1977, a year after "Z" was attacked at Hebron, the Menachem Begin government came to power. At that time some five thousand Israeli settlers lived in the thirty-six settlements. Despite the Camp David Accords of 1978, Israel intensified its campaign to settle the West Bank. By 1985 the number of militarized settlements had grown to 115 with 52,000 settlers. In 1984 a spokesman for the World Zionist Organization declared, "We can reach [a goal] of at least one million Jews in the West Bank by the end of the century." Peace Now, a coalition of Israeli peace activists, called these efforts an "abuse of the principles of both Israeli and international law" which "foments a deep-seated bitterness and hatred toward Israel...."

Each year Israeli occupiers have appropriated more West Bank arable land; today Israelis control 52 percent of the land once occupied entirely by West Bank Palestinians. MCC continues its presence on the West Bank, assisting farmers in reclaiming land, installing irrigation systems, building roads, constructing cisterns, and maintaining a wide network of interpretive relationships.

Israel continues to encroach on the land and civil rights of Palestinians. Harassment of Palestinians also continues but in more subtle forms. A Palestinian is requested by the Israelis to report to the office of the military authority on a given morning. He waits there all day and at the end of the afternoon is told to return again the next morning. The same pattern of waiting follows day after day, week after week. The Palestinian begins to appear to his neighbors to be a collaborator because every day he disappears into Israeli headquarters. Subtle harassment of Palestinians takes other forms as well: Travelers wait for hours at roadblocks where soldiers check their papers; farmers find their source of water cut off; workers stand in line at occupation offices to receive permits for the most trivial of activities. Palestinians know that they are being watched.

In this war of nerves, MCC representatives continue to befriend Palestinians and to establish linkages with concerned Israelis. Questions arise for North American workers placed in this complex and unjust system: How does one identify with the Palestinian people and communicate their stories without being accused of anti-Semitism? Should expatriate workers concerned about the major injustices they see participate in selective acts of civil disobedience? How might MCCers in the West Bank model relationships which will contribute to peacemaking now and in years to come?

18

Caught in the Crossfire:

Lebanon

Life in a warring country is cheap.

Three-and-a-half-year-old Quinton clutched one of his parents and buried his face as each bomb exploded on the Palestinian refugee camp a half mile from his home in Sidon, Lebanon. The eight-month old twins, Emily and John, were oblivious to the 1982 Israeli invasion of Lebanon, but their parents, Phyllis and Ralph Miller, prayed for protection against the danger that they and thousands of others faced. The family had been leaving for church when the first bomb exploded over Ein el-Helwe, the largest permanent refugee camp in Lebanon and home to fifty thousand Palestinians. They dashed back into the house and began to pray. On June 9, 1982, four days after they sought shelter in the basement of their Sidon home, an Israeli messenger warned the Millers and their neighbors, "If you want to live, get out." Ten minutes later they were heading for nine days of safety behind the Israeli line. As soon as the fighting stopped, the Millers returned to Sidon with the other residents.

The Millers' decision to work in a war-ravaged country amid

intense violence, personal risk, and despair reflected their strong commitment to an MCC presence in Lebanon, where little hope remained for peaceful solutions to difficult conflicts. In a nation where government means nothing and armed forces everything, the New Testament mandate to "render unto Caesar that which is Caesar's" poses perplexing choices. Who is Caesar? Political and religious militias and foreign interventionists, vying for power in an area smaller than Connecticut, create a constant shifting of regional control. Learning to distribute relief goods, to do agricultural development, and to share hope in a political caldron is a perpetual challenge for MCC workers in Lebanon.

Ten years before the Millers experienced the Israeli invasion, Lebanon enjoyed a reputation as the "Switzerland of the Middle East." After gaining independence from France in 1943, Lebanon developed into an oasis of prosperity and democracy in a region of authoritarian and militaristic regimes. Lebanon is a tiny, mountainous country, 135 miles long and fifty miles wide, positioned on the eastern end of the Mediterranean Sea. Two mountain ranges running north and south border the fertile Beqaa Valley. Nearly three million people, mostly Arab, live in Lebanon.

The country's National Covenant upholds a representative government based on confessionalism and designed to allow each major religious minority a political voice. Based on statistics from 1932 that showed the Maronite Christians, a Roman Catholic group with ancient Syrian and Lebanese roots, as the leading religion in Lebanon, the presidency was reserved for a Maronite. Sunni Muslims, as the second largest group, controlled the premiership, and Shi'ite Muslims, the presidency of the chamber of deputies. Representatives to this unicameral legislature also included Maronites, Sunnites, Shi'ites, Orthodox, Druze, Byzantine Catholics, and Armenian Orthodox.

This distribution of political power, in appearance arbitrary, nurtured a facade of stability that allowed Lebanon to become

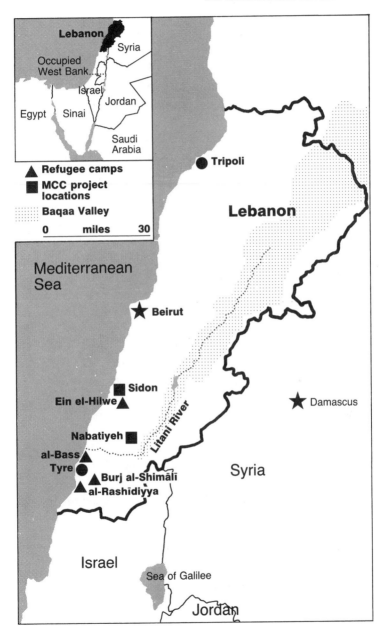

Lebanon

Occupied West Bank
Israel
Jordan
Egypt
Sinai
Saudi Arabia
Syria

▲ Refugee camps
■ MCC project locations
Baqaa Valley

0   miles   30

Mediterranean Sea

● Tripoli

Lebanon

★ Beirut

■ Sidon
Ein el-Hilwe ▲

Nabatiyeh ■

Litani River

al-Bass ▲
Tyre ●
▲ Burj al-Shimāli
▲ al-Rashīdiyya

★ Damascus

Syria

Israel

Sea of Galilee

Jordan

the intellectual, economic, and cultural hub of the Arab world. Free foreign exchange, solid currency, and banking-secrecy laws made the capital city of Beirut a financial center attractive to Arab wealth and encouraged a thriving industry. A higher standard of living paralleled the growth of a middle class, and by the 1970s, Lebanon's literacy rate of 88 percent was higher than that of any other Arab nation. Despite protests against the establishment of Israel as a Jewish state in 1948, Lebanon tried to maintain distance from the Arab-Israeli wars and did not develop a strong army. While the rest of the Arab world mourned the loss of territory and prestige to the victorious Israelis in the Six-Day War in 1967, Lebanon, seemingly unscathed, continued to prosper.

Events in the 1970s, however, proved that Lebanon's position in the Middle East hung in a delicate balance. Internal Lebanese problems corroded the front of social and political cohesion, permitting a certain vulnerability. A gulf between rich and poor, masked by Lebanon's growing middle class, continued to deepen and fester. The government, largely Christian, ignored the needs of the mostly Muslim poor. The Maronite Christians, no longer the largest religious sect, were afraid of losing a political power that was not legitimately theirs. Power struggles between the clans within each faction further hampered cooperation.

The catalyst which finally caused a complete breakdown of Lebanon's delicate order, however, was external. Jordan, threatened by Palestinian militias who used it as a base for raids on Israel, drove out the last Palestinian commando units in 1971. Since the Arab-Israeli war in 1967, Beirut had been a center for Palestinian resistance activities, and with the addition of the expelled commandos in the south, Lebanon became the new base of Palestinian operation and, subsequently, the new target for Israeli retaliation.

This Palestinian presence, with the foreign sympathies and hostilities it invited, was enough to upset Lebanon's fragile social and political system. By April 1975, tensions between the conservative Maronite Phalangist Party and liberal Muslims erupted into a full-scale war. Although a cease-fire in October 1976 officially marked the end of civil war, Lebanon became an arena for much of the Middle East conflict. The violence continues: During the ten years following the outbreak of civil war, more than fifty thousand people in Beirut alone have been killed and thousands of others have been left homeless. Many have fled the country.

But life in Lebanon goes on. Foreigners often express surprise at the "business as usual" normalcy in a country where political chaos and violence have been a part of life for more than ten years. The Lebanese government and military control little more than the few miles of land around the presidential palace at Baabda, outside of Beirut. The rest of Lebanon is subject to feuding internal militias and external "peace-keeping" forces or aggressors. The Lebanese Front, a coalition of rightist Maronite parties dominated by the Gemayal (Phalangist), Chamoun (National Liberal), and Franjieh (Zghorta Liberation) families, seeks to establish an independent Christian state. Overseas Lebanese and rightist Israelis have provided military training for the Front's militias, who have controlled East Beirut since the civil war.

Fighting against the Lebanese Front, sometimes called "the secessionists," is the National Movement, a loose alliance of Druze—a Muslim sect, Shi'ite and Sunni Muslims, a few Orthodox Christians, and leftist parties supported by Iraq and Syria. Besides thwarting the Maronites, the National Movement seeks to establish an Islamic or socialist state. Prominent leaders have included Walid Jumblat, Musa Al Sadr, and Nabi Berri. This alliance is sympathetic to the Palestinian resistance movement, which is fighting for the return of Palestinian lands that Israel now holds. Pitted against the Palestinians in the south are Israeli-backed militias. In the midst of these warring factions have been two occupation or peace-keeping forces: the

Syrians in the north and a United Nations force in the south.

Although MCC has been active in the Middle East since 1948, its work in Lebanon was only intermittent until 1977. In 1958, Ernest Lehman, Arnold Dietzel, Ada Stoltzfus, and Alice Snyder distributed food to hungry children in Beirut, victims of Lebanon's first civil war. In that same year, Menno Travel Service opened an office in Beirut to facilitate travel in the Middle East. When the staff had to be evacuated in 1967 and the U.S. State Department temporarily banned travel to Arab countries, the office closed. In addition to this and a handful of short-term relief efforts in Lebanon, MCC concentrated its programs in Jordan, Israel, and Egypt. MCC's record of thirty-five years of service in the Middle East lends legitimacy to MCC's more recent presence in Lebanon.

The devastating effects of civil war drew MCC to Lebanon in 1977, at first supporting projects of the Middle East Council of Churches (MECC) while looking for a relevant program of its own. MCC decided to direct its resources toward rural development in South Lebanon, a neglected and war-torn area. Farmers became discouraged as Palestinian/Israeli raids and shelling destroyed crops and made it dangerous to go into the fields; many left their homes and farms for northern cities more removed from the border fighting.

In March 1978, only half a year after MCC entered Lebanon to set up an agricultural program, Israel invaded and occupied South Lebanon. This time the Israeli army stopped short of Sidon, but the city witnessed an invasion of another kind: a quarter of a million South Lebanese refugees poured into central Lebanon. With personnel there to see the immediate needs of the refugees, MCC workers responded directly and quickly to the new crisis. Government and international agencies required almost two months to mobilize effective aid. MCC, on the scene, immediately provided food, bedding, basic kitchen equipment, and medicine to refugee camps and clinics.

The MCCers encountered many tragic stories of families separated during the crisis. One worker watched as a two-month-old baby was reunited with his mother after five days of separation. The fleeing mother had placed the baby in a taxi and then gone back into the house for some belongings. She returned to find that the taxi driver had panicked when bombs began to fall and had driven away.

The gradual withdrawal of Israeli troops did not mean the end of occupation for the South Lebanese. A United Nations force moved into the area between the Litani River and a six-mile-wide strip along the border that Israel and the Haddad militia turned into a buffer zone. Slowly, families filtered back into South Lebanon to their homes, although the refugee population remained high. MCC continued to provide relief through the MECC and the United Nations Relief and Works Agency (UNRWA).

After the immediate crisis had passed, MCC concentrated its efforts on rural development, particularly just north of the area Israel had occupied. Unlike the chronically poor countries Bangladesh and Haiti, Lebanon's agricultural poverty stemmed from governmental neglect and years of internal conflict. The government provided farmers in other parts of Lebanon with certain agricultural services but for reasons of security was unwilling to assist the South Lebanese. MCC tried to funnel some of these services to needy farmers in the south, although the government was not always cooperative.

As an alternative to these unpredictable government services, MCC worked to strengthen local initiative and skills and to convince farmers that agricultural investment would be a stabilizing force in an otherwise chaotic environment. The agricultural development program encouraged farmers in the south to stay on their land despite the trying and often devastating interruptions. MCCers distributed fruit trees, forest seedlings, and wheat and barley seeds to favor the production of food instead of tobacco. MCC introduced techniques and equipment in beekeeping, grape trellising, and animal husbandry. Projects such as agricultural cooperatives, forestry education, water conservation, irrigation, and road building and repair benefited the whole community. Outbreaks of violence sometimes disrupted and delayed the agricultural work, but never for more than a few weeks at a time.

Living and working in South Lebanon require a strong commitment because of the personal risks involved. Already in 1978 the United States government urged all Americans to leave Lebanon, but MCC wanted to continue its nonsectarian Christian presence in a country marked with heavy religious and political lines. Although personnel were cautious and tried to avoid high risks, daily work brought them into vulnerable positions. They worked in villages and traveled on roads that were subject to raids, shelling, and terror from various commando units.

The U.N. troops were unable to curb the warring factions and South Lebanon became virtually a no-man's-land sandwiched between Israeli-backed Christian secessionists in the south and Syrian, leftist and Palestinian commandos in the north. Once, the back windshield of a car driven by two Lebanese MCC workers was shattered by what seemed to be a stray bullet. The experience was a disquieting reminder that life in a warring country is cheap. Nor was South Lebanon a haven of security. Commando assailants armed with submachine guns once stole an MCC car and threatened the lives of its occupants. The city was susceptible to shelling by Christian militias or, as in the 1982 invasion, by Israel. MCC workers with U.S. citizenship witnessed destruction and casualties caused by U.S.-supplied weapons.

One incident underscored the danger of poor communication and lack of good information about rapidly changing conditions in Lebanon. Mounting tensions in the spring of 1981, the result of retaliatory attacks between a radical Shi'ite movement and Palestinian commandos, destroyed security in the

U.N. zone. Several MCC workers, not realizing the full gravity of the situation in South Lebanon, drove to a scheduled visit in one of the villages. They were shocked to find Palestinian military barriers just a few hundred yards down the road from the usual U.N. checkpoint. Several different military factions scrutinized them en route. When they arrived in the village they learned that a friend had sent a message warning them not to come. People had been killed in at least three of the villages where MCC worked, and about half of the total casualties in this new outbreak were civilians.

Among other grim stories, the MCC workers heard a report of mutilated bodies found along the roads in burlap bags. They left immediately and arrived at Sidon shaken but safe. Upon hearing of this incident, MCC's Middle East secretary, Paul Myers, assured the workers of support from the home offices should they decide to leave Lebanon, but the MCCers chose to stay and share the hazards of war with their Lebanese and Palestinian neighbors.

During their first five years in Lebanon, MCC personnel worked with staff members Sunnite Abed El Ghani Lazikani, Druze Aref Talhouk, and Shi'ite Hassan Fayad. Their agricultural work touched mostly the poor Shi'ite farmers of South Lebanon; their relief work and later income-generating projects aided many Palestinians. On Sundays, the MCCers worshiped with a Presbyterian congregation in Sidon, and their close ties with the Middle East Christian Council were both work-related and fraternal. This kind of interreligious, apolitical approach was unheard of in Lebanon, where strict factionalism has been the norm. It is hard for the Lebanese to understand that MCC, a North American, Christian organization (both labels that evoke certain political connotations) wants to transcend religious and party lines as it helps those in need.

The tension of trying to be moderate and unbiased in Lebanon became especially apparent after the Israeli invasion on June 5, 1982. It left in its wake an estimated twenty thousand Lebanese and Palestinians dead, over four billion dollars' worth of destruction, and almost half of Lebanon under Israeli control. After the smoke had cleared, Christians and Muslims alike rejoiced in their freedom from Palestinian oppression. The Lebanese overlooked the Israeli violations of human rights. The Maronite government terrorized Palestinians and forcefully objected to their presence. Attempts to aid Palestinians were extremely unpopular and were labeled "anti-Lebanese." The Shatila-Sabra refugee camp massacre in September 1982, which left over one thousand men, women, and children dead, was a tragic reminder to the Palestinians that they were not a welcome presence in Lebanon. Yet among the sixty thousand Palestinian refugees who had been forced to flee their destroyed homes and whose husbands and sons had been arrested by Israeli or Christian forces, MCC found the greatest need for relief and reconstruction. The Millers, joined by Dan Friesen and Ken Friesen in August 1982, continued to work with Palestinians, despite warnings that Christian militias were watching MCC's "anti-Lebanese" activity and that the workers were on the "Kataab's [the Phalangists'] list."

Although MCC workers tried to keep a low profile, they believed that their many foreign contacts increased suspicion of their work and role in Lebanon. The Phalangist armed guards located across the street from the Millers' home in Sidon could not have missed the stream of marked cars from agencies such as the United Nations Relief Works Agency, the International Committee of the Red Cross, or the Middle East Christian Council. In October 1982, a United States Agency for International Development (U.S. AID) representative made an ostentatious visit to the MCCers' home. In addition to six or seven U.S. AID and state department officials, the representative brought with him an American plainclothes guard and seven armed Lebanese guards in uniform who stood watch outside the house. When the U.S. AID representative left, a police van escort outfitted with machine guns roared off behind him. The visit disturbed the Millers, who for five years had worked carefully to keep a low profile and to maintain a distance from the partisan U.S. presence.

MCC workers in Lebanon found hope and encouragement in Wadih Antoun, pastor of the Presbyterian church where the MCC workers worshiped in Sidon. Because he is Protestant, those hostile to the Palestinian presence in Lebanon associated Rev. Antoun with MCC aid to the refugees. Unlike most of the polarized Lebanese Christians, he has been a voice of moderation and has defended MCC's work with the Palestinians. He opposed anti-Palestinian actions, such as attempts by Christians to block housing projects for refugees. During the invasion the basement of Antoun's church sheltered over one hundred Christians, Muslims, and Palestinians: a small mosaic of religious faiths in fragmented Lebanon. Rev. Antoun's affirmation of MCC's work has been a great boost to the program and its workers.

Although the invasion magnified the dangers of MCCers living in Lebanon, it also strengthened their convictions that MCC was an indispensable presence, especially in the south. As part of an American organization, MCCers were relatively free to move about South Lebanon immediately following the invasion. Unlike other relief organizations that wanted to initiate aid, MCC had credibility in the eyes of the Lebanese: during the height of the crisis, MCC workers had endured with their neighbors the terror of the bombardments.

After the 1982 invasion the MCC program took on new dimensions. In addition to starting its own agriculture program, MCC entered into a three-year development program with the Middle East Council of Christian Churches. A six-mile-wide strip along the Israeli border opened for development work in addition to the U.N. zone, and water resources became a major concern. MCC worked more closely with Palestinian refugees, helping families to become self-sufficient through small loans or grants so that barbers, butchers, shoemakers, and seamstresses might purchase needed equipment.

Increasingly, MCCers asked, "When do we speak out on human rights violations?" One worker observed: "We have credibility because people know that we have seen both sides—the PLO and Israel—violate human rights. This impartiality is vitally important." The Sidon MCC guest house was virtually the only stopping point for representatives of international service organizations and foreign correspondents. MCC staff helped informally in gathering data on human rights violations. On one occasion, a series of killings of Palestinians stopped after the killings were exposed in the press.

The violence continues in Lebanon. MCC has carried on its programs despite a situation that appears to be deteriorating. The suicide bombings in 1983 that left sixty-three people dead at the U.S. embassy and several months later killed over three hundred U.S. Marines and French paratroopers suggest that the various "peace-keeping" forces have their foes. In South Lebanon, however, MCC workers have generally respected the pacific efforts of the United Nations forces.

Although the United States eventually withdrew its Marines, MCC has continued its presence in Lebanon. Jill and Robert Burkholder, stationed in Nabatieh, replaced Phyllis and Ralph Miller as country representatives at the end of the Millers' five-year term. Lowell and Jeanette Ewert lived in Sidon, but had to leave when the city became dangerous for foreigners. Rev. Antoun and most of his congregation have left Sidon for areas controlled by Christian militias. In a letter describing the Lebanese situation early in 1985, Bob Burkholder confided to Paul Myers, "It is sometimes difficult to raise morale rather than be dragged down by those around. There are moments of hope and of despair."

In August 1985, MCC's presence in the midst of Lebanon's many wars was affirmed by the quick release of country director Robert Burkholder at the end of a one-day abduction. After questioning him for several hours, his captors urged him not to leave Lebanon but to "continue the good work." They dropped him off near the Beirut hotel of his choice. The abduction could hardly have been a case of mistaken identity, for no other foreigners were living at the time in the Burkholders' community of Nabatieh.

Paul Myers, MCC Secretary for the Middle East, commented after his most recent visit to the region: "In Lebanon political goals have too often been held as more important than lives. Cluster bombs, prison camps, mass graves, and militia checkpoints all speak eloquently of the values of the combatant. By contrast, our work is that of building lives—through better health, more food, giving comfort, reconstruction."

Latin America

In the year of MCC's birth, 1920, the only Mennonite congregation in all of the Western Hemisphere south of the Rio Grande River was an infant church in Argentina planted by missionaries. During the twenties, Old Colony Mennonites from Canada settled in Paraguay and Mexico, and Russian Mennonite refugees entered Paraguay and Brazil. Not until after World War II did Mennonites find their way into twenty additional countries of Central and South America. Today, eighty thousand Mennonites, approximately 10 percent of the world Mennonite population, live in the Caribbean and in Central and South America.

Paraguay has been a center of MCC interest. In 1929-30 in its second major undertaking the young MCC settled two thousand refugees in the Paraguayan Chaco. Into this wilderness MCC introduced development strategies that later influenced its agricultural and community-building efforts in Asia and Africa. Following the settlement of German-speaking colonists, MCC entered into a unique development

partnership, a community building program for nomadic
Indians who wished to settle in agricultural villages. The first
case study focuses on the intertwined but not equally yoked
patterns of community development in the Mennonite and
Indian colonies.

Two other studies address MCC's long-term development
strategies in Haiti and Bolivia, areas of chronic poverty and
political instability. In both countries MCC appointed workers
to serve within other institutions or agencies and later designed
its own development programs in cooperation with nationals.
In Haiti is the story of close ties to Hospital Albert Schweitzer,
a model medical community. In Bolivia MCC has worked
within a master national plan to resettle mountain people in the
lush lowland jungles of the Santa Cruz region. We are grateful
to Mary Sprunger for her contributions on the Bolivia study.

Again, other case studies might be pursued: standing with
the *campesino* in El Salvador, serving on the edge of the Old
Colony settlements in Mexico, or MCC's wartime entrée to the
Caribbean region with a rural program in Puerto Rico.

The case study on Honduras calls for special explanation. In
troubled Central America a strong Honduran Mennonite
Church has developed over the past thirty-five years. Since
1981 MCC has worked closely with the Iglesia Evangélica
Menonita Hondurena (Honduran Evangelical Mennonite
Church). The national church encompasses fifty-eight
congregations with a combined membership of 2,500.

Linda Shelly, country representative for MCC, and Grace
Weber, appointed jointly by MCC and Eastern Mennonite
Board of Missions and Charities, have written a portion of the
Mennonite story in Honduras. Their case study is set in the
context of a growing vision for a holistic ministry of service,
evangelism, justice, and reconciliation. The authors first wrote
the case study in Spanish and invited Honduran Mennonites to
offer their comments. The case study, therefore, reflects a
Honduran perspective and a model of international partnership.

19

Immigrants and Indians in Development:
The Paraguayan Chaco

"In 1951, when we arrived in the Paraguayan Chaco—the 'green hell'—it was called then," Robert Unruh recalls, "the last Mennonite immigrants had arrived from Europe. There in the wilderness were three settlements: Menno, Fernheim, and Neuland, about eight thousand people. At the time there were no more than one thousand Indians in the central Chaco— mostly Lengua and Chulupi." Unruh, who served the Paraguayan colonists for more than thirty years as director of an experimental agricultural station, tells of the native peoples' incredible population explosion: "In 1983, when we left Paraguay, the settlements contained about thirteen thousand Indians. Within the past seven years the number of Chulupi, Lengua, and members of other tribes has surpassed the number of Chaco Mennonites."

Approximately eighteen hundred Mennonite colonists from Canada arrived in the "uninhabitable" Chaco in the late 1920s. Despite difficult pioneering conditions, they established roots in the dry, isolated region. From 1930 to 1932 and from 1947 to

1949, eight thousand more Mennonites from Russia settled in Paraguay as destitute refugees. During the 1930s, the Mennonites' first full decade in the Chaco, they established villages and farms on land where nomadic Indians roamed. During the thirties, as colonists began clearing the land, Indians offered their help in cutting brush, digging wells and cisterns, building fences, chopping wood, herding cattle, and harvesting crops in exchange for sweet potatoes, mandioca, beans, and watermelon. Through daily contact with the colonists the Lengua became steady hired workers, learned to speak the Low German dialect, and began to emulate the Mennonites' social practices. In 1946 Mennonite missionaries in the Chaco baptized seven Lengua men, the first of many converts. The interplay over time of these two peoples, the aggressive, successful Mennonite agriculturists and their native neighbors, provides a unique intertwining of mission and development. The experiment continues to the present with Paraguayan Mennonites in leadership and MCC in a supporting role.

The story of development among the Mennonite immigrants and the native people may be measured by a comparison of the central Chaco that MCCers Myrtle and Robert Unruh first encountered in 1951 with the Chaco they left in 1983. When they arrived in 1951, Fernheim Colony had a colony telephone system and a local radio transmitter, installed by previous MCC workers. But the colony had no indoor plumbing and had electricity for only four hours each day. Mail came up river by boat, with first-class letters from home arriving after three to six months en route. The Mennonite colonists worked the land with horses and oxen. Only two colonists owned a car, truck, or tractor. The entire region had two medical doctors, one non-certified high school, and a colony store with highly limited stock: rice, sugar, coffee, rationed wheat flour, a few yard goods.

By contrast, in 1983 the local cooperatives imported foods to satisfy every taste and sold clothing, stereos, freezers, air-conditioners, cars, and Brazilian-made tractors. The colonies had ten licensed doctors working in modern medical facilities, including a psychiatric center. A vocational school and three high schools served Mennonite pupils, one of which offered two years of advanced (junior college level) courses. By 1983 peanut farming had been completely mechanized and approximately half of the cotton was harvested by machine. In contrast to the fifties, when Chaco Mennonite families farmed an average of twenty-five acres, in 1983 they farmed 250 acres. The powerful jungle-crusher owned by Menno Colony opened expanded acreage.

Between 1951 and 1983, the Unruhs witnessed a transformation of equal proportions among the Indians of the Chaco. Prior to settlement, the Lengua and Chulupi lived at one place for three to four months and moved even more frequently if someone became ill, indicating the presence of inhospitable spirits. They subsisted on what they found in bush and lagoon: armadillo, turtle, fish, eel. They planted small gardens of squash and melons. Men hunted with bow and arrow; women cared for the children, raised food, crafted clothing and hammocks of cactus fiber, and tended the fires.

The settlers from Europe imposed an ecological revolution on the Chaco. As they built roads and fenced out the traditional territories of the Indians, barriers appeared on the nomadic hunting paths. The immigrants cleared the bush and introduced new plants and animals. The centuries-old environment of the hunter and gatherer retreated rapidly in the face of advances by the farmer and rancher. The Indian became a displaced person in a strange, new modern world—a world of less freedom but of more food, medicine, and possessions.

In 1983, settled Indians communicated with Mennonites and Paraguayans in Spanish. Bicycles and tractor-trailers crowded the Indian villages, where families lived in wooden dwellings with roofs of grass, tile, or tin. Farmers cared for approximately seven acres, with some additional pastureland. Indian villages had primary schools, stores with food staples, and ready-made clothing, and tractors as common property. Three or four Indian villages joined together in worship at a centrally located building; thirty such worship clusters met on an average Sunday morning. By the mid-1980s the Mennonite church in Paraguay claimed more than 4,300 baptized Indian members.

For more than fifty years, Mennonites have been involved in settling Indians in the central Chaco. Already in the 1930s, Mennonite ministers from the colonies became concerned about the salvation of their Indian neighbors. In 1935 the ministers organized a mission which they called "Licht den Indianern" (Light to the Indians). The Mennonites attempted to evangelize the Indians, teach them hygiene and child care, and demonstrate agricultural methods.

In 1936 the mission settled a small camp of Lengua Indians on the edge of Fernheim at Yalve Sanga, today the largest Chaco Indian settlement. Mennonite farmers operated a farm at Yalve Sanga to train the Indians to harvest cotton, maize, and kafir fields and to maintain orange, lemon, and guayaba orchards. In ten years the Yalve Sanga population increased to a thousand, but learning the disciplines of agriculture came slowly. The Indians, still relatively small in number compared to the Paraguayan Mennonites, were becoming a significant element in Mennonite colony life. Indian men living in nearby camps came onto the farms to work as seasonal laborers. At crucial harvest times, Mennonite farmers depended on this labor force and in some instances competed among themselves for Indian workers. Many colonists demonstrated concern for the health and welfare of the Indians, as well as distress at the practice of infanticide. As a means of keeping their number in check in a hostile environment, the Lengua killed some of their newborn infants.

By the early 1950s, increasing numbers of Indians were arriving in the vicinity of Menno, Fernheim, and Neuland colonies to seek employment. In 1953 at Yalve Sanga, North American missionaries settled Indian families on half hectare (one acre) parcels in villages modeled on the Mennonite settlements. A major effort to reach out to the Indians began in 1963 with the creation of the Indian Settlement Board, composed of leaders of the colonies Menno, Fernheim, and Neuland, together with representatives of MCC and three Mennonite mission boards. The Indian Settlement Board embarked on a program to settle three hundred families in villages over a three-year period. During the next fifteen years outside contributors spent more than two million dollars on the Indian development program. In addition to MCC, supporters have included Mennonite Economic Development Associates (MEDA), Canadian International Development Agency (CIDA), and Mennonites in Holland and Germany.

Early in the program MCC purchased and set aside more than fifty-five thousand acres of land for Indian families. Start-up costs for settling families were high. Mennonite sociologist Calvin Redekop, in *Strangers Become Neighbors*, emphasized:

> Land scarcity is not the issue.... [But] for the Mennonite the problem is financing the purchase of land; the procurement of the materials, supplies, tools, and implements for settlement; the orderly process of getting the Indian established; and the whole burden of helping the Indian make the transition to agriculture—a process ... which now is to take a primitive culture into the twentieth century in a few years.

Scholars see in the Chaco a unique testing ground for cross-cultural cooperation. The Chaco's three populations—Paraguayan, Indian, and Mennonite—are all prospering, but at various rates. Mennonite colonists are rising to a standard of living not unlike that of their North American Mennonite kin; the Indians and Paraguayans envy their Mennonite neighbors and are seeking to replicate their economic achievements.

MCC observers ask: How long can the tenuous balance between the three cultures last? Will economic rivalry lead to loss of cultural identity? How can the Mennonites encourage an economic and religious transformation of Indian culture which does not erode autonomy and authenticity? In the future the most complex questions may involve the attitude of the government toward both Mennonite and Indian settlers. President Alfredo Stroessner, his authoritarian military regime now in its fourth decade, has supported and encouraged the isolated Mennonite colonists; such governmental stability and benevolence has permitted a "Mennonite commonwealth" to flourish. But the Paraguayan presidency is due for a change, and transitions in leadership may bring into the open submerged Paraguayan attitudes toward the Mennonites. The comparative affluence of the Paraguayan Mennonites, for example, might make them a target of hostility.

In past years the government has been grateful to the Mennonite colonies for "taking care of" impoverished Chaco Indians. Although in 1981, Law 904 provided for the citizenship of native people in Paraguay, their entrée as full-fledged members into Paraguayan society may be a long time in coming. Citizenship is recognized only if the native person is officially registered. A joint Mennonite and Indian agency has been assisting native people in this process.

Researchers have reported that some Mennonites treat their native neighbors as though they were children. In 1972 Paraguayan anthropologist Miguel Chase-Sardi caused an international sensation when he charged that Mennonites were exploiting their Indian neighbors. Protests from Mennonites that they were paying Indians more than national minimum wages did not quell the criticism. Indians from all over the Chaco continued to migrate to the edge of the attractive Mennonite settlements and have increasingly spoken out in their own behalf. Some Christian Indians have requested the same privileges from the Paraguayan government that have been granted the Mennonites, such as exemption for military service. Leaders have negotiated an understanding that Indians and other Paraguayans may attend agricultural school in lieu of military service.

During the years in which the colonists established relationships with their Indian neighbors, MCC worked with the colonies in numerous development projects. MCC assisted the Paraguayans in planning a road across the vast western expanse of the Chaco. By 1962 the Trans-Chaco Highway, 250 miles long, linked the Paraguayan capital of Asuncion to the Fernheim center of Filadelfia; several years later it extended northwest toward the Bolivian border. The United States helped to fund the road, in part through MCC advocacy in Washington, D.C. The highway symbolized the dawning of the modern era for colony Mennonites: agricultural and industrial goods could now be transported directly to lucrative markets in eastern Paraguay.

In 1946 MCC set up an agricultural experiment station near Filadelfia to model the methods and technology appropriate to the Chaco's dry, clay loam soil. In 1947 MCC sent to the Chaco Menno Klassen, the first in a long line of personnel who helped the Mennonites transform the bushland into a productive region. The first requirement was to clear the bush, a task which continues to this day. Robert Unruh, one of Klassen's successors at the experimental station, reports that in 1986 from fifty to sixty bulldozers operated continuously in the Mennonite colonies.

MCCers began a nursery of citrus fruit and shade trees, experimented with peanut, cotton, and sorghum production, and distributed vegetable seeds. During the early fifties, colonists believed that garden vegetables would not grow locally, but MCC workers at the experiment station started plants—cabbage, tomato, eggplant, cauliflower, lettuce—and sold them. Streams of colonists came to the experiment station for tree and vegetable seedlings. Soon the colonies became a land of productive gardens, orchards, and farmsteads.

MCCers and MEDA personnel also assisted farmers with

their livestock problems. Cattle roamed outside the villages. Little barbed wire was available for fencing. MCC brought in equipment to clear the land, and the local cooperative imported fencing. Feeding cattle was difficult since livestock fared poorly on the bitter grasses native to the Chaco. In 1952 Unruh introduced to the region Buffel grass, a sweet pasture grass imported from Texas and native to India and Southwest Africa. Buffel grass proved to be superior in resisting drought, and its importation paved the way for large-scale ranching operations. The experiment station worked with colony leadership in importing quality cattle breeds: Santa Gertrudis, Charolais, Nellore, Brahman, Hereford, Polled Hereford, Brown Swiss, Jersey, and Holstein. Today Menno Colony alone has 250,000 acres of pastureland and 125,000 head of cattle. The widely used Buffel grass, more than any other agricultural factor, has transformed the Chaco bushland into a productive region for livestock.

In the 1950s, MCC explored whether the cooperatives of the Mennonite colonies qualified for credit through the International Cooperation Administration (forerunner of the United States Agency for International Development). As a result, the U.S. program for development assistance—known also as the Smathers Amendment of 1956—extended a million dollars in credit to a Paraguayan bank to be distributed among the colonies. This loan provided capital for the rapid modernization of a variety of colony enterprises.

In the early 1970s the Chaco colonies assumed responsibility for its own agricultural program. As director of the newly organized "Servicio Agro-Pecuario" (Agricultural Services), Robert Unruh oversaw expansion in such areas as livestock health care. Increasingly, as in the case of Paraguayan-trained veterinarian Rudolf Kaethler, qualified Chaco Mennonites joined the staff. Agronomists continued their extension work: delivering lectures on crop rotation and demonstrating peanut combines, disk plows, and other equipment. They assisted farmers in handling plant diseases, insects, and weed control, and demonstrated tillage methods to withstand wind erosion. In 1986 MCC support of the program focused on the experimental use of bushland for crops.

The story of impoverished Mennonite refugees arriving in the inhospitable Chaco in 1930—and in the next fifty years creating a flourishing regional economy—is remarkable. The colonists retained a memory of a "Mennonite commonwealth" in Russia with many institutions for education and mutual aid. They also brought to South America needed artisan and agricultural skills. They shared a common spiritual heritage which affirmed community, hard work, and the vision of a peaceful, productive society. They fashioned two unique institutions for economic development—the *Oberschulze* and his council, and the cooperative—which provided centralized initiative and resources for a pioneer economy of scarcity. The Paraguayan government allowed the Mennonites freedom to experiment, to make their own mistakes, and to reap their profits. MCC assisted with international resources at critical moments.

In their Indian neighbors the Mennonite colonists found able labor for an expanding economy—a factor which, while revolutionizing the Indians' own economy, also submerged their sense of self-direction. In the Mennonites the Indians found employers ready to help them move from a foraging society to a form of modern civilization which incorporated elements of Indian, Mennonite, and Paraguayan traditions. The unusual twist to these development activities—in which MCC and other North American agencies aided the Paraguayan Mennonites in becoming self-sufficient—is the speed and extent to which the Mennonite colonists have taken responsibility for the Indian settlement and development. Mennonites have demonstrated to their Indian neighbors methods of farming, how to prevent disease, how to sing hymns in four parts, and what to believe about God.

Yet the relationship between Mennonite and Indian culture

is interdependent and complex. The Mennonites and Indians are economically dependent on each other and the two groups are becoming more intertwined socially. Indian youths, for example, provide the Mennonites with stiff sports competition: a soccer field stands next to the schoolyard in virtually every Indian village, and Indian teams challenge Mennonites in soccer and volleyball tournaments. The German-speaking Mennonites and Indian Mennonites reciprocate by visiting each other at church-related festivals.

Since 1976, Indians and Mennonites have participated together in the Association of Indigenous-Mennonite Cooperative Services (ASCIM), a wide-ranging program of services including health, social work, education, agricultural extension, credit unions, and marketing cooperatives. Young, progressive Paraguayan Mennonites give leadership to ASCIM. The Mennonite Central Committee together with the International Mennonite Organization (IMO) and other European Mennonite groups have provided substantial support for ASCIM objectives, encouraging, for example, Indian farmers to make capital improvements.

But many Indian farmers are reluctant to take risks on their own land, preferring instead the security of working as laborers on well-established Mennonite farms. The experiment in development continues as Mennonites observe that the Indians, whose parents and grandparents were food gatherers, have not all learned how to keep a tractor in running order, how to care for horses and other draft animals, or how to plan ahead for lean times.

Some observers question whether the Association of Indigenous-Mennonite Cooperative Services, as a social service agency, is taking over the functions which ought to be assumed by the Paraguayan government. MCC Secretary for Latin America Herman Bontrager concludes that government responsibility for Indian welfare is not a likely prospect for the near future. ASCIM, he says, "is one place in Latin America where something good is being done with Indian resettlement."

While MCC maintains limited support for development work in the Chaco and by 1986 had provided approximately three million dollars, observers point out that the importation of North American ideas to the colonies ended more than a decade ago. Colony Mennonites have evolved as a cooperative socialist society, taking responsibility for settling the Indians, who continue to move slowly toward economic self-sufficiency. By 1986 approximately 1,100 Indian families were settled on their own lands and MCC had approved a new five-year plan to settle an additional 350 families.

Herman Bontrager highlights two difficult issues that will occupy the Paraguayan Mennonites in coming years. First, some believe that the social assistance given to the Indians by the Mennonite colonists is contributing to a growing "welfarism." Such dependency may hamper the self-sufficiency objectives of the settlement program. Second, only an estimated one half of the central Chaco Indian residents will become established in community agricultural enterprises, even though the central Chaco depends almost entirely on a farming economy. Some observers of the growing professional competency of ASCIM yearn for the more informal people-to-people programming of an earlier day.

Sixty years after the arrival of the first Mennonites in the Paraguayan Chaco, MCC officials look back with satisfaction on its supporting role in an unusual development enterprise: settling Mennonite agriculturists from Russia, followed by an effort by the new colonists to settle their native Paraguayan neighbors into a farming society. The fruits of the Indian settlement program during the next sixty years, however, will depend on the resourcefulness with which the people of the central Chaco diversify their economy. The future will also depend on the sense of mutuality among Paraguayans, Indians, and Mennonite colonists.

20

Finding Hope Amidst Hopelessness:
Haiti

In Haiti, a land of seven million people in the north central Caribbean, over two hundred Mennonite Central Committee volunteers since 1958 have heard Haitian folk wisdom:

"A bit of God, a bit of the spirit."

"Money in your pocket doesn't make babies."

"The judgment of God comes on a donkey."

The story of MCC in Haiti is one of long-term development. Some have likened the Haiti program to the MCC U.S. program in the hills of Appalachia. Both represent areas of service in unique, rural-based cultures. Both programs take place within exploitative, traditional economic structures which resist change. Both are in areas where many MCCers have come and gone, maintaining a presence to "serve in the name of Christ" where poverty is everywhere. MCC workers learn early that, like the third Haitian proverb cited above, God's judgment and justice seem slow in coming.

Haiti is the poorest nation in the Western Hemisphere. A black nation with a unique Creole language and culture, Haiti draws on the traditions of an extinct native Arakwak Indian population, West African slave culture, and the colonizing powers of Spain (1492-1697) and France (1697-1804). Saint Domingue, as Haiti was called under French rule, was the wealthiest colony in the world, exporting sugar, molasses, cotton, coffee, tobacco, and indigo. The French Revolution set off a chain reaction of uprisings around the world, including the famous revolt of Saint Domingue's blacks in 1791. Former slave Toussaint L'Ouverture led the colony's fight, and in 1804, Saint Domingue achieved independence, reclaiming the name "Haiti." The heroic figure of L'Ouverture is celebrated in Eugene O'Neill's 1920 play, *The Emperor Jones*. Today more than 90 percent of Haiti's population descend from African slaves.

Political chaos has plagued Haiti during its two centuries of self-rule. Eighteenth-century riches made possible through the cruelty of imperialism gave way to nineteenth- and twentieth-century poverty through dictatorship. In spite of its early determination to be independent, the country has been vulnerable to tyrannical leadership. In 1957 physician Francois Duvalier ("Papa Doc") became "President for Life." Since then no elections have been held in Haiti. At Duvalier's death in 1971 he was succeeded by his son, Jean-Claude Duvalier ("Baby Doc"). The Duvaliers grew wealthy at the expense of the poor and kept detractors in line with brutal security forces, the "Tonton Macoutes." In 1986, Haitians rebelled and drove President Jean-Claude Duvalier from power in a bloodless coup.

While MCC seeks long-range solutions to the problems wrought by overpopulation and economic weakness, prospects for the near future are grim. Only one-third of the land surface of Haiti (the Arakwak word for "mountainous") is suitable for agriculture. Situated on the western third of the island of Hispaniola and bordered to the east by the Dominican Republic, Haiti is densely populated with more than 430 persons per square mile. More than 80 percent of the population are rural. Poverty is a way of life for Haitian peasants, most of whom farm fewer than five acres. Haitian wages are the lowest in the Caribbean.

In Haiti more than half of the population are younger than age nineteen. Life expectancy is fifty-one years. The rural population density results in severe health problems—malnutrition, undernutrition, and diseases such as tuberculosis. Eighty-five percent of all Haitians are illiterate. Haitians speak Creole, a language that combines French with West African tongues. In recent years Creole has been associated with black pride; ten percent of the population (usually identified as the elite) speak French. Haitian religion mixes Roman Catholicism and primitivism. Some say that "Haiti is 90 percent Catholic and one hundred percent voodoo."

Into this culture Mennonite Central Committee came in the 1950s and continues to serve. In a visit to Haiti in 1955 MCC's Executive Secretary Orie O. Miller found the sights and sounds of the country unforgettable: "One wonders how we as Mennonites could have been so ignorant and insensitive to Haiti and its needs for so long." Two years later William Snyder and Edgar Stoesz entered Haiti to gather information and concluded that the needs for human development were "almost beyond comprehension." Since then MCC volunteers in Haiti have worked in a variety of areas—public health, agriculture, livestock and poultry, reforestation, developing and marketing crafts, and education and vocational training. One visitor to Haiti described the MCC program as a "confrontation with the insoluable" and concluded that the long-range impact of MCC development programming is less significant than the day-to-day web of people, culture, and affectionate relationships.

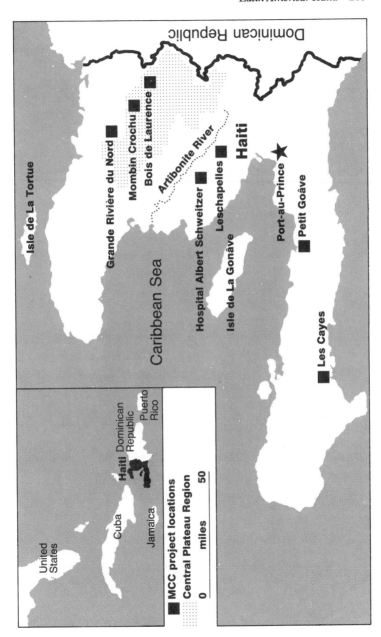

Mennonite Central Committee personnel have served in Haiti primarily at four locations: Petit Goave in the southern peninsula (served by five agricultural workers and a nurse from 1958 to 1963); Hospital Albert Schweitzer in the Artibonite Valley (1958 to the present); Grande Riviere du Nord in northern Haiti (1959 to 1980); and the Central Plateau region, (1976 to the present).

Hurricane Flora devastated Haiti's southern peninsula in 1963, killing as many as four thousand people. Three years later, Hurricane Inez hit the same region. After both calamities Mennonite Disaster Service (MDS) sent carpentry crews and medical workers to Haiti. MDS received immediate permission to enter because the government viewed MCC as a friend of the people. MDS brought to Haiti more than a hundred North American Mennonites who built approximately 340 new homes for hurricane victims.

MCC has also provided medical and agricultural volunteers to staff Hospital Albert Schweitzer in Deschapelles, a community some sixty miles northeast of Haiti's capital, Port-au-Prince. In 1956, W. L. "Larry" and Gwen Mellon built a state-of-the-art hospital near the banks of the Artibonite River. A decade earlier, Larry Mellon, an Arizona rancher and son of the founder of Gulf Oil, was deeply moved by the story of Albert Schweitzer. At the age of thirty-eight Mellon began to study medicine; that completed, he and his wife set out to central Haiti to try to alleviate typhoid, tuberculosis, venereal disease, malaria, and malnutrition in the Artibonite Valley. A biographer later described their vision:

> By detaching himself from politics and working on the personal level, Mellon had found a method that enabled him to help. . . . What Mellon had done was to map out a small section of the island for urgent succor, an area in the middle of the country . . . containing 75,000 people. . . . Just a corner of this land, Mellon told himself, but soon we may "adopt" more. This dream was dashed, for Mellon had to push all his resource to the limit to tend his one tiny province.

The new hospital treated more than ten thousand Haitians during its first year. Most were outpatients; the hospital's fifty-five beds were always filled to capacity. Mennonite Central Committee, while investigating the possibilities for expanding in Haiti, learned of the need for qualified medical staff and in 1958 placed six nurses, two laboratory technicians, and two agricultural workers at Hospital Albert Schweitzer. Other North American staff arrived as well, and the high-quality medical institution continued to grow. The Mellons determined to "operate this hospital in such a manner that we can turn it over to the native Haitians as soon as possible." Less than twenty years later, half of all nurses and doctors were Haitian and the hospital had expanded to more than one hundred beds, with 100,000 patients treated each year in the community clinics. In this flourishing medical community Mennonite Central Committee volunteers conducted Sunday school, supported a weekly community worship service, led Bible study groups, and assisted in youth and community programs.

In 1970 Dr. Mellon, facing poor health, invited MCC to take increased responsibility for the hospital. MCC, concerned that the hospital would absorb too many resources, declined, but continued to work closely with the institution. In recent years North American Mennonites have assumed selected administrative roles, and Haitians have given leadership to a community health program composed of seven dispensaries and more than eighty Haitian health care workers. The fee for a hospital consultation is approximately three dollars; persons who cannot pay are not charged. MCC's Edgar Stoesz reflects that Hospital Albert Schweitzer "has spanned and survived the Duvalier era; in thirty years it has never closed its doors, not even for holidays." He comments further, "HAS has kept its distance from the government while at the same time cooperating with the national health plan and serving as a model of what is possible." In this central Haiti setting, Mennonite Central Committee has maintained one of its oldest partnerships by supporting the preventive medicine model begun by the Mellon family.

MCC's presence in Haiti has also withstood changes in location and emphasis. Its long-term commitment to the country has occasionally meant withdrawing when needs are no longer acute or where Haitians are ready to take full responsibility. When MCC has decided to close out a program, as in Grande Riviere du Nord in the late seventies, it has phased out gradually. As administrator Gerald Shank explained, "We are not trying to put our stamp on the community by establishing institutions that cannot function without us."

Ironically, the departure of MCC from Grande Riviere occurred more than fifteen years after originally expected: early plans at Grande Riviere called for MCC to spend a few years launching a newly built but unused hospital. MCC nurses, doctors, and technicians expected to train Haitians over the next five years and then leave. But in the process, MCCers became deeply involved in life of the community and stayed on for two decades—staffing family planning and preventive medicine clinics, experimenting with poultry and livestock production, offering veterinary services, opening a new library and elementary and vocational schools, supervising a rat eradication drive, seeking better drinking water, forming local crafts cooperatives, and organizing a cannery.

For many MCC volunteers at Grande Riviere, idealism about the effectiveness of "development" eventually became tinged with skepticism. These volunteers acknowledged that the projects they helped start seemed to end in failure more often than in success. For example, MCCers characterized the cannery as "a sluggish institution that somehow cannot seem to get moving, yet never quite dies." After ten difficult years, when as many as eighty Haitians processed pineapple, mango, mayonnaise, chow-chow, and jellies, the cannery finally closed in 1975.

Some MCC personnel conclude that the best contribution

they can make in Haiti is to immerse themselves in its culture. In 1977, Shirley and Vernon King, the program directors for Grande Riviere, reported: "There is no way to substitute money for a good volunteer. MCC has one of the smallest-budgeted organizations in Haiti, but [others] are very interested in what we are doing because we have people there."

At Grand Riviere MCC discovered that "development" is a slow process—community leaders lack the resources to take over health or agricultural or educational programs within a short time. And sometimes foreign development projects have harmed rather than helped the villages for which they were intended. "Haiti has too many in-and-out, short-term programs," one Haitian official told MCC representatives. These transient agencies give charity which often fosters dependence.

For thirty years MCC has observed other foreign agencies come and go in Haiti. While more than two hundred independent religious groups have found their way to Haiti, notes one MCC worker, few are involved in "development at the grass-roots level." Veteran MCCers are skeptical of mission and service efforts done "on the run." As a result, MCC forms a new program cautiously, seeking a niche where its resources will be well used. Even so, MCCers recall the statement by one thoughtful Haitian that MCC "built a lot of roads—but they didn't all connect." In recent years MCC has established closer relations with like-minded groups and cooperated with other Mennonite agencies in Haiti. A 1984 survey found that no less than twenty-one Mennonite and Brethren in Christ groups had missionaries and workers in Haiti. MCC leaders, reflecting on the "confusing kaleidoscope" of evangelical, U.S.-based Protestant programs in Haiti, have deferred planting an Anabaptist-oriented church.

In 1976 MCC joined the Christian Reformed World Relief Council and the Missionary Church in agricultural development in Haiti's Central Plateau region, north of the Artibonite

Valley and south of Grande Riviere du Nord. Here MCC's activities have centered around the communities of Mombin Crochu and Bois de Laurence, where Mennonite Central Committee workers continue to test the concept of development. In these communities volunteers perceive of themselves as "an outreach of the church in Haiti."

In Mombin Crochu MCC is sponsoring a ten-year, community-based development program. More than fifty small groups, motivated by the biblical principles of loving one's neighbor and caring for the earth's resources, generate community income. They plant common gardens, establish fruit tree nurseries, and invest in agricultural supplies. After seven years, MCC-employed Haitian animators (program facilitators) report that participants have experienced an improved quality of life. Local officials believe that people in Mombin Crochu "will not stand for injustices that used to be commonplace, like arbitrary arrests for bribes, or beatings." As in the earlier programs established at Grande Riviere du Nord, volunteers in Mombin Crochu are preparing for the day when MCC will depart, turning over leadership to the Haitians.

Another current MCC program, begun in 1982, focuses on planting trees and conserving soil on the denuded hillsides of the Artibonite Valley. By the end of 1986 volunteers had distributed one million pine, acacia, eucalyptus, and fruit trees to Haitian farmers, emphasizing their value not only as a means for controlling erosion, but also as a source of income through lumber and firewood sales and food production.

The MCC Haiti program is a significant model. Currently, MCC also works with Mennonite Economic Development Associates (MEDA) to increase Haitian employment and income through MCC SELFHELP crafts. In development work MCCers seek to immerse themselves in the Haitians' way of life. In 1985 MCC administrator Herman Bontrager returned from a trip to Haiti impressed that "personnel are dedicated (maybe too much for their own health) and creative." MCC volunteers return to their North American communities with insight about the injustices perpetuated by those who import coffee, sugar, and other cash crops from desperately poor nations.

The MCC Haiti alumni has grown to include more than 230 people who have found in this Caribbean island a training ground for the professions of agriculture, medicine, and education, have struggled with issues of development, and have entered into the unique world of Haitian peasant society. Returning workers speak with affection for Haitian people. Says one, "You can't help but fall in love with them—so very poor, they are rich in the wealth of friendship." These MCC alumni find delight in Haitian folk wisdom and ponder the truths of the proverbs:

"Children are the wealth for poor misfortunates."

"A witch doctor never heals his own sore."

"You can't eat okra with one lone finger."

21

Carving Out New Communities in the Jungle:

Bolivia

Not a day goes by that I don't think about my friends in Villa Amboró.

—Geneva Hershberger

Forty Aymara Indian families pile out of the truck as it stops in a two-acre clearing in the hot, humid Bolivian jungle. They look around anxiously at their new home: a storage building, a well, two primitive shelters. An MCC worker offers them some food and suggests that they begin to organize the evening's meal preparation and sleeping arrangements. No one speaks. They eye each other, waiting for someone to step out and take charge of the strange situation. After some moments of awkward silence, one woman goes over to take stock of the food supplies and directs her daughters to cut up the vegetables. Gradually others begin looking around for something to do: going to the well for water, gathering wood for a fire. Soon the question of division of space for shelters is generating lively discussion. By nightfall everyone has a full stomach and a place to sleep.

During the past forty-eight hours these *altiplano* Indian families have experienced the most radical dislocation of their lives—moving from an arid, alpine world of eleven thousand to thirteen thousand foot elevation in view of the snow-covered Cordillera Real Mountains, down to the five-hundred-foot tropical wilderness of eastern Bolivia. They have left an overpopulated area, where the agricultural base includes potatoes and sheep, for a sparsely populated but lushly productive frontier. In the morning their official orientation begins, but already the colonists have learned something about working together for survival in this new place.

Bolivia's culture and economy is shaped by its unique geography, which divides the country into three distinct regions. Running north and south through Bolivia are mountains and fertile cultivated valleys where Quechua-speaking Indians, descendants of the Incas, make their home. A second region, the altiplano, or high plateau, nestles among the mountains in the western part of the country, reaching altitudes of thirteen thousand feet. Despite year-round cold, scant precipitation, and extreme elevation, these high plains have been the heart of Bolivia for centuries. Sixteenth-century Spanish conquistadors came to "Upper Peru" seeking precious metals and settled on highland estates, forcing the Aymara Indians into servile farm and mining labor. Today, the altiplano is home to the mining industry, the government seat of La Paz, and about 60 percent of Bolivia's population.

The eastern lowlands, or *Oriente*, separated from the altiplano by the rough terrain of the *Valles*, spreads over the eastern two-thirds of Bolivia. In the center of the Oriente is the department of Santa Cruz, site of MCC's program concentration. Sparsely populated and subtropical, Santa Cruz is semiarid in the south, covered with dense rain forests in the north, and full of dry native forests, grasslands, and scrublands in the center. With its high water table and rich agricultural potential, Santa Cruz has been the site of recent colonization activity.

Bolivia has not always been the most impoverished and underdeveloped country of South America. In the sixteenth and seventeenth centuries, the discovery of abundant silver deposits in the Bolivian Andes and the wealth of Indian labor combined to make "Upper Peru" the richest and most densely populated area in Spanish America. By the late eighteenth century, however, Bolivia lost its Pacific coastline to Chile and the silver economy stagnated. Even the advent of mining Bolivia's rich tin deposits a century later failed to put Bolivia on sound economic footing.

Mining wealth has been concentrated among Bolivians of European ancestry (ten percent of the population). Most whites live in the cities, along with Bolivians of mixed Indian and Spanish backgrounds (thirty-five percent). Indians (thirty-five percent) for the most part live in rural poverty. Although tin continues to be Bolivia's biggest export, miners comprise only two percent of the population. The annual per capita income in Bolivia is five hundred dollars. Severe problems with disease, parasites, and malnutrition mean that fifty percent of children in the rural areas never reach the age of ten; the life expectancy of Bolivians is forty-six years.

Since winning its independence from Spain in 1825, Bolivia's political climate has been chaotic. In 160 years of independence, the republic has had 180 governments, many of them military regimes. A country faced with such grim conditions seemed ripe for revolution to Ernesto "Che" Guevara, the famous guerrilla theorist who was deeply involved in the Cuban revolution. In 1966, Guevara organized an unsuccessful guerrilla campaign based in Santa Cruz, then a remote rural area, against Bolivian leader General Rene Barrientos. Guevara had counted on support from the peasants without fully understanding the effects of a major 1953 land reform that had freed the Bolivian Indians for the first time since the Spanish conquest. The peasants, still grateful to the government for their independence and political power, opposed Guevara's attempt to reorder their society. In 1966 Bolivian troops surrounded and killed the guerrilla leader.

The land reform movement emphasized colonization. The

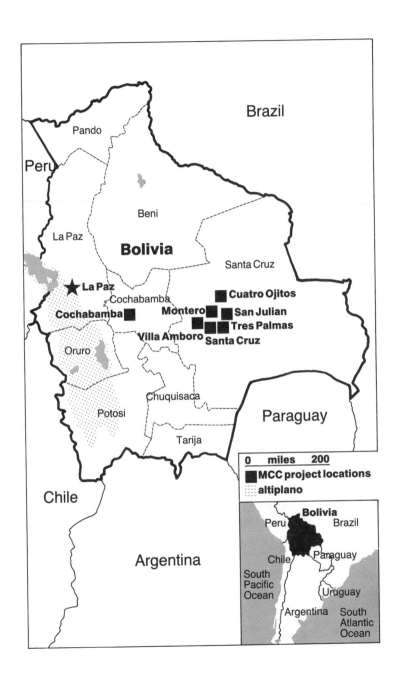

altiplano was overcrowded and unable to produce enough food for its population, while the fertile Oriente was still largely unsettled. The government, hoping to increase agricultural production, invited colonists from other countries and began relocating altiplano Indians into the lowlands. Moving Indians accustomed to a mountain climate and lifestyle to the sub-tropical lowlands has been a radical physiological and social experiment. The altiplano Indians are susceptible to the disease and parasites of the hot, humid Oriente, and for health reasons many of the initial colonists returned to the highlands.

In response to Bolivia's call for settlers, Mennonite colonists, dissatisfied with their economic conditions and communal arrangements in Paraguay, came to Santa Cruz to farm. In 1954 twelve families from the Fernheim Colony in the Chaco started a colony at Tres Palmas, just east of the city of Santa Cruz. Three years later, about twenty-five more families from the Menno Colony settled near Tres Palmas, forming the Canadian Colony. Although Santa Cruz had great agricultural potential, the first pioneer years led to poverty. The farms floundered and some families were destitute and malnourished. The Mennonites desperately needed medical services, health education, and agricultural assistance. Some of the colonists were behind on payments and in danger of losing their land.

MCC first came to work in Bolivia because of these Mennonite colonists. Frank Wiens, MCC director in Paraguay, became aware that the Mennonites were facing many hardships. He gave the colonists a hand in securing farm loans. Recognizing that improved agricultural production was the colonists' only chance for survival, he hoped that MCC could become involved more directly. He arranged to place Paxmen in the colonies under a government program, but in 1960, when these plans fell through, MCC itself placed Paxmen Anton Braun and Waldemar Klassen at the Tres Palmas Colony.

Initial MCC work centered around a Tres Palmas clinic already in existence. MCC personnel offered health care, worked with agricultural improvements, and organized community activities. In 1964 Arthur and Kathleen Driedger arrived to direct MCC's Bolivia program. Besides the few MCCers based at Tres Palmas, other volunteers were "loaned out" to a variety of Protestant organizations in Bolivia, including COMBASE (an evangelical social action committee), the Canadian Baptists, Heifer Project International, Alfalit (an evangelical literacy movement), Wycliffe Bible Translators, the Andes Evangelical Mission, and the Evangelical Union of South America. These contact persons were eyes and ears for MCC's own development planning.

During this time, MCC had a close relationship with the Methodist Church. Beginning in 1962 with Paxmen placements at a Methodist high school for technical and agricultural training in Montero, thirty miles from Santa Cruz, MCC became involved with the Methodists' work in new colonies of highland Indians. Placements at villages like Cuatro Ojitos introduced Paxmen to integrated community development.

For ten years, Tres Palmas was the only independent MCC unit in Bolivia. In the late 1960s, when worldwide organizations were shifting their emphases toward integrated community development, MCC Bolivia began to initiate its own development program. The "loaning" system was becoming unsatisfactory, and personnel felt that they could design a community development program that was as effective as those they had observed.

The transition to an independent MCC program occurred quickly. In 1969 twenty-eight MCC workers served in Bolivia, seven under MCC supervision. By 1970, twenty-five out of forty workers served directly under MCC, and within six years there were no personnel working under other organizations. MCC continued working in the department of Santa Cruz, where new communities of Indian colonists could benefit from development programs. In order to enlarge its community development programs and because most Mennonites had

moved away from Tres Palmas, MCC sold the clinic. In 1968
MCC centered its activities at Cochabamba and two years later
built new headquarters two hundred miles to the east at Santa
Cruz.

MCCers soon discovered the challenge of using appropriate
technology and farming techniques in the Bolivian setting. An
effective development program introduces equipment and
methods matched to the community's expertise and resources.
Thus, promoting animal traction (using oxen, mules, or horses
for farming instead of engine power), drilling wells with hand-
operated equipment, and producing corn and peanut shellers,
windmills and fence stretchers specially designed for small
Bolivian farms all became a part of MCC's appropriate
technology program. The Bolivians were particularly receptive
to MCC's work with animal traction, which increased productivity and enabled farmers to plant two crops a year.

MCC agricultural worker Phil Bender designed a ten-year
plan promoting a holistic farm system that encouraged
colonists to improve the quality of their land. Previously, some
homesteaders saw their lives in the villages as temporary and
exploited the land. But by introducing new crops, livestock,
animal traction, vegetable gardens, fruit trees, sanitation, and
better farm management, MCC helped farm families to
improve their land, health, and community.

MCC attempted to bring essential social services to isolated
communities outside of the national health and education
systems. Sometimes, enabling a village to provide certain services stabilized it to the point that it could link up with a
government program. The MCC Health Promoter Program
trained several persons in each village to provide basic medical
services and to promote general health, sanitation, and nutrition to the villagers, and the Bolivian government came to
depend on MCC's training materials to develop its own health
program. To improve the quality of education, MCC trained
auxiliary teachers in isolated villages where the population was

too small to qualify for a government teacher. Each community was responsible for providing a school building and part of the salary for a villager trained by MCC to teach community children. MCC also placed Teachers Abroad Program personnel in village schools.

Integrated community development became a reality through MCC's involvement in the government colonization projects. In the early 1970s, the Methodists, four Catholic orders, and MCC combined their practical experience and scientific expertise to set up an orientation process for new communities in the colony of San Julian. The government built a road, cleared a living area, dug a well, and constructed several primitive shelters. Then, after the arrival of the families, MCC personnel helped homesteaders learn how to construct and establish homes, work the land, and prepare nutritious meals. The community eventually set up a small health center and a cooperative store. This orientation process helped colonists adjust to a new environment and laid the foundation for a working community that would meet essential economic, social, and cultural needs.

One of the unique features of the MCC program in Bolivia has been the close cooperation with the General Conference and Mennonite Church mission boards since the first full-time missionaries arrived in 1969. MCC has influenced mission direction and policy in Bolivia, stressing the interrelatedness of the two programs. At the same time, MCC personnel have been involved at various levels in evangelism with witness through Sunday school classes, adult literacy courses, Bible studies, and informal personal sharing with Bolivians. In 1965 MCC personnel designed their own project to integrate evangelism into MCC public health work, combining medical care in villages with lectures and classes in literacy, agriculture, health, and religion. MCC requested help from the mission boards when it recognized that some communities were eager for more spiritual leadership than some volunteers were comfortable in giving. After MCC had worked in a village for several years, mission personnel became part of the follow-up phase of development work.

MCC, sensitive to the problem of communities becoming too dependent on missions or development workers, stresses that leadership must come from within the congregation or community. MCC workers have found it important to learn something about a village before approaching the community. MCCers prefer to work with villages of newly settled highland Indians where the people own land, have a relatively stable population, and are located near trade centers or major transportation routes.

Lynn Loucks, who with his wife, Jeanne, served with MCC during the seventies in Bolivia, exemplified community development work. An educator fluent in Spanish, he developed a model for approaching a community and discerning with its residents their needs and aspirations. When Loucks learned that a village might have interest in MCC assistance, he gathered information: Was it an older, traditional village, or a new settlement of people from the highlands? Did villagers own their land or rent from a large landowner? Did it have a stable population or were people leaving for the cities? Was there access to roads and markets?

Loucks sought information from the Catholic priest in the nearest large town, the leader of a nearby Protestant church, and the nearest rural education and public health officials. He rode to the village on his motorcycle, stopped at the general store for a cold drink, and began talking with people. This led to visits with people around the community. With encouragement from village leaders, he conducted a simple census, including the names and ages of all children and their level in school.

At the village of San Julian, he recorded the following information: eighteen families; one classroom where a government teacher had once taught; a second classroom partially completed; twenty-eight school-age children; one soccer field in the center of the village; one public water pump; one small general store; 30 to 50 percent of adults literate but only 5 percent skillful readers; one dollar, the average daily wage; most families earning their income from farming and cutting firewood; two families owning cattle and oxcarts; two horse-drawn buggies in the village; most people owning their own land; an average of four children per family; health problems which included parasites, tuberculosis, and malnutrition; the village located five hours by horse from Santa Cruz.

After gathering this data, Loucks arranged with leaders of the village to hold a public meeting. He drew on the schoolroom chalkboard a horse which he called "Pancho" and told his audience that the horse represented the village. He asked members of the audience to identify all parts of village life and listed each response as a part of "Pancho": head, back, tail, and so forth. The villagers then listed all the things the village needed to be healthy and whole. Loucks asked the San Julian residents to underline those dreams which were within their grasp. The discussion moved toward weaknesses and needs of the community. Villagers in the room became aware that others felt as they did and were eager to act.

After the meeting Loucks summarized for the village leaders the needs which people had identified. He began to negotiate a partnership between the village and MCC. For example, if the village wanted a school, it might agree to complete the second classroom and build a house for a teacher. For its part, MCC might provide a teacher for two years until a national teacher arrived.

Dozens of MCC workers in Bolivia have used development methods similar to this one. Reflecting on his service experiences, Loucks comments:

> What I appreciated about Bolivia is that we volunteers had ownership in the program. Leadership was shared. Then, too,

the Bolivians were so responsive. The highlanders who were resettled in the department of Santa Cruz were resourceful and energetic. They had many needs but were appreciative. I asked a group of them what it had been like five years earlier, and they became excited telling me all the ways their lives had become better. . . . Edgar Stoesz, coming from Akron, helped those of us in MCC to flesh out our development ideas.

Former volunteer Geneva Hershberger tells of her term as an MCC teacher in a village similar to San Julian. Her story is representative of scores of other MCC volunteers. Villa Amboró is an isolated Quechua Indian village in the Bolivian lowlands fifty miles from Santa Cruz. In 1980 she arrived in Bolivia for three months of intensive language study, which, however, did not prepare her for teaching six hours a day in Spanish to Quechua-speaking pupils. After the three months, she gathered notebooks, primers, chalk, and pencils and embarked by bus and by horseback on the two-day trip to Villa Amboró. The village is located off the beaten path; its residents rarely see visitors. Among the obstacles in reaching it is the Surutu River, treacherous to wade across in the rainy season. None of her new pupils had ever travelled to the city of Santa Cruz, a trek she made about once every two months. In Villa Amboró she shared a house with three other MCC volunteers—two agricultural workers and another teacher.

During her first year in Villa Amboró Hershberger taught school in a thatched roof building with low mud walls. She instructed some thirty-five students, ranging in age from six to sixteen, in the first through fifth grades. For the second year the villagers built a simple three-room schoolhouse with a tin roof—two classrooms and one room to house future teachers. Fathers built desks and benches and hung a shiny fabric chalk board. Everyone in the village spoke Quechua; the men and a few women also spoke Spanish.

Villa Amboró had no electricity, no central pump, no general store, and had not been visited by a priest in ten years.

Hershberger's only transportation was the thirteen-year-old MCC horse, "Buzz." One of Hershberger's Indian friends was Cristina, who prepared in the shade of her porch the MCC workers' major meal of the day—mounds of rice and a side dish. She dreamed of starting a store stocked with batteries, food, school, and home supplies. Hershberger says, "She realized her dream. When I left, she was just opening a store on the edge of the soccer field next to the school."

Hershberger has warm memories of the people she learned to know so well. "The Bolivian people are so open—for me, it was a life-transforming experience." As she prepared to leave, a Bolivian arrived to replace her. But like many government-sponsored teachers, he was unprepared for the primitive village life. Since then the village has had difficulty staffing its new school.

When asked what her former pupils might be doing today, Hershberger replies:

> The boys are working with their fathers in the fields. Some probably travel a bit farther to work in the coco fields where they earn higher wages. Some of the older girls may now be mothers. Couples are not really "married" since no one is present to marry them. I'm sure that none of my former students have had an opportunity to leave the village. . . . Not a day goes by that I don't think about my friends in Villa Amboró.

Bolivia continues to be in a state of crisis. National structures for health and education are in shambles. Inflation runs at a rate of eight thousand percent annually. The central government seems powerless, yet in the Santa Cruz area the economy is booming. New construction is on the rise and streets are clogged with automobiles. The country's economic base has shifted from tin to cocaine. Meanwhile, far from Santa Cruz, in village clearings of the jungle, MCC volunteers continue to work with peasants in establishing solidly based, self-reliant communities.

22

A Young Church Awakens to Crisis:
Honduras

The church is ready to suffer . . . and continue working.

> —Executive Committee of the
> Honduran Mennonite Church

Within Mennonite Central Committee one hears talk of the ministry of "word and deed." This concept is called "integral evangelism" in Honduras and is part of the emerging vision for the Honduran Mennonite Church (HMC). Juan Angel Ochoa, who in 1985 served as pastor of the Mennonite congregation in La Ceiba and secretary of the Executive Committee of the national body, explains that witness through word and deed includes proclamation of what Christ has done and is doing, communion within the Christian community, and service. In 1984 the Honduran Mennonite Church formed a Social Action Commission to "share a Christian testimony in an integral way in fulfillment of Christ's gospel for a more just society."

Honduras, a country of four million people, is the size of Tennessee. Next to Nicaragua, it is the least densely populated of the five Central American countries. Neighboring El Salvador, for example, has 560 inhabitants to the square mile compared to seventy-one in Honduras. Honduras exports bananas, coffee, lumber, and meat. Honduras' per capita income, $490, is the lowest in Central America. Honduras has twenty-one thousand Salvadoran refugees. They live in three enclosed camps supervised by the United Nations High Commissioner for Refugees (UNHCR) with whom the Honduran Mennonite Church and MCC cooperate. Honduras provides a base for the U.S.-funded contra forces which have been waging war to overthrow the Sandinista government in Nicaragua.

The concept of "integral evangelism," although only recently identified, has roots in the history of the Honduran Mennonite Church. In 1947, Jacob Brubaker, pastor of the East Chestnut Street Mennonite Church in Lancaster, Pennsylvania, went to New York City on business. While strolling by the wharf to see ships unloading cargo, he was fascinated by the large banana boats and asked where they had come from. "Guatemala," he was told. He began to think about the small churches his congregation had begun in the city of Lancaster. "Why," he wondered, "couldn't we begin a church in Guatemala? One could even travel by banana boat to examine the possibilities."

After consulting with his church and the Eastern Mennonite Board of Missions and Charities (EMBMC) in Salunga, Pennsylvania, he traveled to Guatemala, El Salvador, Nicaragua, and Honduras. Henry Garber, president of the mission board, accompanied Brubaker. Upon their return, they recommended that work begin in Honduras in the area of Trujillo, far from the mission outposts of other denominations. In July 1950, George and Grace Miller arrived in Trujillo as the first Mennonite missionaries in Honduras.

Within a year after the Millers' arrival, they undertook mission activities and established a clinic, operated by a missionary nurse and a Honduran Christian woman. During their first decade in Honduras Mennonite missionaries planted churches in Trujillo and Tocoa. Mennonites also held services in the surrounding villages of Tarros, Santa Fe, San Antonio, Guadalupe, Salamá, Taujica, Zamora, Ilanga, Ceibita, Rio Arriba, and La

Conce. These efforts later resulted in church organizations in several of the villages.

In 1958 the Eastern Mennonite Board of Missions and Charities began sending young people to Honduras to staff community projects. In 1965 the Honduran Mennonite Church established a General Council with eighteen members, eleven Hondurans, and seven missionaries. The council made all decisions regarding finances, pastoral support, and placement of workers. The church grew rapidly in the years following this transition to national leadership. Meanwhile, the church sponsored several programs to train Honduran church leaders. In 1965 it opened a Bible institute in Trujillo. A Christian service committee coordinated social projects and oversaw loans from Mennonite Economic Development Associates (MEDA) to small business enterprises.

During the sixties and seventies the Honduran Mennonite Church sought new ways to become involved in community development. When the government began to provide medical services, the church closed its clinics. The church also transferred a vocational school to the government and a bilingual school to a private board. As the church gave up control of these institutions, it turned toward local short-term projects. In 1970 the Honduran Mennonite Church began sponsoring national teams that traveled to congregations, offering programs on music, health care, sewing, crafts, and agricultural education.

Increasingly, the Honduran Mennonites assumed responsibility for church administration. By 1975, all members of the Executive Committee were Hondurans. Many of the emerging leaders were graduates of the Bible Institute. Educator Damián Rodríguez recalls, "There was an openness on the part of the missionaries for the church to develop its own character."

Meanwhile, Mennonite Central Committee had entered Honduras step-by-step in response to a series of emergencies. In 1965 MCC sent material aid for distribution in hospitals, clinics, and orphanages. Four years later MCC and the Mennonite mission worked together on the island of Roatán where a hurricane had destroyed two hundred homes. In 1974 Hurricane Fifi hit the northern coast of Honduras. Approximately fifty Mennonites from Belize, Costa Rica, Nicaragua, Guatemala, El Salvador, and Puerto Rico joined fellow Mennonites from Honduras, MCC, and the Eastern Mennonite Board of Missions and Charities in an informal international disaster program.

Following this relief effort, the HMC and other evangelical denominations formed an ecumenical organization, the Evangelical Committee for Development and National Emergencies (CEDEN). In 1976 and 1978 Mennonites began smaller projects in response to floods along the north coast. In the late seventies, with Nicaraguans fleeing from Somoza's military despotism, MCC worked with CEDEN in southern Honduras in aiding refugees. Although the national church participated in these projects, much of the initiative, coordination, and resources came from outside the country. But these experiences helped to prepare the church to take responsibility during future emergencies.

In 1980, after terrifying stories of killing and destruction of Salvadoran villages broke into the consciousness of Honduran Mennonites, the HMC launched work with Salvadoran refugees. Presently Honduran Mennonites are responsible for all housing and related construction services for the twenty-one thousand refugees located in camps in Honduras. They work together with the United Nations High Commissioner for Refugees (UNHCR) and four other agencies.

In tiny El Salvador, 60 percent of the population is landless. Most of the desirable land is owned by a small oligarchy known as "the fourteen families." The ruling government has been engaged in a U.S.-supported war to defeat guerrilla opposition in the highlands. One Salvadoran out of every 125 has been killed; 80 percent of the casualties have been noncombatants.

In 1980 the Roman Catholic archbishop of El Salvador, Monsignor Oscar Romero, called the "voice of the voiceless," was assassinated in a church the day after he called for soldiers to lay down their arms and for the government to stop its military repression.

In El Salvador MCC's work is concentrated among the estimated 300,000 people displaced by the lingering war. Including the Salvadorans who have fled the country, there may be a total of one million refugees from this civil war. The Honduran Mennonites' refugee work began when several members of the congregation in San Marcos Ocotepeque, nine miles from the Salvadoran border, contacted the HMC Executive Committee for guidance on how the congregation might become involved. Church members, accompanied by George Reimer, MCC representative in Guatemala, visited the border zones. They interviewed both refugees and Hondurans. Reimer spoke with a Honduran woman who told him, "What can we call the atrocities happening across the border? This is worse than war."

The refugees had lived in small rural communities in El Salvador. They told of soldiers arriving in their villages, entering their houses in search of arms or guerrillas, torturing or killing family members, burning homes, and destroying crops. Survivors fled on mountain trails to the border. They traveled by night, hid by day, and arrived in Honduras malnourished, sick, and scared.

With tears in their eyes they told of horrible sights they had seen: soldiers cutting open a pregnant woman, pulling out the baby, and throwing it to hungry dogs, then strangling the mother with the umbilical cord. A father saw his son crucified by soldiers in the village square. As a means of terror, soldiers sometimes chopped their victims into pieces in front of family members. Even today, six years later, children still draw pictures of people cut in pieces.

In June 1980, the Honduran Mennonites formed a commission to oversee refugee services. Damián Rodríguez recalls: "In

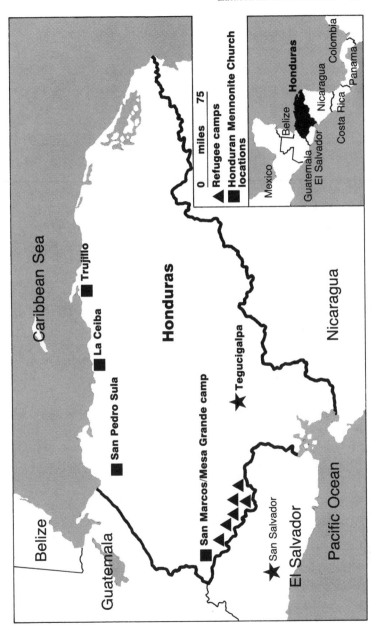

the beginning we saw it as a temporary project. The church wanted to identify with the refugees. We had access to emergency funds from the mission, material aid from MCC, and local Mennonite personnel from San Marcos." In those early days, even the Salvadoran refugees expected their stay to be temporary.

The refugee project grew rapidly and the Honduran Mennonite Church found itself growing as well in spite of frustrations and errors. The HMC had little experience in managing a large refugee project, yet a commitment to learn enabled it to carry on.

The HMC saw its task as "part of the mission of the church." One church leader recalls, "At no time did we think this task would be misinterpreted; rather, we saw it as a privilege to serve the needy." But the refugees, having fled the Salvadoran military, were accused of being subversives. Some Hondurans accused the Honduran Mennonite Church of being subversive for its assistance to Salvadoran refugees. The majority of criticisms came from neighbors and other churches, but even within the national Mennonite body some disassociated themselves from the refugee work.

Aware that any involvement with refugees would be interpreted as political, some Mennonite leaders felt the work was too delicate, too dangerous. Involvement would paint the Mennonite Church as leftist and the HMC might suffer repercussions at the hands of the government. The reality of these risks was confirmed by the deaths of several colleagues who undertook similar work with the Catholic Church. But the HMC Executive Committee decided that "the church is ready to suffer ... and continue working." And the refugee workers trusted in the presence of God.

Challenges in 1984 led to continued reevaluation of the refugee program by Honduran Mennonite leaders. The HMC agreed to support the refugees' decision to refuse a proposal to relocate all the camps to Olanchito, a site deep in the interior of

Honduras. Although the Mennonites took this position to support self-determination for the people they served, others interpreted it as a political stance. Criticism from powerful public and private sectors within Honduras, as well as the UNHCR, placed the whole program in jeopardy. The church began to understand more clearly the risks involved in being faithful.

For six years the church has worked with Salvadoran refugees. Luis Flores reflects: "The church has grown greatly in its understanding of the biblical theology which these times require, especially with regard to the good news for the poor and the oppressed.... The church has seen the problems and the projects of the refugees as a Christian mission."

The Mennonite refugee program has provided a continuing challenge for Honduran Mennonites. Each year church leaders attend a retreat to examine important issues. In May 1984, for example, a pastor at the retreat explained the "spiral of violence," offering his perceptions on the causes of problems in Central America:

> The violence begins with the suffering of the poor, most of whom—despite hard labor and long hours—do not have the resources to support their families. As time goes by, they despair of watching their children die of malnutrition and begin to ask for more opportunities for work and fair wages, health services and schools. Often their pleas are answered with violence on the part of those who have the power to keep them poor. As the poor exert more pressure, factories are militarized and squatters are forced off the land. When people retaliate for injust actions, the spiral of violence grows.

A truck driver in the group rose to his feet and responded: "This description is absolutely true. This is what our people are experiencing.... If we don't want Honduras to follow the route of our neighbors, we need to improve opportunities for the people, not establish a strong military."

Church leaders, realizing that they were growing in their awareness of the injustices which contributed to the refugees' plight and poverty in general, sought a way to communicate their concerns with the wider HMC membership. In September 1984, the Honduran Mennonite Church formed a Social Action Commission to coordinate programs with refugees and poor Hondurans and to educate church members. The HMC has increasingly demonstrated openness to new forms of leadership. Some younger leaders preach a nontraditional theological synthesis. Juan Angel Ochoa reports that the questioning and concern of the church helped him to refine his ideas:

> I was called upon three times by the local church council and the Executive Committee to explain my position. They saw in my teaching the concept of liberation theology. I explained that I preach Anabaptist theology, and that, yes, there are parallels to liberation theology. The starting point is the same: reality. Changes come with birth pains.

When the Salvadoran refugees moved into camps in 1982, the HMC stayed in the border zone and initiated small development projects with the Honduran population. These projects have grown into a newly established church and a development program which includes training in sewing, health, appropriate technology, agriculture, and basic education for adults. In 1984, the HMC through its Social Action Commission began programs in two more areas of the country. In the department of Santa Barbara, the church works with farmers in squatter settlements, coordinating programs in community organization, literacy, and soil conservation. In nearby communities, Mennonite workers seek adequate sources of drinking water. In 1986 the commission began to focus attention on the needs of people in the troubled region near the Nicaraguan border. "We want to see more of our churches practicing integral evangelism," comments Mennonite pastor Ochoa. "We are moving forward."

At a recent MCC retreat, Ochoa shared three concepts with North American co-workers in Honduras:

1. Seek understanding of the political and social milieu. We experience extreme poverty, illiteracy, low wages, and unequal land distribution. The United States is using Honduras as a strategic point to defend its own policies. But the problem in Central America is not communism. Rather, it is an unjust system which has long been present. Some people meet the challenge by saying: "Instead of dying slowly of hunger, let's take up arms."

2. The Honduran Mennonite Church has a ministry to fulfill. We are happy that you are here to work with us. You are foreigners by nationality, but not in God's family. God is the God of all.

3. We can work together, but the vision does not come from North America. Together, we will discover God's will. We must not mix culture with our message; try to incarnate yourselves in our culture.

It is a privilege for MCC to work with a national church with vision, as in Honduras. MCC is challenged to support that vision and encourage its growth without suffocating the initiative of Honduran Mennonites. Bladimiro Cano asserts that the role of MCC is that of a co-worker, "but not one who takes our responsibility away from us."

Cooperation takes various forms. In 1985, five of the twenty-three people working with the Social Action Commission's programs full- or part-time were MCCers. MCC covered 53 percent of the budget for the commission's projects, excluding UNHCR funds for construction. MCC also sent material aid worth $60,750 for the refugee camps. In spite of this assistance, the Social Action Commission of the HMC must have a strong identity within Honduras while MCC maintains a low profile.

"One of the values of the Mennonite presence in Central America," observes an MCC worker, "is that North Americans hear the genuine grievances of the people from the perspective of the church. . . ." In the spring of 1986, North American Mennonites learned of a letter sent by these evangelical Mennonites to the President of Honduras and members of the Honduran National Congress. The church's statement of concern, which follows, appeared in a national newspaper. The statement represents the compassion and growing concerns of Honduran Mennonites in light of their refugee work.

May 15, 1986

Esteemed Senores:

....As Christians we ask the authorities to look after the interests of their people, who in the border zone of the eastern part of the country are being affected by forces and interests which are foreign to our nation.

The Honduran Evangelical Mennonite Church has been in existence for 36 years, and is made up of 58 congregations in nine provinces of the country. Among these there are seven in the Province of El Paraiso, bordering on Nicaragua. However, one of these congregations, which was located in the village of Moriah, has been displaced toward the interior of the country, in search of protection....

In accordance with the commandment of the Lord, the Honduran Mennonite Church, as throughout the world, considers it our duty to abstain from all participation in warfare, direct or indirect.

We exhort governments to reduce their armaments and to seek solutions which will benefit the people, especially those sectors that have been struck by war and impoverished by social neglect. We base our message on the Sermon on the Mount, Matthew 5-7; on the great commandment to hold together love of God and love of neighbor, Matthew 22:34-40; and on the exhortation of the Apostle Paul to overcome evil with good, Romans 12:11-21. We call both ourselves and the authorities to remember that we will be judged according to our treatment of the hungry, the thirsty, the stranger, the naked and the imprisoned, for Christ is to be found in each of them. Matthew 25:31-46

In view of the above, we sense a commitment toward the brothers and sisters of our church, as well as to our brother and sister Hondurans, who have had to abandon their homes due to armed occupation by elements pertaining to the Nicaraguan counterrevolutionary forces. We would therefore wish to call to your attention the following events, which leaders of our church have ascertained to be true:

1. On March 23 armed "contra" forces occupied the houses of the residents of the village of Moriah, and at the same time occupied the Mennonite church building there. They used the church building to store arms for several days.

2. The inhabitants of Moriah, including members of the Mennonite Church, were dispersed as a consequence of the conflict.

3. Four young Nicaraguans who were members of the Mennonite Church in Moriah were forcibly recruited. They are: José Adan Gonzales, 23; Heriberto Caballero; 22, Santos I. Gonzales, 14; José A. Gonzales, 15.

4. Nicaraguan "contra" troops also detained, for one day, the Honduran pastor Germán Rivas.

THEREFORE:
The Honduran Evangelical Mennonite Church presents the following list of petitions:

1. That the constitutional guarantees of the residents of the country's Eastern zone, which have been trampled upon by the counterrevolution, be respected.

2. That aid and protection in every sense be given to the population that has been displaced as a result of the armed conflict in the eastern part of the country which has been provoked by the presence of the counterrevolution.

3. We ask that the good offices [of the government] be exercised so that the counterrevolution will free the four Nicaraguan youth who are members of the Honduran Mennonite Church located in the village of Moriah.

4. We exhort [the government] to respect the principle of nonintervention and of the self-determination of the peoples.

5. We demand the definition of a more coherent policy in accord with our national interests.

6. That the national sovereignty and dignity, blemished by the presence of foreign troops on our soil, be respected.

Respectfully,

Honduran Evangelical Mennonite Church

North America

The Mennonite Central Commitee began as an inter-Mennonite program to meet human need abroad. In 1939 it established a Mennonite Central Peace Committee and the following year it linked hands with the Church of the Brethren and the Society of Friends to administer Civilian Public Service. In the months after the end of World War II, MCC opened domestic voluntary service programs in the United States and Canda, including a teacher-placement program in Newfoundland. Uncertainty surrounded MCC's efforts in voluntary service programs because this had been an area of concentration of the individual Mennonite conferences. However, large inter-Mennonite programs emerged, some, like Mennonite Mental Health Services, controlled by MCC. Others, like Mennonite Disaster Service and Mennonite Indemnity were linked loosely to MCC.

MCC Canada came into being in 1963 and MCC U.S. in 1982. These two national bodies have administered a wide variety of domestic service programs. Some programs date from an earlier era: Appalachia, MCC's witness in Washington, and the thirty-five-year-old trainee program. Some are of more recent origin: the Native Ministries program of MCC Canada, MCC Canada's office in Ottawa, and the Victim Offender Reconciliation Program (VORP). A reading of the annual reports reveals that a variety of additional projects at regional and provincial levels have emerged in response to the awakening consciences of constituency and staff.

Many more case studies could be drawn from the Canadian and U.S. arenas of service: the program after World War II in Gulfport, Mississippi; the development of interracial and urban ministries in such cities as Atlanta, Georgia; the work of Mennonite Conciliation Service in training mediators to assist in community conflicts; settling refugees from Southeast Asia; the developing programs of Mennonites Mental Health Services: Mennonite Disaster Service; and others. Studies have been published on the latter two programs.

23

Becoming Neighbors in the Coal Country:

Appalachia

Three hundred miles west of the national capital lies the Cumberland Plateau of the Appalachians, a mountainous region of flat-topped ridges and steep-walled valleys, richly endowed by nature with dense forests, winding rivers, abundant game, loamy soils, and thick veins of coal.

This is Daniel Boone country, where Indians and then fiercely independent frontiersmen found in these isolated valleys the elements that sustained a vigorous life. Yet it is one of the ironies of our history that many of their descendants live there today in bleak and demoralizing poverty almost without parallel on this continent.

—Steward L. Udall, U.S. Secretary
of the Interior, 1962

Appalachia is an impressively beautiful region of wooded mountains and valleys which stretches from lower New York state to Mississippi. These two-hundred-million-year-old mountains are the oldest in the Western Hemisphere. MCC workers coming to Appalachia soon become enamored with the natural beauty of the region: "The bright yellow of forsythia, the deep pink of redbud, the white of dogwood, and the color of innumerable flowers decorate the hills in spring. Warm rains produce the lush green of summer which yields to the fall panorama of brilliant color."

Appalachia is coal country. In his 1962 book, *Night Comes to the Cumberland*, Harry Caudill, an Appalachian-born-and-bred lawyer, wrote: "Coal has always cursed the land in which it lies. . . . It leaves a legacy of foul streams, hideous slag heaps and polluted air. It peoples this transformed land with blind and crippled men and with widows and orphans. It is an extractive industry which takes all away and restores nothing. It mars but never beautifies. It corrupts but never purifies."

In a twenty-five-county area of eastern Kentucky which includes the concentration of MCC work, coal mining in 1985 remains the sole industry. Coal's "Golden Age," a boom era from 1912 to 1927, collapsed during the Great Depression. In the 1950s miners discovered that their skills were becoming obsolete as the coal industry mechanized with mammoth earth movers and ripped open the landscape with strip mines. The unfortunate result, wrote Caudill, is that "today [the mountaineer] subsists largely on the generosity of the welfare state." Three-fourths of the land surface and four-fifths of the mineral acreage are controlled by absentee owners, an increasing number of whom are multinational energy corporations. In these mountains one finds poverty in visual paradise.

"But the tragedy of the Kentucky mountains transcends the tragedy of coal," declared Caudill. "It is compounded of Indian wars, civil war and intestine feuds, of layered hatreds and of violent death. To its sad blend, history has added the curse of coal as a crown of sorrow."

MCC was drawn to serve in Appalachia because of a growing awareness that beyond the next range of hills to the west of

Akron, Pennsylvania, was "a third world," poor and underdeveloped. In 1962, in his widely read book *The Other America*, Michael Harrington told of from forty to fifty million poor in America: "If these people are not starving, they are hungry, and sometimes fat with hunger, for that is what cheap foods do. They are without adequate housing and education and medical care. . . . This poverty twists and deforms the spirit. The American poor are pessimistic and defeated." Edgar Stoesz, who first surveyed eastern Kentucky as an area for MCC service, wrote, "The needs of Appalachia were highlighted in the Democratic primaries in 1960 when John Kennedy and Hubert Humphrey battled it out, the former with a jet and the latter with a bus, for the votes of the Appalachian people." He added, "Our first trip . . . helped us to see the similarities between the foreign and domestic poor and that poverty is a leveler which reduces people to their minimums." H. A. Penner, MCC-U.S. Program Director, observes that MCC's foremost resource is people: "MCC's response to calls for a 'War on Poverty' was to send people with Christian commitments and technical skills to learn from, interact with, and . . . influence the people. . . ."

Virtually every MCC worker who has gone to Appalachia to serve has read Harry Caudill's hauntingly sad but affectionate portrayal of the joys and sorrows of the mountain people. In 1963 when MCC administrators visited Whitesburg, Kentucky, Caudill and other community leaders encouraged MCC to place workers in the former United Mine Workers hospitals. The following summer, four MCCers arrived, including two doctors to work in hospitals in Whitesburg and in Williamson, West Virginia. By the end of 1964, several nurses and a business manager had joined them. MCC initiated a multifaceted program of medical services, social work, agricultural assistance, and industrial development. The nation's focus on Appalachia peaked in the mid-1960s during extensive press coverage of the "war on poverty." New federal commissions arose: the Area Redevelopment Administration (1961), the President's Appalachian Regional Commission (1963), and the Appalachian Regional Commission (1965).

Idealism abounded during the Kennedy and early Johnson years. Hundreds of Vista volunteers (members of a U.S. domestic "Peace Corps") spread through Appalachia to befriend the poor. Some volunteers became disenchanted with the welfare system which led people to become dependent on government checks. Some could not adjust to the ways of mountain people, sometimes apathetic, sometimes resistant to outside youth ('foreigners") pushing new ideas. Some came for a summer as idealistic volunteers and left a little less idealistic. Many came and went, but the chronic problems remained: high unemployment (35 to 40 percent in some counties), high poverty level, high functional illiteracy, and widespread water contamination.

MCC came to Appalachia and has remained for more than twenty years. In 1986, Central Appalachia, and particularly the Kentucky counties of Harlan, Perry, Knott, Floyd, and Letcher, are home to twenty MCC workers. Until 1981, MCC's program was self-supporting. Salaries of MCC doctors and nurses in regional hospitals flowed into an MCC pool and covered the living expenses of all voluntary service workers and even provided seed money for cooperative businesses and low-cost housing projects. The MCC program in Appalachia required no funds from Akron. Regional hospitals eventually managed to employ local doctors and nurses. With less need for MCC medical personnel, worker-generated income dropped. Moreover, federal aid to the depressed region, made available in large sums since the "war on poverty" days of the sixties, was cut drastically by the Reagan administration. A major target in recent current federal budget slashing has been the Appalachian Regional Commission which in twenty years channeled more than fifteen billion dollars to the area. This withdrawal of federal support, coupled with fewer income-producing jobs for

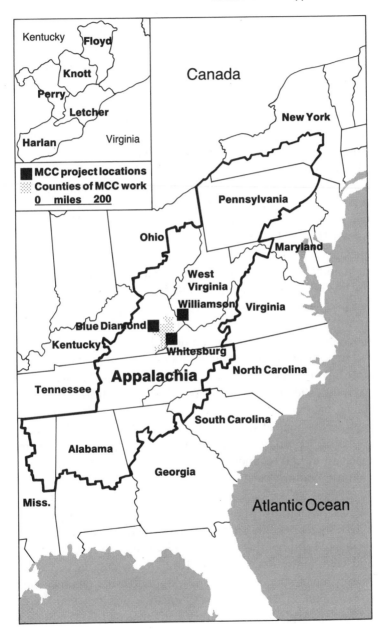

MCC workers, led MCC to reexamine its Appalachia program. In 1986 MCC increased its budget in Appalachia to nearly $116,000. If MCC volunteers are to continue in Appalachia, MCC budgetary support is critical.

Over a period of two decades MCC's program has undergone major shifts. The first decade focused on efforts to stimulate economic activity in local communities. MCC workers tried to initiate opportunities for extra family income. This led to the opening in Whitesburg of Hill 'n Hollow, a marketing corporation for stuffed dolls, baby quilts, and wooden toy cars, and trucks. This craft industry expanded and at its height gave employment to forty producers. In 1976 MCC turned Hill 'n Hollow over to a local employee; it continued to operate until 1981.

In addition to economic development, MCC has tried to influence educational opportunities. MCC had hoped to place teachers in public schools. But because of a "patronage" system in which outsiders were not hired for teaching jobs, MCC made few placements. Sometimes MCC was able to place teachers in adult education positions. Beginning in 1976, as state laws changed, MCC sent more teachers to Appalachia to work in a wide range of educational settings: Head Start classrooms, one-room schools, speech therapy, peace education, and high school equivalency tutoring for persons seeking diplomas. A unique opportunity came in 1981 for two MCC volunteers to teach art to 1,800 elementary students in seven schools in Knott County, Kentucky.

Former MCC worker Karen Grasse has suggested that MCC's program in Appalachia spans several distinct periods: 1964-74, an energetic growth period with as many as thirty-five workers at a time, the biggest emphasis on medical programs and community development; 1974-76, an interim period of reassessment when at one point the number of volunteers fell to four; and 1976-81, a period of creative activity when MCC merged its Appalachia program with that of the Mennonite

Church's Mennonite Board of Missions (MBM).

The interim period was a testing time for MCC. The Vietnam War was ending and the supply of draft-age volunteers dwindled. Moreover, some volunteers had become disillusioned with the concept of large-scale community development work.

Some projects folded when local persons were unable to take over. In 1976, following an outside evaluation of MCC's program, new recruits worked closely with existing local institutions and social programs. The cooperative MBM-MCC program lasted five years, after which the Mennonite Board of Missions withdrew and MCC resumed sole responsibility for the program.

An innovative program recently introduced by MCC is SWAP (Sharing With Appalachian People). In 1986, 538 people volunteered three to six days of service in much-needed repair work on homes in Harlan and Letcher counties. They replaced roofs, painted, repaired floors, and rebuilt homes damaged by fire. The volunteers came from twenty-seven congregations which contributed eighteen dollars a day per worker to cover the costs of room, board, and building materials. In addition to working, the volunteers learned about Appalachia and became friends with local residents.

Since the push in the 1960s and early 1970s for community development, MCC has continued to experiment with cooperative projects by placing workers in existing educational and medical institutions and social service agencies. MCC volunteers continue to ask questions which seem to have few clear answers. With enormous resources of coal energy in these hills, is there any new technology which will permit the coal industry to recover? Can coal make a comeback without leaving a heavy toll of deaths in the mines and without butchering the wooded landscape? Is there a way of liberating people from a system of dependency on welfare checks? Just as the United States admonishes the nations of El Salvador and the Philip-

pines to institute land reform, is it not time to return the land of
Appalachia to the mountain people who have lived there for
centuries?

Can the federal government bring justice to the region and
then radically reduce its bureaucracy and system of handouts?
How can outsiders, sometimes called "foreigners," help people
to find new hope in their mountain communities? The towns
are well supplied with mainline Protestant churches and the
hills are covered with tiny chapels where "fire and brimstone"
sermons are preached to the faithful. Can outsiders breathe
new life into old congregations? Is there a need for the planting
of new Anabaptist-minded congregations?

These mountain people, with all their hurts and with all the
tragedy about them, draw the affection of MCC workers, who
find in the region a way of life that attracts and repels. One
MCC administrator, for example, accompanied Diane, an
MCC social worker, on a visit to the family of one of her clients,
a three-year-old developmentally disabled boy. The administrator recorded his impressions:

> The house was a mountain shack on a small, neat yard. The
> boy's father, a former miner, invited us in. The man was sixtyish,
> with one tooth and one lung. His wife was twenty-seven and
> chewed tobacco. The home was dark; also hot from the coal
> stove fire. A chicken hopped around on the bed and a T.V. sat
> on the shelf. The laundry hanging across the wall looked grimy.
> The father spoke of many things. He admired Diane's way with
> the young boy. The mother spoke little and spit occasionally. I
> felt out of place, but still quite welcome. The clear-eyed, fair
> child, the weathered man and the simple woman would have
> made a beautiful picture, but my camera might have been an in-
> trusion, so I didn't bother.

Some call Appalachia a "national sacrifice area." For
volunteers who come to Appalachia, it has the charms of a
cross-cultural experience. The region has been ridiculed and
caricatured: moonshiners and hard-shell Baptists, "hillbillies"
speaking English with traces of an Elizabethan language, the

feuding Hatfields and McCoys, hoedowns and mountain fiddlers, whittlin' and spittin', cabins up the "holler," and much more.

Increasingly, Appalachian people resent the popularized view of their region. Jerry Gingerich, former MCC worker in Appalachia and currently director of a low-income housing service in Neon, Kentucky, reports that many families are "hardworking, honest, thrifty, clean, God-fearing folk. . . . It is no wonder that these people resent stories that depict Appalachians as either stereotypical hillbillies or as crooks who get ahead by raping their land and exploiting their fellow citizens." Visitors to Appalachia expecting to find nothing but poverty express surprise at the well-tended homes and landscapes they see.

In Appalachia MCC workers have found a gentle, friendly, hospitable people who love to visit and who exhibit a simple, self-reliant way of life. The arts and crafts of mountain people have been recovered and celebrated in the series of *Foxfire* books: broom-making, carpet-weaving, basket-weaving, rail fence splitting, butchering, folk medicines, quilting, storytelling, and a hundred more activities.

MCC workers find delight in people who in adversity draw on inner strength. One MCC visitor asked Tom Gish, editor of the *Mountain Eagle* of Whitesburg, Kentucky, what gives him hope for eastern Kentucky, site of four of the poorest counties in the United States. "The strength of the people," he answered. "They know who they are. A person knows where he comes from, who his father is, who his grandfather is." MCC workers discover a sense of community among the Appalachians. A public official, born and raised in the hills, commented: "There aren't three persons I meet in a day whom I don't know. If something goes wrong around here there are all kinds of people one can call on."

A former MCC teacher recalls a friendship with Della, an Appalachian woman with a "flower garden masterpiece" near

Blue Diamond, Kentucky:

> Della arrived here forty years ago to work in the coal mining general store as a bookkeeper. Today her stories bring the coal mining days back to life. Blue Diamond was a hub of activity since the train stopped daily to collect coal and passengers to transport to Hazard, the nearest large town. Della kept accounts for the miners, who used tokens—a form of credit—to make purchases at the general store. She deducted food, clothing, and other expenses from each one's monthly salary. Unless a miner had a small family and pinched pennies, rarely did he see money at the end of the month. This form of bookkeeping kept Della busy.
>
> As an MCC volunteer I learned to know Della well. She displayed beautiful flowers, both wild and domestic, on the steep hill behind the house and on the long driveway leading to her home. I have always been a nature lover and thus enjoyed the moments spent with Della in her garden.

Most MCC workers stay for a two-year term. This leaves an impression of "an endless flow of MCC workers through the area who leave after spending their terms determining how they can make a meaningful contribution." However, a number of Appalachia volunteers have remained in the region for a second term or have found their own employment as teachers, medical personnel, or community workers. One who developed a particular affection for the people and the culture commented that "being" often wins out over "doing."

An MCC administrator has reflected that volunteers tend to value relationships and this endears them to the people: "MCC workers are highly respected and much appreciated in Appalachia not only because they are addressing human needs but because they are doing so in compassionate, Christlike ways." Karen Grasse, in *We Became Friends*, casts the importance of relationships in Appalachia in a different light: "The challenge has been for MCC to get beyond looking at only the difficulties that are part of life in Appalachia. MCC can also find enrichment and rejuvenation from the people and their culture."

H. A. Penner has reflected on the analogy between Appalachia and Samaria. No group outside mainstream Jewish society is referred to more frequently by Jesus than the Samaritans. Among Jesus' last words are these: "You will be my witnesses in Jerusalem, in all of Judea and Samaria, and to the ends of the earth." Penner asks whether the frequency of the Samaritan references is a possible sign that Jesus' audiences had difficulty relating to the Samaritans. He inquires further, "Is MCC struggling with some of the same issues in relating to Appalachia as Jesus referred to in his teachings involving Samaria?"

24

Empowering Indians:

Manitoba

*"The happiest future for the Indian race is
absorption into the general population and this is
the position of [the Canadian] government."*
—Canadian official
(late 1800s)

*"The people of the south should not come north
only for oil and gas, but also for wisdom."*
—Dene Indian woman (1970s)

*"If the Christian churches of this country should
chicken out on their commitment to Canada's
Native people, then I would not expect any
oppressed group anywhere in the world to trust
us again for at least two generations."*
—Churchman Clarke MacDonald
of Project North (1977)

In 1966 the publicly owned Manitoba Hydro corporation
contracted with the federal and provincial governments to implement a four-billion-dollar diversion project in northern
Manitoba. The plan eventually called for the damming of the
forceful Churchill River, creating a reservoir out of Southern
Indian Lake and diverting water into the nearby Nelson River.

Thus large generators would produce electricity for most of Manitoba as well as for lucrative markets in the United States.

Native communities, particularly the five Cree villages of Nelson House, Norway House, Cross Lake, Split Lake, and York Landing, feared that this massive flooding project would destroy their villages and their livelihood. Canadian church groups joined together to support these Native people. MCC Canada (MCCC) entered the Native rights scene in the mid-1970s as this major conflict heated over the Churchill-Nelson Rivers Diversion Project.

The MCCC Native Concerns program began with one staff person, Menno Wiebe, working with advocacy organizations on behalf of MCCC and focusing the attention of MCCC constituents on problems affecting Native people of Canada. Program Director Wiebe continues to the present day with Native Concerns, which in twelve years has grown to include three staff members in the Winnipeg MCCC office and approximately forty volunteers who interact daily with Native people.

MCC Canada's program of Native Concerns is grounded in the grass-roots involvement of these volunteers who listen to what Native people have to say, assist where services are requested, and encourage Indians in a variety of self-help enterprises. "Native people," observes one MCCC worker, "tend to regard Mennonites . . . not usually as representatives of a small church body or a minority group . . . but as an extension of the overpowering white world." Only after MCCC workers live for a time in Native communities do bonds of friendship and trust develop.

In 1986, ten MCCC volunteers living in Native communities took part in economic development projects: wild rice gathering and marketing, establishing an auto repair shop, managing a retail store, building low-cost homes and training Native crews in the construction trades, developing and marketing Native crafts, and creating jobs through reforestation. During the

summer, nineteen summer volunteers promoted home gardening. A Native conference on alcohol abuse held recently at Al-
kali Lake, British Columbia, in which Mennonite volunteers
participated, led MCCC to join Native leaders in promoting al-
cohol-awareness education as part of community development
programs. Workers observe a high correlation between alcohol
abuse and unemployment.

MCC volunteers who live in Indian communities become
windows of insight for their home congregations and seeds of
conscience for those who shape public policy. In 1986 Wiebe
declared:

> The forty volunteers now working in a number of Native com-
> munities and organizations are . . . made of tough stuff [and are]
> unusually well motivated. . . . The growing acceptance of
> MCCC by Native communities and Native organizations is at-
> tributed largely to the integrity of the voluntary service person-
> nel. That acceptance alone is remarkable in the face of a grow-
> ing hostility between Native and non-Native peoples.

George Erasmus, president of the Dene Nation, has asserted
that "there are no institutions in Canada within which there is
honest participation of Native people." MCCC, through its
Native Concerns program, attempts to take the struggles of the
Native minority population seriously. In northern Manitoba
MCCC and other church-related groups provide a forum for
resolving conflicts between Native peoples and the federal and
provincial governments. MCCC workers believe that on one
hand, "the hour is late [and] there is an urgency about this
work," and that on the other hand, MCCC has made a long-
term commitment to working among Native Canadians in the
hope of affecting structural changes. One MCCC administrator
calls this "ambassadorship in the name of Christ."

The issues MCCC workers face in relation to Native communities are complex. High on the agenda are the questions of
aboriginal (treaty and land) rights. Another major set of
concerns emerge around recent way-of-life upheavals due to

northern Canadian development. MCCC workers in Native communities—nurses, teachers, agriculturists, and social workers—strive to be accountable to the local communities they serve. They resist the established pattern of referring decisions to provincial administrative offices; instead, they encourage Native communities to assume self-government. MCCC personnel "stand with" Native peoples, seeking to be sensitive to a people whose culture predated the Euro-Canadian society.

The Native Concerns program, while similar in some respects to MCC work overseas, faces unique problems. One MCCC administrator observes that the program calls into question assumptions of mainstream North American Mennonites, reflected in such comments as these:

> The goal should be to assimilate Native peoples into Canadian life. They should become good Canadians.
> If they followed our example of industry, thrift, and discipline their problems would disappear.
> Indian customs are delightful but not for the twentieth century.
> Indian reserves and alcoholism go together.

Thus the MCCC Native Concerns Office seeks to inform constituent congregations of the life and concerns of Native people. In one two-week period in 1986 Eric Rempel and Menno Wiebe of the Winnipeg staff spoke to some twenty different groups. Some Mennonites observe that churchwide affluence is resulting in the "numbing of our passion." The experiences of Canadian Mennonites who have become involved with Native communities, however, underscore the need for churches to stand with Native friends in their struggles.

More than four hundred years ago, when whites arrived in the territory which would become Canada, a quarter of a million Indians and Eskimos lived across the vast northern reaches. They came from many different cultural and linguistic groups, including Algonkian, Iroquoian, Siouan, Athapaskan, Kootenayan, Salishan, Wakashan, Tsimshian, Haida, and

Tlingit. Today, following a severe decline in the populations of these ethnic groups, the number of Canadians of native ancestry is rising. Their birthrate is twice the national average. In the Cree communities of northern Manitoba, children below the age of fifteen comprise over half the population.

Not all Native persons are equal in the eyes of the law. The first group, status Indians, are members of a band and hold certain rights under the federal Indian Act. The government considers these persons to be "registered" or "treaty" Indians. More than three hundred thousand persons fall into the "status" category, the majority of whom live on more than a thousand reserves across Canada. Many of the registered bands never made treaties and thus continue to press for land rights.

A second, larger group consists of Métis and non-status Indians. *Métis*, meaning French-Indian, has become the term for all Native persons of mixed parentage who identify themselves as Indian. Many Métis have French, Scottish, Irish, or English ancestry. Non-status Indians are persons who have lost their Indian status for one reason or another—for example, to own land off the reserve. The two groups number over 750,000.

A third group, concentrated in the northernmost reaches of Canada, is the Inuit (meaning "the people"), formerly known as Eskimos.

The history of special privileges for Native people of Canada goes back to the Indian Acts passed in 1868 and 1869. Revised on numerous occasions since, these laws outline national policy for the "Indian problem." Many Indians ceded their territory to the federal government and moved onto reserves, which, officials believed, would serve as temporary holding grounds during the process of assimilating the Indians to another way of life. In the late nineteenth century and into the twentieth century, Canadians expected the Indians to adopt white religion, white values, and white economic structures.

The decade of the 1960s was a watershed for the Native people of Canada. Pan-Indian consciousness rose. They asserted their rights with new vigor. They confronted a government committed to assimilation. "Why not eliminate the special status of Indians?" some officials asked. "Both they and our society as a whole will benefit if we can help them adjust to life as ordinary Canadian citizens." Repelled by this, Native spokesmen called it "cultural genocide."

The Native communities, despite their historic isolation from each other, came together to assert their rights. Three national Native organizations, the National Indian Brotherhood, the Inuit Tapirisat of Canada, and the Native Council of Canada [Métis], formed to assert aboriginal rights. During the 1970s Native activists focused on land rights as well as hunting and fishing rights. But more recently, Native groups have asserted vigorously the right to be recognized as aboriginal nations. Such activity, one churchman observes, "continues to be baffling to those who assume that integration or assimilation is the only road ahead for the Native people."

In the 1970s, several ecumenical organizations gave strong support to the Native rights movement. The Interchurch Task Force on Northern Flooding, based in Winnipeg, dealt specifically with the environmental conflict in northern Manitoba. It educated church groups, lobbied at various levels of government, and supported the Native communities morally and financially. Included in the Interchurch Task Force were representatives from the United Church, Roman Catholic Church, Anglican Church, and Mennonite Central Committee. Another coalition in which MCCC took part, Project North, arose in 1975 with broad church support to address the issues of northern development and Native land claims. Churches worked together to avoid "a further fracturing of remaining Native solidarity."

The four-billion-dollar dam and diversion project threatened the livelihood and survival of the Cree reserve communities and several Métis communities located along the shore of the Nelson River. These twelve thousand Native people relied on hunting, trapping, and fishing to support their families. They asked for government-sponsored hearings. The provincial government declined. Concerned environmentalists and church groups, beginning in 1973, joined them in asking for both public hearings and a halt to the massive diversion project.

In 1974, representatives of the five Cree communities banded together as the Northern Flood Committee, which became their official negotiating body. Throughout 1974 and 1975, concerns of MCCC and others centered on the aboriginal land rights of the Cree; meanwhile, the provincial government refused to recognize these deeper concerns but proposed to settle damage claims. The Interchurch Task Force stood with the (Native) Northern Flood Committee through many months of negotiations and called on the government to publish all documents regarding the project. Eventually the Manitoba government yielded, but the struggle to gain access to more recent documents continues.

In September 1975, the mounting frustration of the Native communities resulted in four days of public hearings sponsored by the Interchurch Task Force. Among the panel members it procured were Native persons and experts in energy development, environmental studies, economics, and sociology. A former chief justice of Manitoba chaired the public hearings, which had no legal force but which were publicized as "open to the public." Menno Wiebe later spoke of the significance of the hearings, held in Winnipeg and in Nelson House, Manitoba:

> The church simply amplified the subdued Native voice because the Indian people had a right to be heard.... Justice is such an easy word to say ... [but] when considering the critical demoralization of Canada's northern Native people then the talk of justice is not enough.

The panel examined fifty-two written briefs and listened to additional oral presentations. The Cree sought compensation for the adverse effects of the Churchill-Nelson Hydro Project on 600,000 acres of their traditional trapping, fishing, and hunting lands. Representatives of the Native communities addressed the panel in eloquent, prophetic cadence. The evidence presented at the hearings ranged from technical impact statements to Native expressions of a unique relationship to water, land, and all creation. In the community of Nelson House, where an estimated two to four thousand acres—including burial grounds—would be flooded, the hearings were packed with Native persons and the presentations took a lively turn.

A Cree translator worked continuously to minimize the language barriers. Among those submitting testimony was seventy-year-old Jerome Nicholas of Nelson House, who told the panel:

> . . . the Creator has created a rainbow to signify and prophesy that the world shall never again perish in the torment of great flood. It is obvious in the present day and age that many a people suffer the agony of great loss and their livelihood and that of future generation, due to flood caused by man. . . . Hydro has flooded all that I have owned and cherished. What will then come of this powerful source that has destroyed our livelihood?

> . . . The Lord the Creator shed his precious blood on this very world, not for one particular race of mankind but for all mankind in this world. Let it be then my fellow man. Let us not battle amongst each other but rather let us set our thoughts and our minds together.

No one from Manitoba Hydro attended the hearings. Also absent were the elected government officials representing the Cree and Métis communities. However, two attorneys associated with the Manitoba government answered questions. Both men contended that Native persons ought to be integrated into mainstream Canadian life. They assured the Native people that they would be compensated for the temporary upheaval and inconveniences. They explained, however, that Native peoples were best served by assimilation. "The overall Churchill-Nelson development is an integral part of the economic development of the Province of Manitoba," they quoted the premier of Manitoba. "The benefits derived provide an essential contribution to the economic well-being of all the province and in particular the north."

The panel, in its concluding report, chided the provincial and federal governments for failing to address the pronounced fear of Native participants that they stood to lose their way of life. The panel stated that the Hydro project, which by mid-1975 had already cost one and a half billion dollars, was too far along to be abandoned. But it recommended that the federal and provincial governments continue to seek ways to mitigate the harmful effects of northern development. Two years later the provincial and federal governments, Manitoba Hydro, and the Northern Flood Committee signed an agreement based in part on recommendations resulting from the church-sponsored hearings.

Many participants believed that the hearings gave courage and support to Native people to stand up and speak their convictions to the government. Native persons demonstrated that they were not rigidly opposed to all development, but that they should be included in decision-making and that "the north should not be regarded simply as a resource warehouse for the south." One Native spokesperson concluded that the hearings were "the only credible thing that happened around the whole hydro project."

Mennonite Central Committee Canada's foray into Native concerns began with this Native struggle in northern Manitoba. The conflict, which provoked a decade-long drama of settling aboriginal claims, continues to involve MCCC in dialogue with government officials and negotiators. By 1986, five of fifteen projected hydroelectric dams had been constructed. In October 1985, the National Energy Board held hearings on the proposed construction of additional dams which would permit the province to export power to the United States. MCC Canada testified that although Manitoba Hydro was strong in technical expertise, it was weak in anthropological expertise. Manitoba Hydro has since sought counsel from MCCC. The Interchurch Task Force on Northern Flooding, of which MCCC is a part, has pressed the government to honor the compensation claims of the Cree and other Native bands.

The Churchill-Nelson Rivers Diversion Project is only one of many Native rights/northern development conflicts which surfaced in the 1970s. In the Northwest Territories and in the Yukon Territory, for example, Native bands disputed governmental pipeline proposals, while in British Columbia the Nishga tribe protested mining activity on its land. The complexity of these issues continues to challenge MCC Canada. Meanwhile, MCCC workers seek creative ways to stand with Native brothers and sisters during what some have called the "rebirth" of Native Canadians. This spirit is reflected in the words of Kwakitul Chief Ernie Willie: "We have what it takes to again become a people."

25

Listening and Speaking:

The Washington and Ottawa Offices

*The Washington and Ottawa offices ... serve as
"listening posts" for constituents.*

Since 1525 Mennonites have stood before high government
officials and submitted their petitions. Delegations have journeyed to cities such as Moscow, Berlin, Jerusalem, Saigon,
Asuncion, Djakarta, Mexico City, Winnipeg, Ottawa, and
Washington, D.C., to make requests, most often in defense of
conscience on issues of peace and war. But only recently have
Mennonites established an ongoing presence near the seat of
government. In 1968 the Mennonite Central Committee appointed Delton Franz as director of a new office in Washington. In 1975 MCC Canada established an office in Ottawa,
headed by William Janzen. Both continue to serve in these
positions.

The Washington and Ottawa offices of MCC U.S. and MCC
Canada serve as "listening posts" for constituents: staff members monitor legislation and publish information, facilitate
contacts with government officials, and organize seminars and
workshops. Both offices engage in advocacy work in behalf of
non-MCC-related groups such as Native Americans, Vietnam-

ese refugees, and Palestinian farmers.

The Washington and Ottawa offices handle a wide range of requests and concerns. In 1985 Janzen, noting that MCC Canada does a large part of its advocacy work through interchurch organizations, commented that the Ottawa Office has received little criticism from Mennonite constituents. He added: "But . . . there might have been more [criticism] were it not for the fact that doing it through such diverse structures makes it difficult to see what all is being done."

The relationship between church and state has long been of interest to Mennonites, who traditionally have shown reserve in civic matters. Today, Mennonites in North America reflect diverse attitudes toward government. Some believe that it essentially provides order for an evil society. They argue that Mennonites should maintain a distance from government: Mennonites should not vote, hold office, or attempt to influence policy. Others praise their nation as benevolent and avoid criticizing it. Some are hopeful that in a democratic society Christians can achieve, political step by political step, a more healthy society. Still others expect less of government in an imperfect society; they work for political changes that contribute to justice and peace but their hope is tinged with skepticism.

Since 1940, U.S. Mennonites have testified periodically before Congressional committees. For generations Canadian Mennonites have petitioned Cabinet ministers and senior officials. In 1970, five representatives of MCC Canada met with the Prime Minister to discuss the Soviet Union and China, MCC's relationship with the Canadian Wheat Board, and the Canada Pension Plan from which Canadian Amish and Old Order Mennonites sought exemption. An excerpt from a transcription of the meeting shows the open exchange between the Mennonites and Prime Minister Pierre Trudeau. The earnest question of the MCC Canada representative and the gracious response of the Canadian leader in this exchange is not

unlike discussions between Mennonites and public officials in
other times and places:

> *C. J. Rempel*: I'm sure all five of us who were coming here, and
> looking forward to it, were deluged by calls: 'What do you want
> to ask for"; "What do you want to talk to him about?" Now, I
> explained it to them that we feel it is only good citizenship [to
> take] time out to discuss government policies, and [to let] our
> convictions be known to the government.
>
> Now, do you appreciate this? ... I know that this is an in-
> fringement on your time How do you look upon this? You see,
> we like to think that we are speaking to basic principles and we
> would like to register them with you so that you know and hear
> [us].

> *Prime Minister Trudeau*: Well, I think I can answer that by say-
> ing that if you were merely a group of 160,000 or less ... want-
> ing to talk to me about [recognizing mainland] China or about
> the Canada Pension Plan, I suppose I would have gotten around
> to meeting you sometime, but I don't think I would have been
> as interested personally. In other words, [because of] the works
> that you are doing in a social sense ... I am interested in the
> spiritual input that you are bringing into this society, as a group
> of people who have a certain faith and who are the leaven in the
> dough....
>
> I hope that there will always be communities in Canada with
> a spiritual input into the society, and no matter how large the
> community or sect, I think it will influence the orientation of so-
> ciety by the righteousness of its ideas and the depth of its faith,
> rather than by merely its particular works in Vietnam or in the
> suburbs or in the slums of Toronto.

Long before the Washington and Ottawa offices existed,
Mennonite organizations promoted draft alternatives for Mennonites. In 1940 Congress established peacetime conscription.
Within weeks MCC, together with the Friends, Brethren, and
others, established the National Service Board for Religious
Objectors (NSBRO), a Washington-based organization moni-
toring Selective Service regulations and providing draft coun-
seling. From 1940 to 1947, NSBRO administered Civilian
Public Service, a program for conscientious objectors. MCC
was an active member of NSBRO and continues to work with

its successor, NISBCO. During World War II Canadian Mennonites concerned about the draft presented their perspective to government officials. The Canadian government terminated conscription at the war's end.

In 1966 members of the MCC Peace Section declared: "Our traditional willingness to testify when our own interests were involved . . . have led to suggestions that we should also be willing to testify when the rights of others are involved." Two years later the Peace Section adopted guidelines for the new Washington Office, which was to monitor issues in six areas: the draft, military budgets versus those of domestic social programs, economic needs of developing nations, domestic poverty, racial justice, and preservation of human freedoms and religious liberty.

The Washington Office of MCC U.S. maintains an official presence near the seat of government, but unlike the Friends Committee on National Legislation with which it works closely, it is not a registered lobby organization. After nearly twenty years in Washington, MCC U.S. is one of forty-three-member organizations of the Washington Interreligious Staff Council. The Washington Office is located on Capitol Hill in the Methodist Building, a few steps north of the U.S. Supreme Court and across the street from the Capitol.

Although MCC Canada's Ottawa Office dates to 1975, its origins date to 1967 when the Board of Christian Service of the Conference of Mennonites in Canada asked editor Frank Epp to serve as consultant in national and international affairs. Epp produced the newsletter *Ottawa Report* and during the next years MCC Canada debated whether or not to create an office in Ottawa. During the turbulent Vietnam War years of 1970 and 1971, Ernie Dick, serving as an MCC Canada volunteer in Ottawa, promoted peace and justice concerns. Some constituents suggested that such advocacy work might be "peripheral" or might "infringe" on the work of the church, while others believed that an office could benefit the organization. In

1971 Daniel Zehr, Executive Secretary of MCC Canada, commented on the controversy:

> In no area [as peace and social concerns] have we done or spent as little and talked and debated as much. While the battle of words about what to do and what not to do in these areas goes on, approximately 150 Canadian volunteers put peace and social concerns into shoe leather around the world.

For several years MCC Canada dropped the issue of creating an office in Ottawa. But in 1974 longtime MCCC leader J. M. Klassen outlined a new proposal, based in part on the experiences of MCC-U.S. staff in Washington. Despite criticism that MCC Canada lacked constituent authorization to be in Ottawa, MCCC decided to begin a three-year trial program. MCCC leaders hoped the new office would promote a "right involvement" in public life. They anticipated new contacts with like-minded Canadian groups. And yet they wondered whether the office would serve to unite—or to divide—Canadian Mennonites.

Beginning in 1975, director William Janzen and other Ottawa staff assisted Mennonites from Latin America of Canadian background (the Kanadier) who wished to come to Canada. As a result of briefs submitted by Ottawa Office personnel, thousands of these people gained Canadian legal status. Several years later the Canadian government and MCCC reached an agreement that facilitated the admission of refugees from Southeast Asia. Other Canadian organizations then used the agreement as a model for making similar ones. Ottawa Office staff have also submitted to government officials substantial briefs on such topics as religious freedom and Canadian foreign policy.

From its beginning the Ottawa Office established relationships with members of Parliament, particularly those of Mennonite background and those with Mennonite constituents. Janzen and voluntary service workers in Ottawa also wrote regularly for Mennonite periodicals on a variety of issues: international development, abortion, capital punishment, arms negotiations, and world hunger. In 1978, Mennonite political scientist John H. Redekop evaluated the "trial program" and concluded:

> The Ottawa Office has become one of the very important ministries of MCC Canada. . . . The long-term involvement with the "Kanadier" [Mennonite immigrants] warrants special mention. It is surely fortuitous that an Ottawa Office was established in time to help hundreds, if not thousands, of socially and politically needy people.

The varied nature of work in the two offices has led to frustrations as well as to satisfactions. An early problem for both offices was the lack of contact with pastors and lay leaders who remained unfamiliar with the work in Ottawa and Washington. Now into their second decade, however, the two offices have achieved a greater degree of public recognition. In part this is due to frequent reporting to Mennonite readers: The "Ottawa Notebook," a collection of short news releases, is sent out biweekly and published in *The Mennonite Reporter; Washington Memo*, a bimonthly newsletter, is sent to six thousand subscribers. Issue-oriented seminars which bring Mennonites from faraway communities to their nations' capitals have also made the offices more visible. The Washington Office in particular has coordinated many seminars over the years, ranging from the status of Native Americans to U.S. policy in southern Africa to international famine crises.

Both offices also engage in liaison work. Both have arranged for returning MCCers and other Mennonites to tell their stories to government officials. The Washington Office has facilitated MCC delegations and Congressional witnesses on such matters as the National Peace Academy, U.S. poverty, and the nuclear arms freeze. An example of such "representation to government" occurred in 1977 when Franz accompanied Patricia Erb, the twenty-year-old daughter of Mennonite missionaries in Argentina, to the offices of key Senators and Representatives. Franz tells the story:

As a university student in Buenos Aires, Patty's field work for the Sociology Department involved her in a social service assignment in a slum barrio. As in other countries under authoritarian military control, such engagements can lead to arrest, imprisonment, and torture—without trial—for being "subversive." Patty's abduction by armed officers from her parents' home in September, 1976, led to fifteen days of imprisonment and torture, after which she was released.

After her expulsion from Argentina, Patty, age twenty, received her parents' and the Mennonite Mission Board's permission to come to Washington. At the request of the Mission Board, the MCC Washington Office made some forty appointments over several weeks for her to share her experience and to ask that U.S. military training assistance to Argentina be terminated. Her torturers had complained at the time of her release: "First your government trains us to do this [at the Army's School of Americas], then your government becomes upset and calls for your release." Patty knew that of the nine thousand to fifteen thousand mostly innocent civilians being held and tortured in Argentine prisons, most would not come out alive.

Two appointments in particular made Patty's presence and testimony in Washington momentous for thousands in Argentina. One was her impact on the late Senator Frank Church (D-ID), chairman-designate of the Foreign Relations Committee. He delivered a speech on the Senate floor describing Patty's experience and sponsored an amendment to halt all U.S. military training aid to Argentina. The amendment passed in the Senate.

The MCC Washington Office also arranged for Patty to be interviewed at the annual seminar of the Catholic Sisters "Network" organization in Washington, attended by nuns from across the country. Patty's input, so moving, resulted in their interest in an amendment to terminate Argentine military aid. The issue became a key focus of their lobbying in scores of offices in the House of Representatives, where a vote similar to the Senate vote had been defeated earlier but would be tried once more. Four hundred and fifty nuns, homework carefully done, fanned out across Capitol Hill to communicate the message of Patty Erb. The vote of 223-180 terminated U.S. military aid to Argentina. The message to Buenos Aires was clear. The number of persons who disappeared into Argentine prisons over the next several years declined and eventually ceased.

Was Patty's voice the only one? No, but it was a significant voice. Furthermore, hers was not the voice of a "Communista" but of a deeply committed Christian.

The staff in the Washington and Ottawa offices meet occasionally with foreign diplomats to explore possibilities for placing MCC service personnel in their countries. Janzen tells of working in 1979 with the Vietnamese Embassy in Ottawa. MCC wanted to reestablish a relief and development program in Vietnam, and Ottawa Office staff members helped to arrange an overseas visit of an MCC delegation. Vietnamese officials, however, refused MCC's request to place resident personnel in Vietnam. Janzen recalls:

> In spite of the differences, an unusual friendship developed. On one occasion we were invited to an elaborate dinner at the Embassy. On another occasion we invited them to dinner. The friendship with the officials also led to their attendance at Bob Koop's wedding. [Koop, an MCC volunteer, served a two-year internship with the Ottawa Office.]

The personnel in both Ottawa and Washington agree that the strength of their offices is due to in-the-field experiences of MCC volunteers serving throughout the world. Both offices, and Washington in particular, rely on MCC's overseas administrators for guidance on which issues ought to take priority. On such a volatile issue as military aid to Central America, for instance, MCC representatives in Washington are careful to take a stance consistent with that of the Central America desk at Akron, Pennsylvania, one which reflects the counsel of MCC workers serving in places like El Salvador, Guatemala, and Nicaragua. Twice a year Delton Franz meets with a coordinating committee composed of MCC area program directors to plan priorities for future work.

The two offices also reflect contrasting patterns of the U.S. executive-congressional system and the Canadian parliamentary system. In Washington, MCC personnel and constituents often confer with Congressional members and their staffs. Washington Office personnel call on constituents to write or call their legislators on important issues. In 1986 the Washington Office, intrigued by the impact made three years earlier by eleven-year-old Samantha Smith's letter to Soviet leader Yuri Andropov, encouraged Mennonite children to write to President Reagan about the nuclear arms race.

By contrast, activities at the Ottawa Office reflect a parliamentary system in which government ministers and civil servants hold proportionately more power than the elected members of Parliament. The Ottawa Office directs the lion's share of its energies to civil servants and their ministers, presenting formal, carefully prepared briefs on specific issues. After ten years of experience, Janzen reports: "We have considerable contact with medium level civil servants." During the 1985-86 fiscal years, MCCC and affiliated organizations sent thirty communications to Canadian government bodies.

William Janzen reflects on the expanding contacts with government:

> ... While we are now deeply involved with government communications, twenty years ago we said virtually nothing on governmental polities, outside of those that affected our people. It is a major change. That does not mean it is wrong. Indeed, it may be that our stance in the current situation is as faithful as the stance of our predecessors in their situation.

MCC Canada does much of its governmental advocacy work through other MCCC programs, such as those responsible for refugees, victims and offenders, native people, and overseas food aid. Often the Ottawa Office assists these other MCCC portfolios. The Office is unusual because most Canadian church bodies conduct their advocacy work through their denominational offices rather than through offices near the seat of government. Since 1970, churchwide activism in Canada on issues ranging from Native rights to victim-offender reconciliation have given birth to numerous interchurch organizations.

By pooling talent, money and ideas, Canadian church groups have worked out a unique and effective system for representing concerns to government. MCC Canada participates in many of these interchurch coalitions.

While many of MCC's constituents look favorably upon witness to Washington and Ottawa, some concerned Mennonites remain unconvinced that the two offices engage in appropriate MCC activity. Some are uncomfortable with what they perceive to be MCC's "critical" stance towards government; they caution against "dictating to government what it should do, rather than petitioning government according to the historic [Mennonite] view."

In 1983 a Beachy Amish delegation visited the MCC headquarters in Akron to protest what they understood to be MCC's openness to liberation theology, nonregistration for the draft, refusal to pay war taxes, and the Peace Section's solicitation of letters from the public to members of Congress. They urged MCC to do its work within "a church basis which is faithful concerning biblical doctrines."

Other Mennonite groups have registered similar protests against Mennonite Central Committee, and specifically, its Peace Section. *Guidelines for Today*, a Pennsylvania-based bimonthly published independently by members of the Mennonite Church (MC), periodically protests the Washington Office's ties with such "liberal pacifist" groups as NISBCO, Fellowship of Reconciliation, and Sojourners. These Mennonites believe that the Washington Office has no business lobbying officials, assisting in peace vigils, or speaking in favor of women's rights.

How does MCC respond to these criticisms? An MCC administrator notes that "We are a pluralistic body . . . . We do not have the freedom to act as an interest group representing a particular point of view . . . . We must constantly work in an environment of diverse views." Another MCC administrator observes that although the Mennonite approach to government may be similar to that of other denominations, "we have a unique flavor growing out of a peace tradition and the experience of *praxis* around the world." He adds that Mennonites are affected by the debate in wider Christian circles as to the appropriate stance toward government.

While personnel in the Ottawa and Washington Offices wrestle with questions of representation, equally difficult questions emerge in response to urgent calls for witness. Should MCC be more assertive in reporting violations of justice of officials and legislative committees? Is MCC enlisting Mennonite constituents to write to their elected representatives on too many issues, issues beyond MCC's competency? Should MCC encourage its workers abroad to report human rights abuses? Is MCC channeling to appropriate officials the body of experience gathered by workers serving in areas of international crisis?

26

Sharing Across Cultures:

The International Visitor Exchange Program

"We're supposed to be enemies—but see how we love each other!"

In the summer of 1986 a college professor, visiting the Mennonite Central Committee headquarters in Akron, Pennsylvania, entered the MCC cafeteria. Eighty-eight international "trainees" had just arrived from many parts of Canada and the U.S. for a four-day reunion and debriefing before returning to their homes. The visitor later described the scene: "Everyone was talking animatedly, the volume of sound turned up high. I sensed that something very special was happening."

The trainees ranged in ages from nineteen to thirty. A year earlier, most had arrived in Akron able to speak little English. Now these friends from twenty-nine different countries, eyes sparkling, described to the MCC visitor highlights of the past year: working on hog farms, in hospitals, in publishing houses; living with rural Mennonite families for one "semester" and adjusting to the fast-paced life of urban Mennonites the next; learning to drive, to quilt, to play guitar; traveling with trainee friends to see more of the continent than most North Americans see in a lifetime. The visitor wished them well on their journeys home and reported later to a friend: "Those young people are higher than kites—they've had marvelous experiences. Doreen Harms, director of the International Exchange Visitor Program, is the dean of an unusually significant program of Mennonite higher education."

MCC's International Visitor Exchange Program (IVEP), begun in 1950, has given nearly 1,800 young adults the opportunity to live and work in North America. From forty-eight countries spread across Africa, Asia, Europe, the Middle East, and Latin America, they have come to serve, to promote peace and cultural understandings, and to strengthen ties of Christian fellowship. The program began when twenty-one Mennonite men from Europe spent a year on American farms. Doreen Harms, Emma Schlichting, Pauline Jahnke Bauman, Elma Esau, and Kathy Penner Hostetler directed the program for various periods from 1950 to 1968. Harms, who returned from Europe in 1968 to guide the program, continues as director of IVEP to the present. Gradually the program has broadened to include men and women interested in a wide range of vocations. To date, the largest numbers of trainees have come from Germany, the Netherlands, Switzerland, and Paraguay; others have come from such countries as Kenya and Korea, Jordan and Jamaica.

IVEP is the oldest and largest of the MCC-supported exchange efforts. Two other programs place North American young people overseas. The Intermenno Trainee Program, similar to IVEP, was begun in 1963 and is administered by European Mennonites. SALT International, begun in 1981, sends U.S. and Canadian high school graduates to developing nations for one year. MCC promotes the SALT program as a way for participants to "test their gifts for future service." MCC has also had a hand in two other exchange programs. From 1971 to 1983 it administered the Polish Agricultural Visitor Exchange Program (now folded into IVEP); currently, MCC supports summer visits by Japanese teenagers to the U.S. through the

Language Laboratory of Japan, a program administered by the Allegheny Mennonite Conference.

Director Harms, based at the Akron office, works closely with MCC's country representatives and Mennonite mission personnel overseas who promote the program, screen candidates, and recommend young people for entry. MCC accepts exchange visitors only from countries where MCC maintains a relationship with national Mennonite church leaders or where MCC or Mennonite mission personnel reside. Each exchange visitor is sent overseas and then welcomed back by his or her home church. Most trainees are Christian but not all are Mennonite. Their home churches view the exchange program as a means of preparing future leaders; many trainees, in fact, have already entered church service before their year abroad. Consider the background of these IVEP participants in the 1985-86 program: Jairus from Zambia, a member of the Brethren in Christ, leads a youth group and hopes to enter the ministry; Paulus from Indonesia is a student of theology; Rosely from Brazil is a musician who translates for a national Mennonite service agency.

The trainees represent a wide range of abilities. Some, for example, are trained as engineers, teachers, farmers, child care workers, mechanics, carpenters, physical therapists, doctors, or nurses, while others arrive in North America with little or no job experience. Harms, assisted by personnel at provincial and regional offices, is always on the lookout for placements within the MCC constituency. The task of placing international visitors in suitable positions is "a venture in faith." Sponsors— businesses, institutions, or individuals—employ the trainees and find families willing to host them. Most trainees divide their time between two six-month placements. Between these "semesters" is a one-week conference during which trainees renew friendships, share their new language skills, reflect on their work assignments, and present programs to area churches. Most IVEP alumni look back on these midwinter gatherings as a highlight of the North America experience. The trainees share a sense of kinship as they tell of the joys and frustrations of their first six-month assignments and come together for singing, drama, recreation, worship, prayer, and Bible Study.

The International Visitor Exchange Program has built up a large body of trainee alumni and sending churches around the world, as well as North American sponsors and hosts, many of whom provide work experience for trainees or keep them in their homes year after year. Indeed, some longtime sponsors have adopted the program as something of a "second vocation." The program's primary emphasis is cultural exchange; vocational development is also important. A recent study showed that between 1969 and 1984, only one percent of all IVEP trainees failed to return home after completing their assignments. The vast majority of trainees returned home to make contributions in their home countries.

MCC's International Visitor Exchange Program aims to be self-supporting. The trainees generate income for the program by working for the sponsors, who furnish room and board, provide spending money for the trainees, and pay a modest amount to MCC for transportation, medical, and administrative costs. In recent years, however, trainees have earned only about 60 percent of the sum needed to run the program; MCC contributes the remainder. In 1986 MCC budgeted $227,418 for IVEP ($95,418 from general MCC funds and the remainder generated from the work placements).

Considering the language barriers and cultural differences between trainees and their hosts, says Harms, IVEP has "significantly few problems compared to the potential that exists for problems...." But since the IVEP staff deals constantly with expectations on the part of sponsors and hosts as well as the expectations of exchange visitors, some problems are inevitable. All visitors suffer pangs of homesickness at times; in rare instances someone returns home early. Romances crop up occasionally, making parting difficult at the end of the year.

Some visitors find the comforts of North American lifestyle irresistible: touch-tone phones, electronically equipped cars, and the like tend to raise materialistic expectations. It is easy to run up a large phone bill simply by touching the right numbers.

Harms notes that the program requires careful planning: "With [international visitors] we cannot take things for granted ... everything has to be highly organized." Sometimes passport offices overseas cause delays, and visas in some parts of the world are becoming difficult to obtain. Moreover, in this people-intensive program some snafus arise out of human error. One trainee lost his passport and had to remain in the U.S.—until, a week later, he found it in his own suitcase.

A year-by-year pattern emerges: arrival in Pennsylvania for the orientation session, the first semester assignment, the midyear conference, the second semester assignment, and a final four-day wrap-up session in Akron. The IVEP office also encourages participants to spend as many as four weeks traveling in North America with their hosts or with trainee friends. Throughout the year these international visitors send a barrage of letters to family and friends at home and to "MCC mother Doreen" at Akron. In a yearbook compiled each summer by the IVEP office, trainees record through prose, poetry, photography, and artwork their enthusiasm and regrets about the year. Paging through the yearbook one senses their delight in things new and their determination to cope with loneliness, cultural differences, and stress. Rewarding moments remain etched in the minds of all participants. Harms recalls the time that trainees Jose and Jeanette of Honduras burst into her kitchen, arms linked with Maritza of Nicaragua. The threesome told her, "We're supposed to be enemies—but see how we love each other!"

Many of the trainees possess deep Christian convictions and see the world through a framework of piety and spiritual rootedness. These young people see the year in North America as a time to grow by participating in the host family's church, by developing devotional life, by coping with cross-cultural adjustments. Here, trainees speak for themselves:

> It is my firm expectation to be able to use all I have learned to benefit and build the church of Jesus in Tanzania.

> I have my quiet time every day.... I read all the Old Testament between August and November.

> Here in Oklahoma something very important happened to me. I became a child of God.

> I still don't feel as comfortable here as in my own church but I do really experience God's being, existence, and love.

> When I can't communicate with people, I am sure God listens to me.

> I'm really ripe with the word of God. It has been forward with Jesus. No turning back, no turning back. It is really wonderful.

Trainees take every opportunity to educate new North American acquaintances about their home country:

Piere-Andre from Switzerland
My first assignment was in northern New York on Dave and Tippy Zehr's farm.... I worked on the 180-acre dairy farm to feed cows, heifers, and sometimes milking (when the family was blessed with a baby). I tried to be an assistant in everything.... Dave took a lot of time to teach me things about cattle care, veterinary programs, etc.

Jennifer from India
For my first six months I worked on a poultry farm in northern Alberta in a little town called Bluesky. The population was probably around two hundred, quite a contrast for one coming from [Calcutta], a city of about nine million. It sure was quite an experience working with the chickens!

Laurette from France
By working in the nursing home I discovered the fantastic world of the old people.

Novelette from Jamaica
I have a lovely group of three-to-four-old kids in my Sunday school class. They're the most adoring and loving little children

I've ever come across. I've learned so much from them each
Sunday we meet.

Jean-Luc from France
My work was fixing cars and nice big trucks in Bergey's Garage.
It was a good experience in mechanics . . . but I had a hard time
to learn the "inch system" which still doesn't make sense to me!

Uwe from West Germany
I worked at a huge woodworking factory. . . . My working place
was in the church pew departments. All the time we were working with heavy solid oak.

Portia from Hong Kong
First, I was very scared of my working performance for I had
never worked in any field of mental retardation . . . . The staff
constantly assisted and gave much opportunity for me to learn
through the practical working with the retarded adults. . . . I
began to love the retarded.

Irene from Brazil
My sponsors publish a magazine entitled *Mennonite Family
History*. A highlight of the year was when they helped me
prepare an article on my grandfather: "Immigrant Bernhard
Friesen from Russia to China to Brazil."

Here the trainees speak of culture shock and difficult adjustments:

Elfriede from Brazil
Sometimes we wanted to give up. We felt like children, dependent and often lost. But you understood us and what we
were going through. . . . You had admitted the stranger into the
privacy of your home and that was a risk. . . . Humor was especially important to us during this time.

James from Bangladesh
We have to adjust to different environments and to different
situations. We need to think about every matter from a different
point of view because everyone's way of thinking is different.

Elly from the Netherlands
I had a hard time getting used to praying aloud. In Holland . . .
praying is done silently. [But in the church I attended here]
everybody seemed to pray for every little thing in life. . . . I felt
completely lost.

Jose from Honduras
Sometimes I turned rebellious and complained about the things I considered an injustice.

Neftali from El Salvador
My second six months I spent in Pennsylvania where everything was much easier for me, especially making friends. In the second six months I had confidence to speak English.

Strange food and differences in lifestyle provoke commentary:

Ashit from India
One problem was food, because I am used to very spicy food. I had never eaten beef before I came to America.

Sutanto from Indonesia
I eat at the Eastern Mennonite College cafeteria for lunch and supper. Flowing ice cream, a salad bar which never stops, nine kinds of beverages and different kinds of food, which you can have as much of as you want, threaten my getting fat.

Andrea from Brazil
I appreciated seeing the old people. How strong they are!

Margrith from Switzerland
I lived with a nice family. . . . It was too bad they were busy all the time, so they couldn't show me much of the beautiful country [in the area].

Ciro from Brazil
I didn't know what Halloween was. . . . but later on discovered why all those wizards and butterflies were pushing wheelchairs.

Joachim from West Germany
My second assignment was opposite from the first one. I moved from the protected family life of a lovely farm in Nebraska to Voluntary Service life and the big city of Philadelphia. . . . I enjoyed my second assignment as much as the first one.

Trainees form international friendships to last a lifetime:

Saskia from the Netherlands
[At] the conference in Denver. . . . everyone looked healthy and

happy.... The program of the trainees in the church included the song, "Let There Be Peace On Earth and Let It Begin with Me," which will always be my favorite song.

Josue from France
When I meet someone the first question that they ask me is, "Are you anxious to get back?" And the only thing I can answer is, "Well! I am going to leave a lot of friends behind me here."

Gisela from Switzerland
The three weeks when all the trainees are together [impressed me]. I'll never forget the unity and love .... We are one in the Spirit. It is a little bit like heaven.

Matthias from West Germany
We had lots of fun, Sergio, Beata, and me. I still see us in that little red brick church playing blues on Sunday afternoons. And on the one after my birthday party, I committed my life to the Lord.

Shizuo from Japan
[My father] lost his mother and older brother by an atomic bomb while he survived.... Even though thirty-nine years have passed, many Americans do not know what happened in Hiroshima and Nagasaki.... I have talked about Hiroshima at churches, at schools and meetings [and] have taken part in a number of peace rallies.... I have learned a lot from American peacemakers.

A frequent theme is gratitude:

Tomler from Nigeria
The generosity of the Mennonites fascinates me so much.

Faith from the Philippines
With both my first and second hosts I attended Bosslers Mennonite Church. The church has enriched my life in many ways, especially through its Paul-Timothy [program] and share group meetings.

John from India
I lived with Omar and Sara ... in the Amish country. I really had a very nice time with them. They treated me like an older son.... Their children treated me like a brother. I could write a book about their hospitality.

Tabitha from India
I relished the icy but gentle kiss of new fallen snow. It was a fun and new experience to go tubing and sledding.

Margarita from Uruguay
Late in December snow came and I was so happy. . . . When I touched it I was filled with emotion. I had made many plans while expecting the snow, like rolling around the yard or making a snowman. I finally made one with big donut eyes and a bright carrot nose.

Elizabeth from India
Both families I stayed with were very nice. I will never forget the teasing and the kidding, the discussions at suppertime. Mrs. Stutzman knows my local dialect, Chatisgarhi, because she was born in India at Champa. So we cooked Indian food many times.

Silvana from Brazil
I didn't know what to expect with my first semester host family. I was so scared! But when I saw Carmen, she came and gave me a hug with a beautiful smile and welcomed me.

Lilia from Argentina
My first impression of the host family was not too good. They were too young. . . . they sure weren't mom and dad, and at that moment I felt I needed a mom and a dad. Anyway . . . I got to love Karen and Larry, my "parents" in Ontario, so much.

Learning to communicate in a new language is one reason many trainees desire to live in North America; stories abound of moments both trying and humorous:

Maritza from Nicaragua
My first negative experience was having to eat in the cafeteria at MCC with no one to talk to. Many times I was afraid if someone talked to me I would not be able to answer them because of my poor English.

Shefali from Bangladesh
At our first orientation in Blooming Glen . . . it was very interesting to me when Doreen started to talk to us. She talked very slowly so that we could understand. I wondered how she could know each of us personally!

Jose from Honduras
When I arrived at the [repair shop] I felt myself in the situation of the tower of Babel (Genesis 11:9) since all workers at the shop spoke to me in English without mercy, and I did not understand. Nevertheless, I enjoyed my job. . . .

Christine from Uruguay
After my first day of English class . . . the [four children in my host family] expected me to come home speaking English fluently. They were surely disappointed.

Ingrid from Paraguay
I had a lot of fun with [host family children] Angela and Gerald and won't forget them. One day Gerald called to me and said, "Ingrid, come and watch this TV program. They're talking your English." I went to hear, and of course, they were speaking in Spanish!

Helen from Taiwan
I went to California with Susanne, Hermine, and Silke for two weeks of vacation. We drove the car 4,400 miles all the way. We sang, prayed, sight-saw, and paid the speeding tickets together. . . . I really enjoyed those three lovely European girls. They were talking in English because of me. I really appreciated that.

Margarette from Haiti
Now I know many expressions which I will never forget: "You bet," "Oh boy," and "No kidding." I was very happy and surprised when the students gave me a T-shirt as a souvenir, with "Swift Current Bible Institute" on the front and "No kidding" on the back.

Trainees take every opportunity to educate new North American acquaintances about their home country:

Wilmer from Colombia
I learned to enjoy the silly questions people used to ask me about my "poor country." . . . . Nevertheless, I indeed showed the real Colombia through chats, discussions, and pictures.

Aaltje from the Netherlands
Just before Christmas I talked in church about how we celebrate Christmas at home. (And it sure beats Christmas in Canada.)

Not because I was homesick, but because of the abundance of gifts people get here and the impersonal way of opening them.

Adele from South Africa
I hope to have shared not only the pain of my country but also the hope that resides within the lives of the many South Africans who thirst for justice. . . . We are indeed an international community.

Each August, as trainees reunite in Pennsylvania for their farewells, they share these and many other thoughts with each other. Some will see each other again in future travels, others will eventually welcome their North American host families to their homes in such faraway places as India, Poland, or Bolivia. In the summer of 1985, Sonja of West Germany told this children's story to her friends before leaving for home:

> "The men where you live," said the little prince, "raise five thousand roses in the same garden—they do not find what they are looking for."
> "And yet, what they are looking for could be found in one single rose, or in a little water."
> "Yes, that is true," I said.
> And the little prince added: "But the eyes are blind. One must look with the heart. . . ."

Sonja concluded that the story of *The Little Prince* symbolized for her a year of "seeing behind the small happenings, . . . in every person, the unique, single rose with its message of peace, freedom, joy, eternity, which God meant to be."

An MCC observer acquainted with the program throughout its thirty-five year history has reflected: "Surely no one attending the first MCC meeting in 1920 ever dreamed that this fledgling relief program would later bring ninety or more young people to North America each year for transcultural experience." Some ask whether this is the kind of work in which MCC should be engaged. If one asks the trainees, they respond with a unanimous "yes."

27

Reconciling Victims and Offenders:

VORP

*In Clovis, California, Ron Classen, director of the
Fresno County Victim Offender Reconciliation
Program (VORP), answered the phone. The
woman on the line was a rape victim. She told
him that she had learned that the rapist was
being sentenced to approximately twenty years in
prison. The teenage offender was not someone
she knew personally, but she was concerned
about his stiff sentence. "Can your program do
something more constructive?" she asked. "I'm a
strong person and I'm going on with my life. I
want to see this boy helped. I can't imagine that
all that time in prison is going to help."*

*Classen suggested that she call a community
agency and ask if it was willing to suggest an alternative sentence that would include victim-offender reconciliation. She agreed and in the next
weeks met with the agency's staff. But after extensive discussions, the agency decided not to become involved due to the seriousness of the crime
and the history of the offender. Classen then told
the victim that VORP might become involved if
she wished to pursue alternative sentencing and
was willing for VORP to arrange a meeting
between her and the offender.*

Victim Offender Reconciliation Program, or VORP, is a community-based mediation program whereby trained volunteers help to restore relationships between victims and offenders. Usually VORP is used as an alternative process for sentencing criminal offenders; at other times it serves victims and offenders outside of the judicial process. Grounded in a commitment to reconciliation, VORP seeks to help both parties live in the community without fear.

VORP deals mainly with cases involving theft, burglary, shoplifting and vandalism, although some programs also take on criminal cases involving personal violence. VORP is used by some judges as an alternative to a prison term; by others, as part of a sentence which may include time in prison. While VORP may be ordered as part of a probation condition, the referral is not pursued if either the victim or offender is unwilling to participate. Observers of the criminal justice system report that VORP is having an undeniable impact in criminal justice circles: VORP language and concepts are appearing in legislation and are cited frequently during debates about the present "retributive" model of justice.

The program works this way: An offender is usually referred to VORP by the court or by the probation department following a trial. After the VORP office receives a referral, it determines whether the case meets certain requirements, for instance, that the offender has admitted guilt. If so, VORP assigns the case to a volunteer trained in mediation. A VORP staff member or volunteer contacts both the victim and the offender, explains the program, discusses the consequences of the offense, and invites each to participate. If they agree, the VORP representative arranges for the two to meet to discuss the case. At this meeting the victim and offender negotiate restitution and in most cases sign a contract stating the amount of restitution. Some offenders agree to pay the victim for damages; others agree to work on behalf of the victim or the community; still others agree to combine payment and work.

This face-to-face encounter gives both parties the opportunity to present their version of what happened and to ask questions of one another. Reconciliation is always a goal of VORP meetings, and while it does not always take place, some form of reconciliation often does occur. After a meeting, the VORP mediator submits a written summary and a copy of the contract to the VORP office, which forwards the contract to the court or probation officer for approval and enforcement. VORP volunteers stay in contact with the victim until the offender completes the terms of the contract.

Indiana-based journalist John Bender traces the origins of VORP to a 1974 incident in Elmira, Ontario. Interested Mennonites first tested the VORP concept when two youths of that community went on a one-night vandalism spree that resulted in more than two thousand dollars' damage. The vandals were caught and charged with criminal conduct. Beginning in the late 1960s, Mennonite Central Committee Ontario had begun to search for alternatives to incarceration. The provincial office, based in Kitchener, developed a close relationship with the Waterloo Region Probation Department. MCC volunteers began serving with the department, organizing a network of community volunteers to work with offenders on probation. When the nearby Elmira vandalism case surfaced, probation officer and former MCCer Mark Yantzi had a novel idea, "Why not initiate a meeting between these two young men and their victims?" Neither of the youths had a previous criminal record. Could Mennonite volunteers intervene in the case and negotiate a settlement which circumvented the usual legal process?

Assigned to the Elmira vandalism case, Yantzi suggested to the judge that it might be "therapeutic" for the youths to become acquainted with their victims. After initial hesitation, the judge agreed and asked Yantzi, together with Dave Worth, to supervise the meetings. Worth, then MCC's coordinator of volunteers for the probation program, tells the story:

There were twenty-two victims. The two youths had been angry one night about what they thought was some unjustified hassling from a local official about a loud muffler on their car. They took it out on their neighbors, smashing windows, slashing tires, breaking a cross off a church sign, denting fenders, and puncturing car radiators.

We decided on a very simple procedure. We met the youths in Elmira and retraced the route they had taken on that night a few months earlier. We instructed them to go up to the door, introduce themselves, and explain why they were there. "We'll be behind you all the way," we told them. All of the victims were surprised. One or two expressed real anger at what had taken place and a few expressed genuine concern for the two offenders.

As a condition of probation, the judge ordered the youths to pay the victims for damages, and three months later we repeated our door-to-door trek. This time the youths distributed certified checks to the victims. As a result, the two young men felt they could hold up their heads in the community, the victims felt something had been done, and VORP was born.

Within a year Yantzi and Worth submitted a formal proposal to local law-enforcement officials. By mid-1976, the new Victim Offender Reconciliation Program had accepted sixty-one cases. Forty-eight of these resulted in meetings between victims and offenders. The widespread support of judges, social service agencies, and church groups allowed MCC to form a partnership with the Ministry of Correctional Service for processing VORP cases.

Organizers of VORP quickly learned that the structure of the program was crucial. How could Christians, committed to the ideal of reconciliation, work with a justice system which rarely gave voice to either victims or offenders? Organizers had to convince attorneys and probation departments that this alternative program could work. To others interested in starting VORP in their communities, Mark Yantzi commented, "We see ourselves as being in the system but not of the system."

Another early program, in Elkhart County, Indiana, originated through the interest of Mennonite probation officers and seminary students. The fledgling VORP began in the juvenile

section of the probation department, where problems soon
arose. The overworked juvenile probation staff, lacking the
time to train volunteers, handled the mediation process themselves. They found themselves in the awkward position of jug-
gling two roles—acting as "neutral" VORP mediators in addition to serving as criminal justice officials. In 1979, the VORP
program became a private nonprofit organization aligned with
an Indiana-based umbrella organization, Prisoner and Community Together, Inc. (PACT).

The evolution and experiences of the Elkhart program—
which refined the VORP concept and provided a viable
model—resulted in international publicity in *Newsweek*, the
New York Times, and network news programs such as NBC's
Today. Local VORP leaders viewed the media scrutiny as a
mixed bag. Certainly, kudos from the secular press helped the
Victim Offender Reconciliation Program gain acceptance
among MCC constituents and resulted in inquiries from many
quarters. But organizers worried that broad media coverage
might create false expectations and that the program's quality
might suffer if the VORP concept spread too rapidly. One
VORP organizer, pleased by the public embrace of the
program but concerned about the need to provide sound
educational materials, concluded, "We can't *own* an idea."

The interest displayed by the press, as well as MCC's commitment to share information, transmitted the VORP idea into
many medium-sized communities and some large cities. The
spread of VORP is not unlike the growth of Mennonite Disaster
Service and MCC relief sales. VORP is a grass-roots program,
independent of administrative decision-makers in Akron and
Winnipeg. Beginning in 1979, Howard Zehr directed local
VORP and Prisoner and Community Together, Inc. (PACT),
programs in Elkhart, Indiana. Zehr also gave leadership on
wider criminal justice concerns through MCC's Offender
Ministries Program, which in 1982 became the MCC U.S. Office of Criminal Justice. The MCC office cooperates with the

Michigan-based PACT, which sponsors a national VORP Resource Center and distributes MCC-related material on VORP. In Canada, Edgar Epp first directed MCC's Victim Offender Ministries Program and promoted a wide range of justice issues in addition to VORP. In 1983 Dave Worth assumed leadership of the MCC Canada program.

Most of the fifty programs in the U.S. and twenty programs in Canada modeled on VORP began without direct MCC support, although they have used handbooks and other materials published by MCC. In Great Britain, the term VORP is used for victim-offender meetings in prisons modeled on programs in the United States, and increasingly, other European programs are springing up based on the reconciliation concept.

Part of the reason for the program's growth is its low cost. Dependent on church and community resources and private foundations, most VORPs are staffed largely by trained volunteers. A local VORP may be operated with an annual budget of from twenty thousand to forty thousand dollars, or in some cases, less. Comparative program costs per offender are striking: several hundred dollars for offenders in VORP, versus fifteen thousand to twenty-five thousand dollars per year for offenders serving prison terms. The United States alone has over 600,000 persons in prison, collectively a huge tax burden.

As new VORPs form, some Mennonites argue that the Victim Offender Reconciliation Program should have an explicitly *Christian* base. In many communities VORP organizers strive to work closely with justice and government officials while rooting the program in local churches. One VORP organizer expresses gratitude that others "show openness to our perspective . . . shaped by our biblical approach, our convictions on violence, our experiences historically as a church."

The guiding principles of VORP are simple, yet they turn traditional notions of administering justice upside down. VORP organizers believe that reconciliation is the most important goal of the program. They emphasize the importance of "per-

North America: VORP 349

sonalizing" the crime so that an offender is faced with the human dimension of his or her act. Given the complexities of the existing court system, victims and offenders frequently are bewildered, frustrated, and depressed. Getting the "run-a-round" after a crime occurs is a common experience. Through the process of meeting, talking, and listening, however, the parties may eventually resolve their conflict.

Criminologists have sometimes criticized VORPs for being too hesitant in serving as an alternative to prison sentencing. MCC's Howard Zehr points out that VORPs need to take on cases more serious than misdemeanors in order to achieve credibility as a substitute for imprisonment. Yet VORP organizers know how seldom judges are willing to use the reconciliation program alone as an alternative to prison sentencing. VORP organizers debate the issue among themselves, since reconciliation and punishment (that is, providing a substitute for a prison term) can be conflicting goals. If VORP case workers—intent on achieving credibility—begin to accept only the most serious cases, they miss opportunities to work at reconciliation between victims, and offenders in a wider range of cases.

Related to this issue is the tendency of judges in the U.S. (and to a lesser extent, in Canada) to fill prisons to maximum capacity. While offenders who participate in VORP tend to draw reduced sentences, the program's presence in a community does not affect the number of people sent to prison. Dave Worth of Ontario concludes: "To my mind, VORP is not an alternative to prisons. . . . The important thing about VORP is that it proves to the church and the secular world that reconciliation is possible."

Organizers emphasize the frequent "spin-off" effect of VORP, and note that its concepts are applied frequently outside of established programs. In one case, a woman realtor was assaulted in the dark basement of an empty house. Her male assailant fled after knocking her to the floor. Two years later, after becoming involved in a Mennonite church, the man expressed remorse to his new pastor. The pastor, an acquaintance of the realtor, wondered, "Can anything good come out of a meeting between a violent offender and his victim?" After consulting with a friend familiar with VORP, the pastor arranged for a meeting in his study, where the small group prayed for the presence of God's Spirit. The offender, sharing the pain of his past deeds, faced the woman and said, "I'm sorry—I didn't mean to hurt you." The woman replied softly, "I forgive you."

Victim Offender Reconciliation Programs provide unusual opportunities for both victims and offenders. Although VORP volunteers remain neutral in the dispute, they are trained to empathize with the victim. One of the challenges facing VORP is the emerging victim rights movement, which has criticized the church for failing to care for victims. VORP is concerned with offenders, too, particularly the needs for healing. VORP personnel emphasize, however, that their programs are not an "easy way out" for offenders. Meeting one's victim is frightening, and some offenders with prison experience report that they prefer to face a prison term rather than meet a hostile victim.

Through VORP, concerned Mennonites have moved from prison ministry work to developing methods of conflict resolution for victims, and offenders. The services offered by the MCC U.S. Office of Criminal Justice and MCC Canada's Victim Offender Ministries reach beyond Mennonite circles to a wider constituency. Interest in justice issues has led MCC to address such issues as domestic violence, ministry to families of prisoners, the needs of crime victims, and capital punishment, MCC's partnership with others in victim/offender reconciliation permits entrée into new areas of service. Howard Zehr, for instance, is chairperson for the National Coalition Against the Death Penalty, a consortium of more than one hundred organizations.

Continued international interest in VORP provides MCC with opportunities to educate the public about justice issues.

VORP often brings issues of justice and injustice close to home. One VORP organizer notes that "the area of crime provides/demands an opportunity to be involved in peacemaking very directly in every community and congregation. . . . We do not have to wait for a war to take a stand against violence."

28

Providing a Link to a Separated People:
'Die Mennonitische Post'

Canadian Mennonite Abraham Warkentin, editor of a unique German-language newspaper, recalls this encounter with some modern-day pilgrims during a recent trip to South America:

> When I was at the Santa Cruz, Bolivia, airport recently, waiting for my flight home, a Mennonite couple with ten children arrived. They were from Mexico and were returning there after only a few months in Bolivia because of the unrest. I was able to assist the family in a few small ways at the airport and was moved by the experience. . . . I helped the children, toddler to eighteen years, drag their huge boxes, suitcases, and flour bags full of belongings across the tarmac to the waiting plane.
>
> . . . . The tired, frustrated mother, the nervous father who couldn't fill out the customs declaration forms, the children who were again being uprooted, the thousands of dollars wasted and the incredible attitude of these people who trust that somehow they'll pull it off again against pretty big odds—this all made me think how representative it was of our people who are forever

moving somewhere, always looking for a place where they can put down their roots, farm, and raise their large families.

In Latin America there is a large body of Mennonites who have no conference headquarters, no biennial or triennial sessions, no position papers, no hospitals, no high schools or colleges, no mission boards, no delegates to the Mennonite World Conference. These people, whom Warkentin characterizes as "our forgotten brothers and sisters," are not Amish or Old Order Mennonites. They are colony Mennonites, or the "Kanadier," members of settlements in Mexico, Paraguay, Bolivia, Belize, and Costa Rica.

For three generations they have lived in a Hispanic culture; most men speak some Spanish but few women do. The Mennonites established colonies because they wanted to educate their own, yet today many Kanadier can barely read or write. They are a more populous people than most North American Mennonites imagine: 100,000 strong and growing. According to one estimate the colony Mennonites in Mexico have the highest birthrate in the world. In Belize they comprise four percent of the country's total population. This is the highest percentage of Mennonites anywhere in the world.

The term "Kanadier" refers to descendants of Mennonites who immigrated to Canada from Russia in the 1870s. Fifty years later, seven thousand of these conservative Mennonites chose to leave southern Manitoba and central Saskatchewan rather than to send their children to Canadian public schools as the provincial governments then required. After years of negotiating and paying large fines, they sought new homes in Latin America. Beginning in 1922 they settled in the Chihuahua province of northern Mexico; in 1926 they entered the Chaco of Paraguay. In Paraguay, government officials granted the Mennonites a "Privilegium" allowing them to administer their own schools and colonies. Other countries have granted privileges less extensive than Paraguay's.

Following the spread to Mexico and Paraguay, new colonies formed in Bolivia, Belize, and the United States. The movement between these many colonies continues. As a result of loosened immigration restrictions during the post World War II years, a steady stream of Kanadier moved back to Canada. Two of the most recently settled Canadian colonies are in Nova Scotia, home since 1983 to German-speaking "Kleine Gemeinde" Mennonite families from Belize, and in southern Argentina, where more than 150 Mennonites from Mexico and Bolivia have settled.

Despite the return flow northward, the numbers of Mennonite colonists in Latin America continue to grow. Presently an estimated fifty thousand live in Mexico, twenty-two thousand in Paraguay, seventeen thousand in Bolivia, five thousand in Belize, and several hundred in Costa Rica. The majority of these Mennonites are Old Colony; the rest include Sommerfelder, Kleine Gemeinde, Chortitzer, Bergthaler, Reinlander, and other small Mennonite groups. The Old Colony Mennonites pursue a way of life separate from the more than twenty-five thousand Spanish- and Portuguese-speaking Mennonites in Latin America and progressive Russian Mennonite groups in Mexico (General Conference and Kleine Gemeinde), Belize (Evangelical Mennonite Mission Conference and Kleine Gemeinde), and in Paraguay (General Conference, Mennonite Brethren, Evangelical Mennonite Brethren, and others).

What is the link between Mennonite Central Committee and these conservative, agrarian Mennonites who have shied away from modern technology and outsiders? In 1977 MCC Canada formed the Kanadier Mennonite Colonization Committee. The latter serves as an advisory body to MCC Canada which publishes *Die Mennonitsche Post (The Mennonite Post)*, a German-language semi-monthly newspaper. The paper has several goals: to provide a vehicle for education, communication, and spiritual growth, and to foster a sense of identity among the colony Mennonites.

Colony leaders acknowledge that their communities, although separated from compromising influences of the world, have serious internal problems: illiteracy, alcoholism, family stress, and a loss of Mennonite identity. By publishing *Die Mennonitische Post*, MCC Canada hopes to make a modest contribution to strengthening these Mennonite communities.

The twenty-page *Post* includes Bible verses, inspirational articles, news from community correspondents, and special pages for children. But it is best known for publishing letters from its readers. During its first eight years of operation the *Post* published eight thousand letters—often fifty or sixty per issue. The letters section serves as both family newsletter and community bulletin board. Typical is this comment from a reader in Cuauhtemoc, Mexico: "Since our relatives are scattered throughout North and South America, we always read the *Post* right through to see if there may be news from one of them." Another enthusiast wrote, "It felt as though an old friend, one who had been away for many years, had finally arrived."

Older persons are avid fans of the paper. For many of them the *Post* takes the place of an earlier publication, the *Steinbach Post*, founded by Jacob S. Friesen in 1913 and published until 1966. Because of its uniquely international readership, the Steinbach German-language paper failed to attract advertising ("Who wants to advertise cars in a paper going to five different countries and read by people who cannot or will not drive them anyway?"), and finally folded. Since 1977 the *Post* has provided a much-appreciated reading supplement. Today the *Post* has about 6,500 subscribers and more than thirty thousand readers in six countries. Colony Mennonites are frugal; in some isolated areas a copy of the *Post* makes its way from one end of the village to the other.

This international enterprise poses some difficulties for the Canadian Mennonites responsible for the paper. Always there are logistical problems: the many currencies used by readers, the different languages and scripts used in letters to the editor, and transportation of the paper to remote corners of Latin America. There is also a baffling ebb and flow of subscriptions. MCC Canada has hesitated to subsidize the paper since it wants colony Mennonites to feel ownership of the *Post* and hopes that someday they will assume publishing responsibilities.

Another problem for the *Post's* publisher concerns the paper's content. In 1981, MCC Canada decided to introduce new sections on agriculture, health and development, and women's concerns. But the *Post's* editor learned that some readers, particularly preachers and elders (*Ohms*), were critical of articles which went beyond devotional material. Notes one Canadian contributor to the *Post*, "Some believe they can read their Bible at home; no one outside need preach to them about lifestyle."

The advent of the semimonthly newspaper, however, has created some spin-offs which are bringing even more reading materials into the reach of Old Colony Mennonites and other Kanadier. During the early 1980s, MCC Canada began to sponsor additional projects: running a bookstore in Mexico, publishing pictorial books and German-language histories of the Kanadier Mennonite people, and distributing records and tapes. Mennonite Central Committee Canada personnel moved to Mexico and Bolivia to promote *Die Mennonitsche Post* and to assist with other concerns.

In 1981, MCC Canada sent George Reimer to Cuauhtemoc, Mexico, to serve in a new position under the auspices of *Die Mennonitische Post*. In addition to other duties, Reimer edited a German-language supplement for readers in Mexico, *Beilage fuer Mexiko*. *Post* editor Warkentin cites Reimer's dedication to the paper:

> He is probably the only Mennonite who has the patience to wait out entry clearance at the Mexican border lock-up rather than

pay a bribe. He feels the books he takes over the border for our
bookstore and library in Cuauhtemoc are exempt from duty by
Mexican law and refuses to pay bribes. If held by officials he
fortifies himself with sunflower seeds and waits until the officials
realize they cannot get blood from a stone, and let him go.

In 1985 a new chapter in the story of *Die Mennonitische
Post* began. MCC Canada and colony Mennonites in Mexico
began negotiating the transfer of responsibility for the *Beilage*
supplement. Also in 1985, the first issue of *Beilage fuer Bolivia*,
a four-page insert produced by Mennonites in Santa Cruz, appeared with the *Post* in Bolivia. As new opportunities arise,
MCC Canada and the Kanadier Mennonite Colonization
Committee reemphasize their conviction that *Die Mennonitsche Post* aids Kanadier Mennonites in their quest for
cultural and religious identity.

Die Mennonitische Post is a program of Mennonite Central
Committee Canada that is rather different than the conventional image of MCC service. Sponsorship of the *Post* reflects
the diversity of MCC activity more than sixty years after its
founding. Some ask: Is this legitimate work of the MCC? If
not, what other Mennonite agency ought to do it? How broad
is the MCC charter in a world of varied needs?

Some North American Mennonites see the mission of *Die
Mennonitische Post* as opening a window for these Mennonite
brothers and sisters who have lived in relative isolation. MCC
Canada, however, emphasizes sensitivity. "We must not see
the Old Colony Mennonites as Mennonites with cultural lag,"
cautions one administrator. Abraham Warkentin points out the
educational value for North Americans who learn to know the
Mennonite people of the colonies: "If we smile with amuse-
ment at their coveralls and buggies and large families, those
smiles must fade when we are confronted with questions about
our own lifestyles and luxuries."

People Support

Mennonite Central Committee is referred to variously as "a service agency," "a church organization," "a resource for meeting human need," "a mission board," and "a Mennonite bureaucracy." MCC is also a movement with ten times as many unpaid volunteers as salaried staff.

Throughout its history MCC has invited volunteers to process material aid for overseas needs. Groups in cutting rooms and material aid centers prepare fabric for congregational sewing projects and sort and bail clothing. Families assemble school kits, layettes, and Christmas bundles to be dedicated by congregations prior to shipment. Volunteers join in canning, soapmaking, and grain-bagging projects. Workers load trucks and freight cars with relief supplies.

People of all ages participate in community walks for MCC and CROP. Children deposit money for overseas projects in MCC cardboard banks. In some years as many as six thousand volunteers have served for one or more days with Mennonite Disaster Service teams working in tornado, flood, or other di-

saster-stricken areas. Thousands have made use of psychiatric
centers coordinated by Mennonite Health Services. Other
thousands have made travel plans with Menno Travel Service,
once an MCC agency but now independent.

A thousand workers serve continuously in MCC in North
America and overseas. MCC workers write home to their
families and congregations about their work. Some family
members go abroad or visit domestic programs. Many MCC
supporters have hosted international trainees for six months or
more. The emergence and growth of MCC shops illustrates the
initiative of MCC constituents. The first shop opened in
Altona, Manitoba, in 1972; in 1986 between seven and eight
thousand volunteers served in 120 MCC shops in North
America. Some shops retail only MCC SELFHELP crafts
made by producers in thirty countries, while others sell only
contributed items. Most shops offer a combination of the two.
In 1986 Canadian and U.S. shops provided through thrift and
SELFHELP sales more than three million dollars, 12 percent
of MCC's total income.

Grass-roots or people-based programs are described in case
studies on MCC relief sales and the Canadian Foodgrains
Bank, both of which illustrate the broad peoplehood strength of
Mennonite Central Committee. MCC is not only a resource for
meeting human need but it also brings people together in new
patterns of service and fellowship. With the passing of time
MCC has grown from being a temporary committee to an in-
clusive and complex institution that continues to draw strength
from the loyalty of the people.

Additional topics call for study: The mobilization of business
talent in Mennonite Economic Development Associates
(MEDA); the marketing of international crafts through MCC
SELFHELP: the emergence of more than 120 MCC shops.
Case studies could also be prepared on MCC personnel policies
and practice (recruitment, selection, and maintenance) and on
decision-making patterns and administrative styles.

29

Organizing Festivals for MCC:

Relief Sales

*The act of gathering for a day or two . . . is not
too different from when rural Mennonites
worked together in barn raisings, hog butchering,
and threshing rings.*

Relief sales, like meat canning, thrift shops, and Mennonite Disaster Service, are expressions of desire among Mennonites to do something concrete to help those in need. These sales, which numbered thirty-three in the United States and Canada and raised more than $3,100,000 in 1985 for MCC, demonstrate that MCC is a people's movement. From the first publicized relief sale in 1957, held on a rural Pennsylvania farmyard near Morgantown, the idea of contributing money through organized sales came not from the MCC executive committee or staff, but from Mennonites in local congregations looking for ways to serve and to give.

In some respects, the act of gathering for a day or two to promote and support a common, benevolent cause is not too different than when rural Mennonites worked together in barn raisings, hog butchering, and threshing rings. Although these communal activities are now practiced only by the Amish, memory of them lingers. Perhaps MCC relief sales enjoy widespread popularity and success because they are somehow reminiscent of these earlier community experiences.

Mennonites who participate in modern relief sales do so at least in part because they are fun and festive. Although Mennonites have traditionally been wary of pleasure for pleasure's sake, many embrace the opportunity to enjoy themselves while doing something productive. Relief sales embody several things dear to the Mennonite soul: a deep desire for togetherness and camaraderie, celebration of family, church, tradition, and service, and the impulse to help others. Relief sales represent a grass-roots movement. Many sales began through the initiative of local committees, which drew on statewide networks of Mennonites but which had little or no access to area MCC offices.

The spontaneous beginning of the relief sale movement and the fact that sales have remained relatively autonomous may be two key reasons for their success. Their history does not include efforts to centralize or add professional staff. Relief sales share several other characteristics with material aid efforts, Mennonite Disaster Service, and MCC SELFHELP/thrift shops. North American Mennonites, experiencing affluence in recent decades, have sensed the gulf between their standard of living and that of the world's poor. They have sought creative ways to channel their riches to service, relief, and development. Mennonites also relish being "personally involved." Through relief sales they have come to feel more partnership in MCC work than when they simply place money in an offering plate.

A striking aspect of relief sale planning is the effort to give the sale a particular regional flavor. A 1970 newsletter sent to relief sale committee members contained this advice: "Every sale has a character of its own. Efforts need to be made to establish that character early in the sale. Once established, the sale can proceed." Sale-goers have expectations of what they will experience: quality antiques at the California/West Coast sale, hand-crafted furniture in Ohio, the emphasis on quilts in Pennsylvania and Indiana, the "traveling quilt" feature initiated at the Nebraska sale, a mass men's chorus in Kansas, a women's chorus begun in Ohio. Always there are food specialties: dried fruit and New Year's cookies, borscht and zwiebach, shoofly pie and funnel cake, pancakes and sausage.

The architects of the first well-publicized relief sale in 1957 could not have foreseen the prairie-fire-like expansion which would result from their efforts. At the Ralph Hertzler farm half a mile south of Morgantown, Pennsylvania, Mennonite families spent a Saturday afternoon in March buying and selling used items. The sale promoted by Hertzler and two fellow church members, Ford Berg and Milford Hertzler, called on neighboring Mennonites to "scour your attics, basements, closets, barns for items which you can spare and other people may care to buy." The purpose was to raise money for distribution of surplus food to impoverished countries. To encourage people to contribute, the proponents of the sale distributed an inventory of common items found in attics, garages, and homes, and added, "The Lord loveth a cheerful giver." In addition to a noon meal, they promised an event of "friendship, fellowship, and helpfulness" with all proceeds to be designated for relief.

The seed idea of relief sales may have been planted a decade earlier in eastern Lancaster County when in 1946 or 1947 a group of Mennonite farmers gathered harvest produce, quilts, and farm items for auction and gave the income to MCC. This harvest relief auction was first held on the Leon Sommer farm, later at the Gap Firehall, and still later at an Intercourse auction barn. Willis Umble served as treasurer. The first news item about this sale in the Mennonite press did not come until 1962. The sale, known as the Gap MCC Relief Sale, is held biennially.

During the 1960s, relief sales grew rapidly as Mennonite groups in Indiana and Illinois borrowed the idea from the Morgantown community. By the end of the decade, annual sales had been established in Ohio, Michigan, Virginia,

California, Kansas, Ontario, and Manitoba. Increased giving to MCC accompanied the geographic spread. In 1967, eight sales netted $100,000 for MCC; three years later, relief sales contributed nearly three times that amount. During the 1970s, relief sales contributed about one-fourth of Mennonite Central Committee's total income from constituents. From the first publicized sale at Morgantown through 1986, a total of 400 sales in Canada and the United States have netted $28,500,000.

Occasionally, MCC officials sought to redirect the fund-raising exuberance of local relief committees. In 1970, for example, the media publicized war and hardship in Nigeria, and many Mennonites, accordingly, designated their gifts and relief efforts for aid to that distressed country. MCC intervened by asking local and statewide sale organizers to promote the needs of countries such as Brazil, Bolivia, India, and Jordan alongside the obvious need in war-torn Nigeria.

One participant and observer of many relief sales has remarked: "If one wanted to bring relief sales to a halt, it would not be easy. Too many people are finding deep satisfaction in the sales." He highlighted the lively participation of those responsible for sharing ideas and making decisions, particularly some who might not be as involved in other church-related activities: "In no Mennonite conference do I hear women talking up as much and being listened to as intently as at these relief sale planning sessions." Certainly, the opportunity for persons to serve on planning committees has underscored special talents and interests: quilting, hog butchering, auctioneering, public relations, mass meal planning and preparation. People create networks and friendships they might not have the opportunity for otherwise.

Relief sales also build relationships through their ecumenicity. In Kansas, for example, sale participants include eight different Mennonite and Brethren in Christ groups. In all, a celebrative "grass-roots" spirit prevails with enthusiasm for "doing the Lord's work."

Relief sales are coordinated by geographic areas, with only the most informal of networds linking them to the MCC headquarters. John Hostetler, Material Aid Director for MCC, has throughout this history of the sales served as the primary resource person from MCC. During the early years of sale activity, Hostetler often answered questions about MCC's work overseas and explained how money raised at the sales would be used for relief. His role has been one of "information sharing," with the development in more recent years of a newsletter sent to all relief sale committee members. In this way, promoters of sales in different states and provinces have been able to communicate thir ideas with others. Hostetler also aids such cooperative ventures as the annual meeting of relief sale organizers held at different locations each year.

On the state or regional level, sale coordinators work with different committees to see that all aspects of the sale are carried out. The impulse and major planning may come from an enthusiastic "core group," which takes responsibility for setting goals and inspiring others to make the sale become a reality. The core group generally looks for a contact person from each participating congregation who will provide information, solicit workers, and make specific assignments to local volunteers. Committees with representatives from all over the state or province are formed to work on certain aspects of the sale. These include coordination of food, quilts, antiques, facilities, and publicity.

Those who are most active in the planning find it helpful to travel to other sales and to the annual meeting. And once relief sales are established, they have a tendency to grow, partly because of the exhilaration experienced by people who participate. One person has noted that "the enthusiasm of the sales committee has a sort of missionary quality. The participants want other communities to have experiences similar to the ones that they have enjoyed."

The role of the Mennonite Central Committee administration has been characteristically low-key regarding sale activities. John Hostetler feels that many questions raised during the past two decades are important. In one newsletter, he encouraged sale committee members to discuss ten important issues:

1. How do workers, customers, and visitors feel about sales?
2. Do the MCC relief sales strengthen the local congregations?
3. How important is the feeling of worker satisfaction?
4. Have we sought and listened to the critics and dissenters?
5. Are the original goals and assumptions adequate today?
6. Are the sales efficient in the use of human and fiscal resources?
7. Do sales help people understand more clearly what it means to be a Christian?
8. What are the significant results or by-products of the sales?
9. Do the sales pose any kind of a threat to other local efforts?
10. Is the time and effort allocated to sales in harmony with Christian priorities?

During the late 1960s, when relief sales were spreading rapidly to new states and provinces, some persons discussed the validity of the sales in response to an editorial in a March 1968 issue of the *Gospel Herald*. The editor had written a page-long essay on his uneasiness with relief sales as a money-maker for the church. Among other concerns, he highlighted the question regarding consistency of Christian priorities. "Do sales for relief," he asked, "undercut the stewardship teaching of the church and Scripture which stresses free, voluntary giving out of gratitude for God's grace?" He pointed to the tendency in church money-raising projects toward commercialism, which he felt compromised the church's commitments to spiritual, sacrificial giving.

The editor's critique drew responses from many readers. Some expressed dismay at what they felt was a dubious practice—Mennonites receiving food and goods as a motivation to give. One reader wrote, "Let us not go any further in the direction of needing a social event in order to give of our abundance to the physically distressed throughout the world." Other readers defended the sales. A veteran worker commented that she supported the sales because they raised a significant amount of money, created a way to allow people to give of themselves, fostered cooperation, and offered a positive witness of Mennonites to the community.

Following the *Gospel Herald* debate, some churches and individuals continued to question the legitimacy of the sales. One Mennonite leader, who acknowledged never having attended a relief sale, commented: "These spontaneous grass-roots movements ... extend the dependency of the old missionary era and reincarnate the old but comfortable giver-receiver syndrome. ... The pervasive attraction of feeding the hungry and doing good is producing a ... cultural and religious paternalism." He raised the question of whether relief sales generate pressures on the MCC to do work that is inappropriate to the needs of the poor and the hungry.

Another criticism surfaced in the mid-1970s when patterns for North American consumption came under scrutiny among some Mennonites who argued that the sales did little to promote a responsible Christian lifestyle. They asked whether Mennonite Central Committee should be more active in heightening awareness of alternative lifestyles for North Americans. This concern led to an emphasis on information and interpretation centers at the sale sites. After the publication of *The More-with-Less Cookbook* and its companion book, *Living More With Less*, a number of sales featured booths presenting ways in which North Americans might limit consumption. At about the same time, SELFHELP craft items began appearing regularly, which lent an international flavor to each local sale. Finally, some observers noted the undue emphasis on food, and suggested that sales raising funds to meet world hunger needs should stop selling various kinds of "junk food."

Promoters of the sales acknowledge that the danger of commercialism is an ongoing concern. Some who are interested in encouraging a wider public to attend the sales have turned to media coverage, including the production of television commercials to advertise upcoming sales. Local television and radio talk shows are one way of bringing MCC concerns to a wider audience. At some sales one sees buses bringing people from cities a hundred to two hundred miles away for the relief festival. Many sales have sold products advertising the program: custom-designed belt buckles, yardsticks, T-shirts, and caps. Some filmmakers have produced documentaries of the sales. Many sale organizing committees have used MCC-produced films and filmstrips about the work of MCC. Films are used at sale sites to educate the public and at planning meetings to inform the volunteers. One calls the sales "the Mennonite version and prototype of 'Live Aid' and 'Hands Across America.'"

"Kick-off dinners," one of several recent developments related to the sales, have been a means of covering all overhead expenses before a sale begins. Sale promoters have sought to cover all costs in advance so that they can say on the day of the sale, "Each dollar raised goes directly to MCC for helping needy people." In some areas, one or more banquets are held prior to the sale. In Kansas, the idea of MCC fellowship dinners has become popular. Church members sign up as either guests or hosts, and on a designated Sunday host families serve a meal to guests from other churches who have been assigned to them. In return for the dinner, guests pay a certain amount to help cover the cost of the sale. In 1986, 179 Kansas hosts served dinners to 855 guests from fifty-nine churches for a total of

$12,727. Additional money was raised from pledges by individual churches and Sunday school classes.

Nearly all Mennonite and Brethren in Christ congregations in the area of an MCC relief sale find some way to participate. In 1985, 22 percent of U.S. constituency giving for MCC came from the twenty-one relief sales in the U.S. One MCC leader observes: "The sales illustrate how MCC is owned by the constituency. Akron has little to do with relief sales." The question lingers, "Is this a good way of gathering gifts for MCC?"

30

Storing Grain in the Good Years:
Canadian Foodgrains Bank

*And let them gather all the food of these good
years that are coming, and lay up grain under the
authority of Pharaoh for food in the cities, and let
them keep it. That food shall be a reserve for the
land against the seven years of famine which are
to befall the land of Egypt, so that the land may
not perish through the famine.*

—Genesis 41:35-36

In 1975 a group of Canadian Mennonites who had served
with MCC overseas, concerned about famine in areas of the
world and the specter of famines yet to come, promoted the
idea of Canadian farmers donating part of their wheat crops to
a central reserve for emergency needs. They invoked the Old
Testament example of Joseph, who prepared for famine. They
pointed to MCC's experience with food distribution and
asserted that the MCC constituency was deeply involved in
food production as well as concerned with the ethics of national
food policy.

Arthur DeFehr, who a year earlier had returned to Canada
after serving as MCC country director in Bangladesh, helped to
launch the program with a nine-page "proposal for an MCC
Food Bank." MCC had enjoyed a high level of support from
Canadian Mennonites, many of whom had benefited after

World Wars I and II from MCC relief efforts in Europe. The time seemed right for such a program, which some heralded as "the most creative idea to come out of MCC in a long time."

During early discussions, farmers responded enthusiastically to this plan for helping to alleviate world hunger. They could grow grain with the knowledge that it would benefit persons in dire need. In some ways, the food bank plan did for farmers what the MCC Teachers Abroad Program in Africa had done for teachers a decade earlier. It allowed a segment of the MCC constituency to link Christian compassion with a particular livelihood and expertise. It served North American constituency needs to give; it met particular immediate overseas needs for food.

The food bank plan evolved as a result of discussions in 1975 and 1976 with Mennonite Central Committee Canada (MCCC), based in Winnipeg, Manitoba, and with Mennonite Central Committee, Akron, Pennsylvania, which served as the center for overseas relief and development programs. Winnipeg and Akron administrators encouraged the food bank idea, acknowledging MCC's previous involvement in emergency food distribution. Some saw it as a timely development, coinciding with international concern about food crises in Biafra, India, Bangladesh, and Cambodia. In Mennonite circles, world hunger concerns had moved to the top of the agenda when representatives of MCC gathered at their 1974 annual meeting in Hillsboro, Kansas. There delegates called for a reexamination of North American patterns of consumption. They also called on MCC to strengthen rural development, family planning, and nutrition programs in poor countries.

Yet in 1975, some MCC administrators who worked closely with international programs expressed caution. "How will a food bank mesh with our commitment to long-range food production programs overseas?" they asked. "For the past twenty years MCC has shifted from an emphasis on relief to an emphasis on development. Will a food bank program, with its goal of giving away large quantities of food, inhibit long-term agricultural development in areas where it is consumed?"

This concern about the value of emergency relief versus agricultural development has produced an ongoing tension within MCC during the ten-year history of the food bank program. In 1976, the same concern prompted North American and overseas MCC personnel to convene in Minneapolis to establish guidelines for the new program. Despite these early efforts at reaching consensus, the grain storage program has, according to Canadian Mennonite journalist Harold Jantz, "created great strains within Mennonite Central Committee, especially within MCC Canada, where it had its birth." The program's history illustrates the emergence within a church organization of radically different philosophies of helping people, styles of administration, relationships to churches and government—as well as the more emotional issues of personality, power ("who calls the shots"), and sense of territory. "Nothing I have worked with in all my years with MCC," commented one MCCC executive, "has been as emotionally and mentally taxing [as the struggle over the Food Bank]."

The original Food Bank came into existence in the fall of 1976. Under the program, farmers grew the wheat and delivered it as usual to the Canadian Wheat Board (CWB) at local elevators. The farmers signed over to the Food Bank their tickets representing the initial CWB payment, and the Canadian International Development Agency (CIDA) matched the farmers' contributions at a three to one ratio, so that the Food Bank could purchase the grain from the Canadian Wheat Board. CIDA's matching funds covered expenses such as wheat purchase, storage fees, handling costs, and the cost of international transportation to designated ports. Eventually, the farmer received payment for the delivered wheat representing the final price obtained by the CWB on the world market. MCC Canada, as a "parent" agency, provided support services and guidance to the Food Bank Board. Finally, the Akron-based MCC provided the overseas distribution system.

The Food Bank Board administered the program, keeping track of the number of bushels procured, the amount shipped overseas, and the number of bushels in reserve. Under a five-year trial plan, the Food Bank agreed to deal solely with wheat and to limit the "bank account" of wheat in storage at no more than two million bushels at any given time. Donors were gratified with the plan: "Here is stewardship at its best—each dollar gift is matched by three dollars of government gift."

At first, some MCC personnel expressed concern with the involvement of the government agency CIDA. They wondered whether dependence on government financing would weaken the financial support of MCC's Mennonite constituency. Others cautioned that CIDA might offer funding with strings attached: for example, putting subtle pressure on the Food Bank to aid countries which MCC considered only marginally deserving. The fear that the Food Bank might become a political tool was based in part on earlier MCC encounters with the United States Agency for International Development (U.S. AID). But as the Food Bank evolved, MCC staff who worked closely with CIDA felt little or no political pressure from the agency. For its part, CIDA commended the Mennonites for taking the lead in the unique grain storage program.

The Food Bank was only partially dependent on CIDA, however. Initially, Executive Director John R. Dyck and a ten-member Board of Directors appointed by MCCC ran the program. During the Food Bank's first years, its leaders carried on prolonged negotiations with the Canadian Wheat Board about restrictions imposed by the wheat quota system. These problems were eventually resolved to the benefit of the farmers and the Food Bank. In 1977, farmers contributed to the Food Bank fifty-three thousand bushels of grain at a cash value of $146,000.

Sister Christian service agencies followed with intense interest the Food Bank development. During the late seventies, the United Church of Canada and the Lutheran Church sent observers to Food Bank board meetings in Winnipeg. Their presence foreshadowed the eventual involvement of half a dozen non-Mennonite church agencies. However, one MCCC executive reflects back with a feeling of uneasiness that "they were persuaded into joining."

Early in 1978, the first shipment, eleven thousand bushels of wheat, left Vancouver for Calcutta, India. Ironically, the first shipment was designated not for emergency aid but for development: MCC and Lutheran World Services used the wheat in food-for-work programs which they administered jointly. Distribution overseas, however, often posed sticky problems. Many areas of the world in need of food were unaccustomed to a wheat-based diet. An MCCer working in Africa expressed the frustrations of overseas workers acquainted firsthand with the problems of distribution: "I am sitting here wishing that Kansas Mennonite farmers had decided to bring something besides hard wheat with them from the Old World, say, sorghum or millet."

Some within MCC questioned whether the Food Bank supply was even necessary, given a world economy which by 1977 was characterized by abundant harvests. An MCC India worker noted, "In view of the surplus food situation we do not feel it is appropriate to import large quantities of food grains." MCC reminded Food Bank Board members that "production is cyclical. Let's not now push too hard."

Food Bank advocates and MCC personnel overseas were of divided opinion on the matter of food aid. Most in MCC agreed that food shipments were necessary in disaster and emergency situations. Many other agencies, with highly publicized programs, channeled large shipments of emergency aid. Field workers believed that MCC should focus its efforts on development programs, helping people to grow more food close to where it would be consumed. A second issue was size: How deeply did MCC want to commit itself to a large-scale material aid program? MCC had traditionally shied away from very large programs because of concern for quality control. MCC preferred to move material aid through the smaller conduit of church organizations rather than through cumbersome government channels. A third issue centered on authority: MCC perceived the Food Bank as a bank which managed an account and transferred a commodity on request. The wheat in reserve belonged not to the Food Bank but to MCC (or another partner agency)—for eventual shipment to destinations deemed worthy by MCC. Problems arose when Food Bank staff and MCC staff failed to agree on where, to whom, and how much to ship.

In the spring of 1978, the Food Bank appointed a new executive director, C. Wilbert Loewen, who promoted the program aggressively among Mennonite constituents. Under his direction, support for the Food Bank program grew to include some sectors—for example, colonies of Hutterites—that had rarely identified with MCC programs. To Loewen and others the "banking" concept as defined by MCC was too narrow. They saw the Food Bank as a prophetic yet practical model of what could be done to alleviate suffering in the world, albeit on a small scale. Food Bank personnel were enthusiastic in their promotion of the program to Canadian Mennonites, to the discomfort of some MCC administrators who cautioned that "hard promotion" was not in keeping with MCC standards and that constituency relationships were the parent agency's (MCCC's) task.

MCC administrators were also concerned that Mennonites might be so attracted by the prospects of multiplying their dollar power through the CIDA matching program that they would channel more of their giving to the Food Bank rather than through MCC to the less glamorous, long-standing development programs which depended on cash gifts rather than grain. MCC knew that farmers had been attracted to the Food Bank program precisely because it made relief aid tangible; farmers could go to the docks to see their wheat off to a faraway famine area. Likewise, generous farmers returned from Food Bank-sponsored trips to Asia enthusiastic about seeing the fruits of their labors.

MCC, however, sensitive to issues of food production, nutrition, and education in developing countries, saw Food Bank personnel and Board members taking a direction of their own apart from the total MCC program and policy. Independent decision-making by the Food Bank, MCC leaders feared, would harm MCC's image among constituents, damage fragile church and government relationships overseas, and twist program priorities. Through the late 1970s and early 1980s, MCC and the Food Bank negotiated various points of tension. These tensions led a Food Bank Board chairman to resign in protest over a variety of issues: mandate, style, and understanding of the role of the binational office in Akron in overseas programming.

Meanwhile, after a slow start, the Food Bank began to receive a volume of wheat far beyond initial projections. From 1978 to 1980 the Food Bank sent wheat to India, Zaire, Upper Volta, Chad, Vietnam, Zimbabwe, Kenya, and Nicaragua. Beginning in 1978, it also began major shipments to Ethiopia. For the first time in the history of the Food Bank, major news headlines focused daily on the hunger crisis. Worldwide press reports of starving millions, and in particular news coverage of the famine in Ethiopia, validated the grain storage program. In 1980 the Food Bank shipped nearly eighteen million pounds of wheat overseas.

By the 1980s, the Food Bank had created tremendous momentum among Canadian Mennonites. Members of the Food Bank Board of Directors favored restructuring the program to include broader participation. In 1983, after much discussion between MCC, MCC Canada, and the Food Bank, the program was transformed from a small-scale "pilot program" to an umbrella organization which served six Christian agencies or "partners" in addition to MCC Canada. Each denominational partner was responsible for promoting the program within its own constituency, and each partner allocated its grain resources and handled its own distribution overseas. Each partner, including MCCC, had an "account" of its own in the bank.

The restructured organization, named the "Canadian Foodgrains Bank" (CFB), was designed to operate for three years, after which the charitable, nonprofit organization would come under review by MCCC. MCCC had the power to renew, modify, or cancel the program. The Canadian Foodgrains Bank dealt in millions of dollars of grain and became an even more popular vehicle for giving among Canadian farmers.

Yet some close to the CFB continued to express concern over the agency's widening scope. They cited *Against the Grain*, a recently published book by Tony Jackson of the British relief agency OXFAM. Jackson argued that in most cases food aid undermined local production and was more harmful than helpful. He spoke of a "narrow slot" in which food aid was appropriate in fostering development.

While MCC believed that the careful process of reorganization had helped to eradicate some of the problems associated with the original Food Bank, tensions continued. Again, questions centered around size, authority, administrative style, and the nature of development. The CFB existed on the basis of new guidelines designed to insure that MCCC's concerns would be recognized: namely, that CFB was to be a bank rather than an operating agency. The CFB Board consisted of eight members from MCCC and two from each of the new partners.

By the summer of 1982, MCC's overseas secretaries, based in Akron, were disconcerted with the operations of the Canadian Foodgrains Bank. They expressed strong reservations about what they saw as its emphasis on "going big." They argued for the use of food aid in smaller, targeted areas. CFB personnel, on the other hand, argued that MCC had shown a lack of interest in food aid. In the give-and-take of these discussions, overseas secretaries and personnel emphasized that they were committed to CFB as an appropriate resource. One MCCC executive commented that CFB was "too preoccupied with the resource and not enough with the need, too supply driven, and too promotion focused." He added that on "too many occasions it [did not behave] as a servant of the partners."

During the mid-1980s, distribution fiascoes overseas plagued the program. Several shiploads of corn and wheat from Canada arrived in the ports of Mozambique on Africa's eastern coast. The grain had been seriously damaged during the shipping process and had arrived in inferior condition. African relief agencies criticized MCC for its handling of the shipments. One MCC administrator declared: "MCC has always committed itself to sending a quality product, even when the cost is slightly more. Why has this criterion been breached?" He also expressed displeasure that the Canadian Foodgrains Bank had dealt directly with the Mozambique government, rather than through MCC's usual channel, the Christian Council of Mozambique. He concluded: "Mozambique is in a desperate situation with reference to food. We have food resources on hand. Because of our own administrative bungling . . . we have jeopardized an important relationship."

Constituents were scarcely aware of these institutional tensions; meanwhile, the Canadian Foodgrains Bank continued to commend itself to a widening Canadian public. In 1985, at the close of the agency's first three-year mandate, MCC Canada received from an eight-member review committee a candid evaluation of CFB based in part on interviews with farmers, agency representatives, staff members, and MCCC personnel. The committee affirmed the Foodgrains Bank concept and program which "had alleviated much hunger and saved many lives." It approved of this "opportunity for Christians of different church affiliations to work together." It added that having reserve grain or money to buy food for an emergency was "practical and efficient." It affirmed the CFB's goal of helping food relief recipients to "achieve independence from food aid." It acknowledged that MCCC had been perceived as "heavy-handed in its relationship with CFB." The review committee recommended that the CFB continue, but advised that the partners (never the CFB) should distribute the food overseas as part of their total programs.

The review committee recommended nine structural changes. Of these, the following three had particular significance:

1. That the chairman of CFB be an elected non-salaried officer with responsibility to chair the Board and Executive Committee and that a new salaried position be created, the Chief Executive Officer (COE), who will carry responsibility for policy, inter-partner relations, and general oversight of program. The Chief Operations Officer (Manager) will be responsible to the COE for the management of operations.

2. That food grains or cash received directly by the CFB—rather than by one of the partners—are to be dispensed through the member agencies.

3. That when a partner receives grain for distribution, but does not have a program, the partner will approach a fellow partner for assistance in the utilization of the resource. This will remove CFB from the role of overseas distribution and programming.

MCC Canada submitted the review committee's recommendations to the CFB Board. The partners agreed with the recommendations and proceeded to introduce the structural changes. MCC Canada reduced its membership on the Board from eight to two, thus giving MCCC the same representation as the other partners.

A year after these changes were implemented, CFB and MCCC staff members acknowledged that while much of the troubling atmosphere surrounding the CFB had cleared, some tensions remained. Reg Toews, Associate Director of MCC and a member of the review committee, reflected recently: "The Canadian Foodgrains Bank story illustrates how a good Christian organization can get into serious trouble and—with courage, stick-to-it-iveness, and caring—can overcome. We regret, however, that some persons were deeply hurt in the process."

Former MCC Canada Executive Secretary J. M. Klassen, who was involved in the development and subsequent trials of the food aid agency, adds this observation:

> The degree to which personalities played into the tensions is hard to separate out from the organizational and functional aspects. It's amazing how messy administrative structures and relationships can be tolerated as long as there is trust and confidence in and among the personalities involved. If this is true in the micro MCC/CFB structures, how much more is it a factor in national or international relations?

For Further Reading

General Books and Publications

Dyck, Cornelius J., ed. *From the Files of MCC*. Scottdale, Pa.: Herald Press, 1980. First in a series of five volumes on the history of MCC; contains historical documents on MCC origins, refugee and relief work.

_____. *Responding to Worldwide Needs*. Scottdale, Pa.: Herald Press, 1980. Second volume; contains documents on MCC's entry into Europe, the Middle East, Africa, and Asia.

_____. *Witness and Service in North America*. Scottdale, Pa.: Herald Press, 1980. Third volume; contains documents on the growth of peace witness, mental health work, voluntary service, and Mennonite Disaster Service.

_____. *Something Meaningful for God*. Scottdale, Pa.: Herald Press, 1981. Fourth volume; collection of fifteen biographies of MCC workers.

Epp, Frank H. *Mennonite Exodus: The Rescue and Resettlement of the Russian Mennonites Since the Communist Revolution*. Altona: D. W. Friesen and Sons, 1962. History of the Canadian Mennonite Board of Colonization, founded in 1922.

_____. *Mennonites in Canada, 1786-1920*. Scottdale, Pa.: Herald Press, 1974.

_____. *Mennonites in Canada, 1920-1940*. Toronto: Macmillan of Canada, 1982.

Hiebert, P. C., and Miller, Orie O. *Feeding the Hungry: Russia Famine, 1919-1925.* Scottdale, Pa.: Mennonite Central Committee, 1929. Earliest published history of the work of Mennonite Central Committee.

Juhnke, James C. *Becoming a Denomination.* Mennonite Experience in America, Volume 3. Scottdale, Pa.: Herald Press, 1988.

Mennonite Central Committee Workbooks. Annual reports of the activities of MCC, MCC U.S., and MCC Canada, published each January. A rich directory of information including summaries of overseas and domestic programs and the latest statistics on SELFHELP and material aid.

Mennonite Quarterly Review. July 1970. Eight scholarly articles commemorating the 50th anniversary of MCC, with a bibliography compiled by Melvin Gingerich.

Toews, Paul. *Mennonites in America, 1930-1970: Modernity and the Persistence of Religious Community.* Mennonite Experience in America, Volume 4. Scottdale, Pa.: Herald Press, scheduled to appear 1989.

Unruh, John D. *In the Name of Christ: A History of the Mennonite Central Committee and Its Service, 1920-1951.* Scottdale, Pa.: Herald Press, 1952. A commissioned history documenting MCC's first thirty years, with annotated bibliography.

Additional Reading on MCC-Related Topics

Bender, Urie A. *Soldiers of Campassion.* Scottdale, Pa.: Herald Press, 1969. History of conscientious objectors serving through MCC's Pax program in the 1950s and 1960s.

Development Monograph Series. Akron, Pa.: Mennonite Central Committee, n.d. Booklets emphasizing grass-roots work from the MCC experience.

Eby, Omar. *A House in Hue.* Scottdale, Pa.: Herald Press, 1968.

Epp, Frank H., ed. *Partners in Service: The Story of the Mennonite Central Committee Canada.* N.p.: Mennonite Central Committee Canada, 1983.

Fretz, J. Winfield. *The Meda Experiment, 1953-1978.* Waterloo: Conrad Press, 1978.

————. *Pilgrims In Paraguay: The Story of Mennonite Colonization in South America.* Scottdale, Pa.: Herald Press, 1953.

Gingerich, Melvin. *Service for Peace: A History of Mennonite Civilian Public Service.* Akron, Pa.: Mennonite Central Committee, 1949.

Glick, Helen. *Spiritsong: Mennonite Central Committee's 25 Years in Bolivia.* Akron, Pa.: Mennonite Central Committee, 1987.

Grasse, Karen. *We Became Friends: A History of Mennonite Central Committee in Appalachia.* Akron, Pa.: Mennonite Central Committee, 1983.

Hess, J. Daniel. *From the Other's Point of View: Perspectives from North and South of the Rio Grande.* Scottdale, Pa.: Herald Press, 1980.

Horst, Irvin. *A Ministry of Goodwill: A Short Account of Mennonite Relief, 1939-1949.* Akron, Pa.: Mennonite Central Committee, 1950.

Klassen, James. *Jimshoes in Vietnam: Orienting a Westerner.* Scottdale, Pa.: Herald Press, 1986.

Martin, Earl S. *Reaching the Other Side: The Journal of an American Who Stayed to Witness Vietnam's Postwar Transition.* New York: Crown Publishers, 1978.

Neufeld, Vernon H., ed. *If We Can Love: The Mennonite Mental Health Story.* Newton, Kans: Faith and Life Press, 1978.

Redekop, Calvin. *Strangers Become Neighbors.* Scottdale, Pa.: Herald Press, 1980. Sociological perspective on the development of Native Indian groups living near Mennonite colonists in the Paraguayan Chaco.

Shenk, Wilbert. *An Experiment in Interagency Coordination.* Elkhart, In.: Council of International Ministries, 1986.

Smith, Willard. *Paraguayan Interlude.* Scottdale, Pa.: Herald Press, 1950.

Stoltzfus, Elaine. *Tending the Vision, Planting the Seed: A History of MCC in Haiti, 1958-1984.* Akron, Pa.: Mennonite Central Committee, 1987.

Wiebe, Katie Funk. *Day of Disaster.* Scottdale, Pa.: Herald Press, 1976. The story of Mennonite Disaster Service.

Information Services of MCC

News releases published by MCC appear in a wide range of constituent newspapers and periodicals, most frequently in *Mennonite Reporter* and *Mennonite Weekly Review.* Each year, MCC distributes new and updated audiovisual materials interpreting its programs. A resource catalog, listing current printed and audiovisual materials, is available from all MCC offices.

Archives

The files of MCC offices and personnel remain in Akron for ten years and in Winnipeg for five years. The largest collection of MCC documents is located in Goshen, Indiana, at the Archives of the Mennonite Church, the depository for MCC records. The depository for MCC Canada records is the Mennonite Heritage Center in Winnipeg, Manitoba. Other Mennonite research centers, such as the Mennonite Library and Archives in North Newton, Kansas, also have substantial holdings pertaining to the Mennonite Central Committee.

Countries and Dates of MCC Service

Countries of MCC Service (In addition to the United States and Canada)

Country	Periods of Service
Russia	1920, 1921-27
Paraguay	1930-
England	1940-47, 1978-
France	1940-43, 1946-
Poland	1940-42, 1947-49, 1971-
India	1942-
China	1943-51, 1981-
Egypt	1943-45, 1968-
Puerto Rico	1943-50
Ethiopia	1945-51, 1975-
The Netherlands	1945-68
Italy	1945-51, 1976-
Austria	1946-68
Belgium	1946-50, 1965-
West Germany	1946-
Philippines	1946-50, 1977-
Brazil	1947-
Hungary	1947-48, 1978-
Mexico	1947-57, 1967-75, 1981-
Indonesia	1948-
Formosa (Taiwan)	1948-56, 1987
Lebanon	1948-49, 1958-59, 1976-
Pakistan	1948-50, 1959-76, 1981-
Argentina	1949-66
Japan	1949-58

Uruguay	1949-65
Switzerland	1950-
Hong Kong	1950-52, 1958-76
West Bank	1950-
Korea	1951-71
Greece	1952-77
Peru	1954-63
Vietnam	1954-
Nepal	1957-
Liberia	1957-62
Morocco	1957-78
Algeria	1958-78
Haiti	1958-
Bolivia	1959-
British Honduras (Belize)	1960-63, 1981-1984
Chile	1960-61, 1985-
Congo (Zaire)	1960-
Thailand	1961-63, 1975-76, 1978-
Kenya	1962-
Burundi	1962-68
Tanzania	1962-
Zambia	1962-
Malawi	1962-81
Nigeria	1963-
Dominican Republic	1963-76, 1979-
St. Lucia	1965-68
Guatemala	1965-66, 1976-
Yugoslavia	1966-71
Jordan	1967-82, 1985-
Turkey	1967-
Botswana	1968-
Sierra Leone	1969-75
Bangladesh	1970-
Jamaica	1970-
Swaziland	1971-
Sudan	1972-
Chad	1973-
Lesotho	1973-
Laos	1975-
Burkina Faso	1975-

Niger	1976-79
Colombia	1976-
Grenada	1976-82
South Africa	1978-
(The Transkei)	
Dominica	1979-81
Nicaragua	1979-
Ireland	1979-
Uganda	1979-
Kampuchea	1979-
Somalia	1980-
Zimbabwe	1980-
El Salvador	1981-
Romania	1981-
Honduras	1981-
Angola	1981-
Mozambique	1982-
Portugal	1985-
East Germany	1986-
Costa Rica	1986-

The Authors

Robert S. Kreider   *Rachel Waltner Goossen*

Robert S. Kreider received a Ph.D. in history from the University of Chicago. He has taught history and peace studies on the faculties of Bluffton College, Bluffton, Ohio, and Bethel College, North Newton, Kansas. He has served with the Mennonite Central Committee in a variety of assignments, including one in Europe, 1946-49, and as a member of the Executive Committee. He was director of the Mennonite Library and Archives, North Newton, Kansas, and editor of *Mennonite Life*. Kreider and his wife, Lois, live in North Newton, Kansas.

Rachel Waltner Goossen is a historian and free-lance writer. A native of Newton, Kansas, she graduated from Bethel

389

College and received an M.A. in history from the University of California, Santa Barbara. Goossen served a one-year internship with the Mennonite Library and Archives and subsequently taught courses in historic preservation and community history at Bethel College. She is the author of *Brick and Mortar: A History of Newton, Kansas* (1984), *Meetingplace: A History of the Mennonite Church of Normal* (1987), and *Prairie Vision: A History of the Pleasant Valley Mennonite Church* (1988). She has also contributed articles to *Mennonite Life* and to *The Mennonite Encyclopedia*, Volume V.

Goossen and her husband, Duane, live in Goessel, Kansas. She is a member of the Goessel Mennonite Church and serves on the Historical Committee of the Western District Conference.

The Mennonite Central Committee Story Series